Marie d'Agoult

Marie d'Agoult

The Rebel Countess

R I C H A R D   B O L S T E R

Yale University Press   *New Haven & London*

Designed by James J. Johnson and set in Perpetua types by Tseng Information Systems,
Durham, North Carolina.
Printed in the United States of America by R.R. Donnelley & Sons Company,
Harrisonburg, Virginia.

Library of Congress Cataloging-in-Publication Data

Bolster, Richard.
Marie d'Agoult : the rebel countess / Richard Bolster.
p.   cm.
Includes bibliographical references and index.
ISBN 0-300-08246-0 (alk.)

1. Stern, Daniel, 1805–1876. 2. Authors, French—19th century—Biography. I. Title.
PQ2152.A38 Z8454   2000
848'.709—dc21
[B]   99-055838

A catalogue record for this book is available from the British Library.

The paper in this book meets the guidelines for permanence and durability of the Committee on
Production Guidelines for Book Longevity of the Council on Library Resources.

2   4   6   8   10   9   7   5   3   1

To Allison

Contents

Preface

Marie d'Agoult became well known in the France of Louis-Philippe for her elopement with Franz Liszt and then as a writer under the name Daniel Stern. She wrote fiction, articles on literature, music, art, and politics, and the *History of the Revolution of 1848*. In her unfinished memoirs, she left a vivid account of her early life in a succession of homes. All have been demolished, but we can see them in our imagination: the old wooden house in Frankfurt, the country mansion in the Loire Valley, the house by the Seine from which she viewed the revolution of 1830. Marie d'Agoult lived through an exceptional period in French history, one that began with the empire of Napoleon and was marked by many dramatic changes of regime. Her letters and other writings reflect the intellectual life of France over several decades.

She was the daughter of a German mother and a French aristocrat who had fled the Revolution. Rich, beautiful, and talented, she seemed to have been born under a lucky star. Her bilingual education enabled her to acquire an extensive knowledge of French and German culture; she would also become well versed in Italian literature, music, and art. In her youth the works of Chateaubriand, Byron, Lamartine, and Hugo charmed her. Throughout her life, she became acquainted with many important figures, including Charles X and his prime minister, Jules de Polignac, who precipitated the revolution of 1830. She was courted by Vigny, Sainte-Beuve, and the press tycoon Emile de Girardin. George Sand became her friend and then betrayed her by giving Balzac information he would use in his novel *Béatrix,* which contains cruel and thinly veiled allusions to Marie's relationship with Liszt. Her passion for music had brought her into contact with this brilliant young performer, who became the love of her life. The idea of emancipation was in the air, and Marie decided to seek personal fulfillment by leaving her husband in order to live openly with Liszt. They moved to Italy and stayed there happily for a time. After five years, during which she bore him three children, their idealistic romance degenerated into conflict and disenchantment. Marie then devoted herself to the life of the intellect. She returned to Paris, where she established a salon frequented by distinguished names such as Michelet, Littré, Taine, and Renan. In addition, her writings won her a reputation as a journalist and historian. Her published books include *Nélida, Esquisses morales, Essai sur la liberté, Histoire de la révolution de 1848, Dante et Goethe,* and *Mes souvenirs, 1806–1833.*

I am grateful to the University of Bristol, which has provided financial support for my research. I also wish to thank Mariarosa Maranzano for her valuable comments on my typescript and to pay homage to Jacques Vier and Charles Dupêchez, who have contributed so much to our knowledge of Marie d'Agoult. Translations of letters and documents from the original French are my own.

CHAPTER 1

A Soldier's Daughter

THERE is an old saying in Germany that a child born at midnight is influenced by dark forces which show themselves in dreams and premonitions. Marie de Flavigny would often recall this superstition, because she was herself a Midnight Child who came into the world in late December of 1805. Her place of birth was the ancient German city of Frankfurt, on the river Main. Her mother, Maria, belonged to a prominent local family which owned the leading bank in the city. The Bethmann bank enjoyed high status and was engaged in major financial operations throughout the continent. The decades of conflict started by the French Revolution of 1789 had led the kings of Europe to borrow heavily in their attempt to overthrow the new regime in Paris; to the Bethmann family in Frankfurt the war had brought great wealth.

Marie's father was an exiled young French aristocrat whom the accidents of war had brought to Frankfurt in 1796.[1] The early life of Count Alexandre de Flavigny had been one of ease and privilege before the Revolution. He had been a page at Versailles, the magnificent palace of Louis XVI and his charming consort, Marie-Antoinette. When the Revolution of 1789 began, Flavigny was twenty-three and a lieutenant in the artillery, an élite corps whose officers possessed mathematical and scientific skills and looked down on the cavalry, just as the cavalry felt superior to the infantry. Like many officers who had sworn an oath of loyalty to their king, Flavigny left France and made his way to the German town of Coblenz. There he joined an army of French royalists led by Prince Condé and supported by the major European monarchies. Condé and his men were preparing to invade France in order to restore the king to power. In June 1791 Louis XVI and his wife had escaped from Paris disguised as middle-class travelers. Unfortunately, they were recognized and recaptured at Varennes before they could cross the frontier into Germany. The king whom Flavigny had sworn to serve was now a prisoner of the revolutionaries and was suspected of complicity with those who planned an invasion of his country.

The years from 1789 to 1791 had brought profound change to the easy life of Marie's father, who was now a soldier in earnest and playing a part in one of the great dramas of European history. His first major conflict would be the battle of Valmy, which took place on 20 September 1792. Condé's army was part of a large alliance of Prussians and contingents from other German states, and the invading royalist forces were so certain of victory that crowned princes such as the king of Prussia and the duke of Weimar had accompanied them to observe the battles and were already imagining their triumphant entry into Paris. Early events tended to confirm this expectation as they took the fortified towns of Longwy and Verdun without difficulty and advanced quickly from the German frontier toward Paris. Condé's aristocratic officers had assured their German allies that the new French army opposing them was made up of ill-trained rabble and that the majority of the population would receive the invaders with open arms.

The first French troops encountered by the allies lived up to their reputation for indiscipline and incompetence, as they were mostly raw volunteers who had been repeatedly driven back. In a desperate last effort to defend Paris, the French commander Charles Dumouriez decided to make a stand on a small plateau at Valmy in spite of the risk of being surrounded. Rejecting advice, the young king of Prussia then ordered an instant attack by the allies. To their astonishment, they were confronted by regiments of well-trained regulars, determined fighters who were eager to defend their country and its new regime.

For Alexandre de Flavigny and his royalist comrades the defeat was shocking and unexpected. Marie's father left no written record of his experiences or thoughts on that memorable day, but a vivid account was recorded by Goethe, who witnessed it all in the company of the duke of Weimar.[2] He recalled that great demoralization spread quickly through the invading armies, who only that morning had assumed they would chase the French off the plateau. As night fell, Goethe was in the company of a wet, hungry, and mostly silent group, without even a fire to cheer them. He tactlessly expressed the opinion that they could console themselves with the thought of having participated in a great event in world history. It is likely that Alexandre de Flavigny felt no such consolation. A few days after the battle the grave news arrived that France was now a republic and that the former king awaited trial on a charge of treason. At this point the exile must have realized that his return to a privileged position in his homeland was seriously in doubt and that the precarious life of a soldier would be his for some time.

In the years which followed, Flavigny continued to experience the dangers of war in Condé's army as it fought with initial success at the battle of Wissembourg on the northern frontier between October and December 1793. The French royalists distinguished themselves in the allied army, which captured twenty kilometers of fortifications from the republican forces, only to lose them again.[3] For the next few years Flavigny and his comrades were in the vicinity of the Rhine, awaiting the next stage in the continuing war between the French Republic and the old monarchies of Europe. In 1796 Marie's father, who now held the rank of colonel, was sent to Frankfurt with the important mission of raising an additional regiment for the next campaign. The necessary funds were coming from Britain and were to be dispensed by the Bethmann bank. Thus it was that the young French aristocrat met his future wife.

Maria Bethmann was then a twenty-four-year-old widow and the mother of a six-year-old daughter, Augusta. The circumstances of this early marriage were not exceptional at the time, though they may seem strange to us. At the age of seventeen Maria had accepted the hand of Jakob Bussmann, a business partner of her father's and exactly twice her age. In the wealthy classes such marriages between young girls and older men were seen as a sensible arrangement in that an older man could provide a better home, including servants and a carriage, and could be expected to have a certain knowledge of life, including sexual matters. Teenage girls were physically nubile and usually eager for the status provided by marriage, a social condition which freed them from a highly protected existence. Naturally, such unions were not based on calculation alone, and common sense prescribed that some element of affection and esteem was needed, though the realities of courtship and marriage were far from the notion of passionate love found in sentimental novels. Little is known about the years Maria Bethmann spent with her father's business partner, but later events would indicate that they left her dissatisfied with arranged marriages.

When the young widow met Alexandre de Flavigny, with his charm, blue eyes, fair hair, fine uniform, and aristocratic name and manner, she liked what she saw. This man was clearly different from Jakob Bussmann. The problem was that the qualities she found irresistible did not arouse enthusiasm in her family. He was a foreigner and an exile. He was a soldier who might be killed in his next battle. He was an aristocrat and they were commoners, proud of their own class and status. To cap it all, he had no money and few prospects, whereas Maria was already a rich woman who had inherited the estate of her husband, to say nothing of her share of the Bethmann fortune. The theme of star-crossed lovers that had inspired many a play and novel was in this case a reality.

To Maria the decision seemed simple. She wanted Flavigny, she had enough money for both of them, and her situation as widow had emancipated her from family authority. Unfortunately this stance was not accepted by her domineering mother, Frau Bethmann, who, determined to prevent the match, called on Maria's older brother, Möritz, the head of the family firm. The Bethmanns could do very much as they pleased in Frankfurt, so the pair decided to thwart the lovers by getting the authorities to serve an expulsion order on the French officer for an alleged irregularity in his passport. When he refused to leave the city, he was promptly locked up as an undesirable alien. Maria, who considered Flavigny to be anything but undesirable, angrily countered the plot. She asked to be driven to the prison, where she entered his cell and remained alone with him for a sufficient length of time to tarnish her reputation. She next went defiantly to her mother and brother and asked whether they would still try to prevent the marriage.

As she was now technically dishonored unless she wed Flavigny, the family withdrew its opposition. It was clear that Maria's quiet manner masked a rigid determination. No doubt she felt she had paid her tribute to duty in the years with Bussmann and that the time had come to grasp at happiness. It is a remarkable fact that in years to come both of Maria

Bethmann's daughters, Augusta Bussmann and the future Marie d'Agoult, would become famous for similar acts of folly inspired by love. In 1807, when Augusta was sixteen, she decided to marry the poet Clemens Brentano in spite of his reluctance. She invited him to go in her carriage for a ride in the country one evening and when he entered the vehicle he found her wearing a wedding dress and accompanied by two witnesses. The horses took them at breakneck speed to Kassel, where everything necessary for a wedding ceremony had been prepared. One can imagine Brentano's misgivings, but he went ahead with the marriage and lived to regret it. When the stormy relationship became unbearable, he more than once tried to leave Augusta, but with little success. It is clear that Maria Bethmann had passed on her passionate nature to her daughter, and equally evident that intensity of emotion is no guarantee of future bliss. Indeed Augusta was to have a tragic end.

By contrast, the marriage of Maria and Flavigny would bring them many happy years. The wedding took place in the town of Solothurn, Switzerland, in September 1797, after which the couple moved to Vienna, as dictated by Flavigny's military career. Their first child, a son, did not survive infancy; a second son, named Maurice, was born in 1799.

The remnants of Condé's army were now gathered under the colors of Austria, whose emperor was continuing the struggle against the French Republic. Flavigny's last experience of war with his royalist comrades was to be the battle of Hohenlinden, which took place near the river Inn in Austria in 1800. When the Austrian force advanced, the army of the French Republic had made a tactical retreat through the forest. The Austrian army imprudently followed them and became entangled in a difficult narrow passage leading through the trees. The French army was waiting, its regiments deployed on the small plain in front of the town of Hohenlinden. As the first Austrians emerged, one French section carried out a frontal attack, while another attacked the flank of the Austrians still in the forest. To add to the confusion, snow was falling, making visibility difficult as hand-to-hand fighting took place among the pines. Many of the Austrians were killed, wounded, or captured, or simply fled in disorder; the result was another severe reverse for the French royalist cause. The empire of the Hapsburgs found itself obliged to accept defeat. Weary of the dangers and disappointments of war, Flavigny was ready to hang up his sword. Like some of his comrades, he might have taken up service in the armies of the Russian czar. He was theoretically under sentence of death in his own country, as were all Frenchmen who had fought against the Republic, and it seemed impossible that he could ever return. Recovery of any family property also appeared improbable, in that the estates of exiled nobles had been confiscated. The best plan was therefore to settle in Frankfurt, the home of the Bethmann family, leaving behind the insecurity and hardship of military life. Flavigny had fought loyally for his king, but the cause seemed lost; the time had come to think of his young family and of his own future.

Like many German cities in these troubled times, Frankfurt had a community of French exiles, and Flavigny had only to look around him to see how fortunate he was. Many of these uprooted French had a difficult life and were dependent on the help of the local aristocracy. Some made a little money by giving French lessons, doing clerical work, or even working as cooks and gardeners. Most were young and did their best to maintain the atmosphere of gaiety and conviviality which had been typical of their class. Others had assumed false names and made a clandestine return to France, where nobody troubled them once the fanatical persecution of the Terror was over. Then in 1802 France ordered a general amnesty for all exiles except those still active in foreign armies. From this time on, Marie's father was free to return to his native land. Nonetheless, he chose to remain in Frankfurt rather than become a citizen of a French Republic now ruled by the remarkable Napoleon Bonaparte, whose title was first consul but who was known to royalists simply as the Usurper.

Frankfurt was a fine and prosperous city, and the Bethmann family was generally admired. Maria's brother, Möritz, was a man of outstanding ability and progressive ideas, one of which had been the creation of a college for Jews—this at a time when the city authorities still maintained a ghetto which was closed off by gates at night. Möritz was known for his skill with people and his understanding of the power of money. It is said that when the French army stood at the gates of Frankfurt, he saved the gold and silver treasures of the city's churches by rushing to Paris and bribing the appropriate minister. He took on this mission even though he held no office in the Frankfurt city council and in spite of the fact that the council did not have the ready money, which meant that he had to advance it himself.

Möritz Bethmann had a pragmatic mind, and it seems that he accepted Flavigny into his well-to-do family without difficulty. Differences of wealth and social rank were forgotten, or at least not mentioned; in addition marriages between poor aristocrats and rich young women from the middle class were not uncommon. It is probable that Flavigny could not speak German well, in spite of his years in exile, though, like all educated people at the time, the Bethmanns could speak French. Language was therefore no problem; Marie and her brother spoke German to their mother and French to their father. This gave them a fluency in both tongues which in years to come would afford them an intimate knowledge of two literatures and a broad cultural perspective. These were the unusual but happy circumstances into which Marie de Flavigny was born in the winter of 1805. Her parents had wealth, charm, personality, good looks, and intelligence: it was a good start in life.

The city in which Marie lived her first years was like many fortified towns which continued to live in expectation of war. Space was scarce within the protective city walls, and life was noisy and intimate in the crooked and narrow cobbled streets, some of which were barely two meters wide, making it impossible for two horse-drawn vehicles to pass each other. Most streets had no underground drains, and any heavy rain made pedestrian life difficult. The narrowness of the streets prevented sunlight from reaching the lower level of houses, where cobblers, tailors, milliners, and other artisans could be glimpsed through small windowpanes as they bent over their work. On the ledges of the higher windows were boxes filled with geraniums, honeysuckle, and sweet pea. The most desirable living quarters were those on the middle floors or those with the luxury of a spacious inner courtyard. On the steep roofs were the nests of storks, which were believed to bring good luck.

From the window of her first home, on the corner of the Gallienstrasse, Marie de Flavigny could look down on the lively Horsemarket, full of dealers, buyers, and tossing manes. Farmers traveled to the nearby city each morning to sell their fruits and vegetables as well as live hens, ducks, and piglets, which were a source of entertainment for young eyes. Marie later recalled that in cities at this time, when the rich had servants and industrialization had not rearranged the urban and mental landscape, different classes often lived under the same roof. They knew each other by name, and it was customary for the wealthy to offer hospitality to poor neighbors at times of family celebration. On summer Sundays Marie was taken to the cool gardens of the Bethmann country house, a magnificent villa which would have the honor of being used by Bonaparte during one of his campaigns. Winter too had its outdoor pleasures on good days, as she and Maurice sat warmly wrapped in furs while a trotting horse pulled their brightly painted sleigh through the magic of snow-covered forests. The world seemed a fine place to this child protected by wealth and loving parents.

Marie de Flavigny was still too young to understand the events of the time, but they were keenly noted by her father and history was moving on. French and German armies now moved across Europe in a seemingly endless state of tension punctuated by battles. Flavigny viewed the expanding power of the French Republic with dismay. Its success in 1804 would have seemed unbelievable a decade earlier, when it had been struggling merely to survive. Strangest of all was the fact that this once fanatical regime which had sent Louis XVI and Marie-Antoinette to the guillotine had been replaced by a virtual monarchy in which Bonaparte held the title of emperor. With disbelief, the nations of Europe read press accounts of the crowning of Bonaparte. His prestige in France was now so great that he had even convinced some republicans that the best way to prevent a return of the Bourbon kings was to create a new dynasty, on the principle that a system could not be fully destroyed until it had been replaced.

To the mortification of Frenchmen loyal to Louis XVI, Pope Pius VII had consented to take part in the ceremony, and was charmed by Napoleon when they met. The event had taken place with much pomp in the cathedral of Notre-Dame in December 1804, after a magnificent parade of cavalry had preceded the imperial coach on its way from the Louvre Palace under a pale blue winter sky. A large crowd observed Napoleon, who was very much at ease in a sumptuous costume of purple velvet and gold. His wife, Josephine, looked radiant in a white satin gown sparkling with diamonds, on her head a diadem of pearls and other gems. With a gesture representative of the manner in which he had achieved power, Napoleon had not allowed himself to be crowned by another but had taken the symbol of royalty in his own hands and placed it on his head. He then laid the crown of empress on the head of Josephine, in a scene recorded by the painter David. Night had fallen by the time they left the ancient edifice, and twenty thousand torchbearers accompanied the new monarchs to their palace. Along the route they were cheered by an immense crowd, while the royalists sat at home in despair.

An equal source of discomfort for Marie's father was Napoleon's continuing military success, despite some setbacks. In the year of his coronation he decided to conquer Britain, which had been saved from earlier invasions by the powerful British navy. He gathered a large army and a fleet of barges at Boulogne, while frantic efforts to prepare resistance were under way throughout southern England. He had been frustrated by the victory of the British fleet at Trafalgar, where Nelson had been killed by a sniper as he stood unprotected on the deck of his ship. When news came that the Austrians and Russians were once more advancing on him, Napoleon changed his plans and quickly marched east. Once more his military genius won him a rapid and resounding victory as he defeated the armies of both nations on a frozen landscape at Austerlitz, and Napoleon's soldiers had one more reason to believe that their leader was unbeatable on land.

So it must also have seemed to Marie's father, who knew that every new victory of the Usurper made the return of the old French kings less likely. Napoleon's continental power was plain to see in Frankfurt, as Flavigny now found himself living in the capital of a new confederal state which was a satellite of France. Called the Confederation of the Rhine, it had been created by a treaty signed in July 1806 by Napoleon and the rulers of no fewer than sixteen German states. The agreement was that the French emperor would keep an army within the boundaries of the confederation, which would be part of his protection against Austria and Prussia. This was a new blow to the Austrian empire, defeated yet again and stripped of several provinces. Next it was the turn of Prussia. The army which had been such a fearsome weapon of war under Frederick the Great was shattered at Jena in

October 1806. The rout of the badly led Prussians was so complete that the battle ended like a hunt, as remnants of the army desperately fled before the French cavalry. Flavigny must have noted, however, that not all Germans were displeased by the outcome, as some admired the new French regime for its progressive ideas, such as religious tolerance.

It is not surprising that Alexandre de Flavigny now considered returning to France with his family. By means of the Confederation of the Rhine, Napoleon's power seemed firmly established over a great territory extending from the North Sea to the Adriatic and far into central Europe. Not only was he emperor of a vast new France and king of Italy, but he had placed his brothers on the thrones of Holland and Spain, had made his brother-in-law, Joachim Murat, king of Naples, and had created new kingdoms in the German states of Bavaria, Würtemberg, Saxony, and Westphalia. His rise appeared almost miraculous, and had Flavigny not been a rationalist in the manner of the eighteenth century, he might have agreed with those who believed it had all been accomplished by the hand of God. They might as well live in France as in Frankfurt, he reflected; the French officers he had met could confirm that the country was stable and that Napoleon was favorably disposed toward the old nobility, wishing to attract able individuals into his armies and administration.

Although Marie's father would never compromise on his royalist principles, he did return to his native land in 1809, exactly two decades after the great Revolution which had shaken the world. The impact on French society had been profound, bringing the eclipse of the aristocracy and the rise of a new class made wealthy by speculation. Under Napoleon a new administrative and military elite had also been created, based on ability and not on birth. In spite of this, he had set up a nobility of his own, creating new princes, dukes, counts, and barons. Only a few years earlier, the term *aristocrat* had been an insult and a death sentence; now the wheel of fortune had turned full circle. Count Alexandre de Flavigny therefore decided the time had come to end his exile. He would pull up his roots for one last time and return to France with his wife, Maria, and his children, Maurice and Marie, then five and four, respectively.

There were practical reasons for the move, as the Flavigny name would be of more use to Maurice and Marie in France than in Germany. It is also probable that Madame de Flavigny readily agreed to a change which would put her out of range of her interfering mother. There was also the agreeable prospect of a town house in Paris and a country estate in some pleasant French province. She had the money, and her husband knew how to spend it with style.

CHAPTER 2

The Fall of Napoleon

T HE journey from Frankfurt to Paris was a major undertaking in
1809, even for the rich. The section from Mainz to the French capital alone took five days, despite the fact that the roads were well
maintained because of their military importance. For reasons of safety, a
speed limit was in force: coaches were allowed to bring their horses only
to a trot, not a gallop. An unexpected rut in the unpaved roads could easily
cause vehicles to overturn, with disastrous consequences for the passengers.
Travelers in France at this time had a choice of guidebooks providing information about major routes. These books, such as the recently published
three-volume *Itinéraire complet de l'empire français,* by Hyacinthe Langlois,
listed interesting monuments and landmarks such as hills, rivers, villages,
and factories. Most important, however, was the advice concerning inns
along the way, in particular the problems related to bedding. In addition
to checking that the sheets were dry and clean, it was recommended that
one protect against vermin by spreading a large square of leather, preferably
the skins of two stags sewn together, between the sheet and the mattress,
where the insects lurked. This barrier could also be improved by the judi-
cious use of camphor in the bed. But nothing could alter the fact that the
long hours of being shaken in a coach followed by unpleasant nights proved
tiresome and exhausting. Even worse, bands of armed robbers had not yet
disappeared from the countryside, in spite of increased patrols by mounted
gendarmes. Although travelers were advised to defend themselves with a
double-barreled pistol, many meekly handed over their money to robbers,
who were bound to be better armed and were often ruthless deserters.

Because of their wealth, the Flavignys were able to avoid the cramped discomfort of public stage coaches, traveling instead in their own two car-riages, one of which carried three servants. As they proceeded, they en-countered French soldiers, strong young men on their long march toward their military posts in the German states, and carts loaded with munitions and equipment for distant French armies. Like those traveling by coach, the Flavignys stopped every twenty or thirty kilometers to change horses at staging posts. The postmasters who supervised these stopovers made a good living from the hire of horses and enjoyed a high status, as shown by their tricorne hat and fine uniform with silver braid.

Marie's parents knew that it was important not to be caught in the dark—forests in particular were places to fear. The family reached the Meuse River without incident, however, and then crossed the gently un-dulating region of Champagne before arriving in Paris. There they rested temporarily in an apartment provided by friends of Möritz Bethmann.

Soon after, they looked for a suitable property in a green and pleas-ant area near Tours, in the Loire Valley, a region whose winters were mild compared to those of Frankfurt. It also appealed to Flavigny because it had remained a bastion of royalism (even though the movement was mostly in-active at that time). In addition, there was a feeling of safety in this region, which, unlike Frankfurt, was not a corridor for the armies of Napoleon marching across Germany. On 28 May 1810 an estate named Le Mortier, near the village of Monnaie, was purchased by Madame de Flavigny for two hundred thousand francs.[1] As their carriage left Paris and rolled west later that summer, Marie and Maurice saw the ancient cathedral of Chartres rising from the sea of wheat. After passing through the picturesque town of Vendôme, on a winding tributary of the Loire, they finally arrived at Le Mortier. A new life was to begin for these two city children.

Their large house had had a troubled history since the Revolution, hav-ing first been confiscated from its noble owners and then sold and resold five times to various speculators within less than twenty years. The building was finely proportioned, with tall chimneys and a slate roof. Dense woods framed the property, and some decorative birch trees stood at the front. It took the wealth of Marie's mother to pay for a proper renovation of the mansion, with its stables and barns. Like many country houses, it had a bakery, the vestige of recent times when lords of the manor had a legal monopoly on the local production of bread. The estate consisted of four farms which could be rented out or managed by the owner, but Flavigny was not eager to devote himself to work of this sort. He liked the estate because of its suitability for other activities that interested him. A hunter's paradise, the region was full of deer, wild boar, partridge, and hare.

Marie soon felt at home in Le Mortier as she and Maurice eagerly explored the big house fronted by lawns which sloped down to a stream. Country life was there to be discovered, and she was soon captivated. As an adult, she reflected that a childhood spent in a city which is a stage for significant historical events is a better intellectual stimulus for a young mind than one spent in the country, but at that moment she was content with a rural life which changed steadily with the seasons. This new existence was not without excitement. There were tales of wolves following evening travelers like shadows, though it was said they would not attack, and on winter mornings the fresh marks of their paws could be seen in the snow.

Alexandre de Flavigny fitted easily into the life of a country gentleman, roaming the woods on horseback with his gun and dog. After the evening meal, the family would eagerly read the paper for news of political and military events, attempting to detect the truth within a censored press. Marie's mother found this new life very quiet after Frankfurt but consoled herself with thoughts of visits to Paris and with the belief that their house would not be occupied by a passing army. (Time would prove her wrong.) She spent much of the winter season in the French capital, where she began to build up a circle of acquaintances, both for her personal pleasure and to prepare for the entry of Marie and her brother into high society. She well knew this was the route to fine careers and prestigious marriages.

For Marie, the next five years were a time of freedom and happiness. She sometimes played alone, and sometimes with the village children. Her aviary was filled with colorful local birds such as chaffinches and bullfinches, and every summer when the meadows were scythed, farmhands brought her abandoned partridge chicks which she tried to raise, without much success. On the other hand, a pair of rabbits, one white and one black, produced an endless family of piebald offspring. Her most unusual pets were two piglets of a wild boar, which were brought home by the gamekeeper. They were fed milk from a bottle, then put out to graze with the lambs under the eye of a shepherd girl, until they finally grew into fearsome creatures with great tusks. In the shady woods, Marie collected fascinating insects such as cater-pillars, which she brought home and kept in a box. Then, through a micro-scope, she and her father, who encouraged scientific exploration, would watch their transformation into butterflies. Marie later believed that this early experience with nature showed her that continual change is central to all existence, including the life of society.

From her childhood years in the country she would always remember seasonal activities like cutting the wheat, gathering the grapes, and giving gifts to the poor at harvest time. She experienced the great domestic event of the twice-yearly washing of clothes, for it was the custom in rich fami-lies to own enough linen for the operation to be done after long intervals. An army of local washerwomen would be employed, and the yard would resound with their chatter, mixed with the slapping sound of sticks beating the wet linen. She was fascinated by the mysterious activities of the char-coal burners, who worked deep in the winter woods while the wind sighed in the empty branches and the crows called overhead.

In Marie's remembrances of these childhood years, the name which re-curs most often is that of her father, the person she loved and admired above all others. Round him her idealized memories would later form like crys-tals. Now in his early forties, he had a youthful air, in spite of his prematurely white hair. He had retained his military bearing, tempered by the graceful manner of one who had lived at court, and his blue eyes and his smile had not lost their warmth and charm. Sensitive to physical appearances, Marie never tired of looking at her father and was filled with pleasure when any-one commented on their likeness. One notes that in years to come her great love, Franz Liszt, would also be tall with fair hair and blue eyes.

Marie's involvement in nature continued despite the coming of winter. She once created a miniature garden on a bed of clay, using twigs and pebbles to form tiny forests and mountains. Shells brought from Martinique by a neighbor became deep caves lined with moss, and a piece of broken mirror mimicked a lake. Her father, who sometimes participated in his daughter's activities, cut little farmhouses out of cork and carefully painted them. They placed a fisherman's hut by the lake and a château lit internally by candles on high ground, as this imaginary land faithfully represented the class divisions of real society. The additions went on for weeks, and in later life Marie would recall this happy episode with her father.

Life in the mansion was not a matter of games alone, for her formal education had to be considered. Moreover, there were two languages to be maintained and two cultures to discover. Marie was still fluent in German, which she spoke with her mother and a nursemaid brought from Frankfurt. The household staff also included a German footman dressed in the Viennese manner, with a feather in his cap and a cutlass in his belt, and an an Austrian cook, Adelheid, a genius in the art of pastry. Breaking all the rules, she would give cakes to Marie between meals, thereby winning the gratitude of the little girl and her friends. Marie read in German the fables of Christian Gellert, which had charmed generations of children, and she had learned to play simple pieces by Haydn and Mozart on a piano made in Vienna.

The German influence on Marie was strong in these early years, and in time she would immerse herself in the works of Goethe. With her fair hair and dreamy blue eyes, she looked the part of a Germanic maiden. Her father, on the other hand, had no inclination for music or wistful northern sentiment. Life in Frankfurt had not made him receptive to the culture of Germany. His ironic attitude toward it was typical of a generation of French who were still convinced of their nation's cultural superiority. His favorite authors were Rabelais, La Fontaine, and the witty Voltaire. He also loved the great tales of ancient Greece and recounted them to Marie so often that she knew more about the adventures of Hercules and Persephone than she did about Christian mythology. She later reflected on the difference between the easy skepticism and tolerance of her parents and the Catholicism which would again become such a strong feature of French life in the early nineteenth century.

At this point in her life, an unfortunate event occurred associated with the name Minerva, the goddess of wisdom. At about the age of nine, Marie began growing so fast that she developed a stoop and adopted a posture unsuitable for a young lady in high society. Her neck seemed almost too long, as if weighed down by the mass of hair on her head. No doubt the proper cure would have been exercise, but in deference to contemporary theory Marie was made to wear a contraption known as a Minerva. It was a velvet-covered metal frame with a long shaft which extended up the back, followed the curve of the head, and extended down to the chin. It would surely make Marie acquire the habit of holding her head in a regal manner, reasoned her mother.

Strangely, she soon grew accustomed to the apparatus, later claiming that this was an indication of her docile nature. It was certainly proof of the persuasive skill of her parents, who had convinced her that the contrast of black velvet and fair hair was highly attractive. Her liberation came unexpectedly one day when her mother was playing waltzes on the piano. Dancing to the music on a polished floor, Marie slipped and fell into the fireplace. Fortunately it was empty except for the andirons, one of which gave her a deep cut on the right cheek. The scar remained with her for the rest of her life, which explains why her portraits always show her left profile. She was never again asked to wear the Minerva and promised herself that if one day she had a daughter she would not restrict her freedom by using such artificial devices.

The year that Marie and her family settled in France had been one of apparent prosperity for the regime of Napoleon, but there were still storm clouds on the horizon. A new alliance with Britain had given Austria the confidence to make one more attempt to overthrow him, and in April it invaded Bavaria. Napoleon quickly marched into Austria, where he had the impertinence to take up residence in the royal palace of Schönbrunn, hurriedly abandoned by its rightful occupants. In late May reports reached France that the invincible commander had been beaten at Essling, even that he had been captured. The rumors spread quickly, causing consternation among the supporters of the regime and bringing sudden hope to royalists. Then in July details reached Paris of the greatest battle recorded in military history. Three hundred thousand men had fought at a place called Wagram. The French and their allies from the Confederation of the Rhine had surprised the Austrians by rapidly crossing the Danube under cover of darkness. When the summer sun rose on the massed regiments, the cavalry were an impressive sight as they galloped through fields of tall wheat, their swords flashing. Napoleon himself had marched on foot with his legendary regiment of guards, and his soldiers had once again shown themselves ready to die for their charismatic leader. The victory he won that day was memorable, but it was costly, and he would never know another one like it.

As the years went by, Marie's parents continued to observe the evolving situation in France. In Paris there reigned a feverish atmosphere peculiar to those extraordinary times. Those who benefited from the regime were living life to the full while they waited and hoped for favorable events.[2] The latest victory at Wagram seemed to be a final consolidation of Napoleon's power, as he again imposed financial and territorial penalties on Austria. Then came the astonishing news of a marriage between the French emperor and an Austrian princess. This meant that two states which had fought each other with such determination would now be allied. Nothing could have been worse for the political hopes of the royalists than this acceptance of the Usurper by Europe's oldest monarchy, and Marie's family seemed ever more doomed to a life of social exclusion and quiet mediocrity.

To make matters worse, the unlikely marriage between Napoleon and Marie-Louise had quickly produced a son. This opened up the prospect of a new dynasty which might sit on the throne of France for generations. Napoleon soon became attached to his young wife, who was of average looks and intelligence but affectionate and sensual. To please this princess from an ancient royal family, he again made efforts to entice members of the old French aristocracy into his court. The wedding celebrations had been impressive, and an enthusiastic crowd had greeted the emperor and his bride when they appeared on the balcony of the Tuileries Palace. This was the high noon for Napoleon's empire, and Paris had never seen so many crowned heads together at one time. The royalists watched sardonically as the members of the new aristocracy with their diamonds and finery threw themselves into a life of pleasure and display. It was as if they felt their good fortune could not last, being doomed to end suddenly on some battlefield.

Superficially there seemed to be less probability than ever of a change of regime, but Marie's father waited and hoped. Although Napoleon was powerful, hidden opposition still existed within France. The continuation of hostilities brought hardship to all regions, even to the Loire, which was far from the fields of battle. Public opinion was repressed and manipulated by Napoleonic propaganda, but the more thoughtful members of the nation

felt growing alarm as France continued to be at war with so many countries. The only real allies of Napoleon were small states like Bavaria and
Saxony and other members of the Confederation of the Rhine who saw
France as a protection against the ambitions of Prussia and Austria. On the
other hand even Napoleon's opponents admitted that he had imposed discipline on France after years of political and financial mayhem. In the army
and the administration his regime promoted individuals of merit from all
sections of society. Class animosity had decreased, and the old aristocracy
was less hated by the peasantry, which had been freed from its former tax
burden and obligatory work on estates. Napoleon still wanted able officers
for his armies, and more than once Flavigny was approached to take up the
sword again and put on the uniform of the empire, with the promise of high
rank and rich rewards.

Marie's father continued to refuse, but his patriotic feelings must have
been aroused as he saw the growing stresses of war around him. Military
service was a recent invention and was deeply resented by the farming community, a sentiment that was not surprising given that most soldiers were
recruited from the country because city dwellers were rarely strong enough
for long marches and other hardships. Military service now lasted five years
and would be extended to seven as French defeats began. The countryside
soon got used to the sight of flying columns of soldiers looking for deserters. These columns were so numerous in some regions, especially the west,
that bands formed, and many a peasant family hid a son in a barn or in
the woods or sent him away under a false name in the hope of saving him
from the army. To make up for the absent farm workers, German prisoners
of war were sent to France, where they could be seen trudging along the
road, often without a guard. Marie's future friend George Sand would one
day recall how as a child she was touched by the sight of thirsty prisoners
and gave them food and drink to help them on their way.[3] Some of these
exiles came to like their new home and even married into the families of
the French farmers on whose land they came to work. Like some protesters
of our time, they wanted to make love, not war.

During these events the Flavigny family continued to lead a quiet life,
enjoying social contact with royalist neighbors in Paris and near their country home. They observed the great bread shortage which followed the bad

harvest of 1811, when July thunderstorms had reduced the crops in their region. Eager to maintain peace in the capital, Napoleon had done everything to maintain the supply there, but this had made things worse in some provincial towns and in March 1812 a bread riot took place in Caen. Growing signs of discontent could be seen, and people again began to ask themselves what political change might come. Public opinion had been much affected by the massive conscription of soldiers in 1812. There was ominous news that they were to march to Russia, though little was known about the potential dangers of the vast country or its climate. Even Napoleon's opponents believed that he would win another victory, but at what cost? A few months later it became clear, despite the evasions in official reports, that a major disaster had hit the army. The truth was revealed by the few survivors who struggled home from the frozen plains of Russia.

There were now too many empty places at the fireside, and a growing section of the nation felt a great weariness. With each passing year, fewer people believed that Napoleon was safe on his throne. Soon it would be apparent that the battlefields had reached French soil, though the press still proclaimed that the empire was invincible. The nation began to fear plunder and rape as news came that the armies of Prussia, Austria, and Russia were advancing on Paris from the east and the north. The generals of the invading forces did not want to alienate the civilian population of the provinces affected, but the Russians and Austrians had little control over some units of irregular troops like the Croats and the Cossacks, whose only pay was what they could take by force. The mounted Cossacks caused most fear, because they could thread their way through woods, swim across rivers, and appear without warning in a village, which they would then plunder.

Quickly the suffering provinces were laid waste by the armies of France and those of invaders. Driven to desperation by exhausting marches through roads blocked by snow or trodden into mud, the soldiers of all nations became pitiless in their treatment of the population. Villagers fled to the woods with what few possessions they could carry and often found their homes burned when they returned. Some enraged civilians retaliated by killing sick or wounded soldiers separated from their units, an action that brought violent reprisals. The horror of the situation was increased by the packs of wolves which came out of the woods to eat the bodies of men and livestock. The French were now feeling the hardships which their own armies had inflicted on the rest of Europe.

Marie's family remained in the relative safety of their country home and congratulated themselves for having chosen one far from the eastern frontier. Had they remained in the capital, they could have witnessed the precipitate departure of the empress Marie-Louise: on the morning of 29 March 1814, bystanders watched in silence as the young woman in a brown riding costume got into a coach with her infant son and rode off accompanied by a cavalry escort to protect her from roving bands of Cossacks. At the same time most of the civil authorities left the capital, carrying police files and the crown jewels. Napoleon was in the country trying to increase his forces, some of which were surrounded and besieged. Secret orders were sent to commanders by means of trusty agents who hid them ingeniously in the sheath of knives or in the collar of dogs, but it was to no avail.

A few days later a battle between unequal forces took place just outside Paris. The defense did not last long against the superior numbers of the Prussians and the Russians, and the city saved itself from destruction by a timely surrender once the attackers had taken the heights of Montmartre. That night the inhabitants of Paris saw the surrounding countryside covered by thousands of watch fires lit by the victors, and for the first time they could measure the power of the armies sent against them. In recent months the official newspaper Le Moniteur had been highly economical with the truth, and on the day of the attack, it chose to provide an account of events in ancient Troy. The true situation could not be kept from the country for long, however, and reports of the fall of the capital soon spread to the provinces. When the news reached Marie's father, he celebrated the event by telling the gardener to plant white lilies. This flower was the symbol of the old French monarchy, which was presumably now to be restored after two decades of unprecedented events.

In reality this outcome could not yet be anticipated with certainty, since the majority of the nation was indifferent toward the deposed royal family and longed for peace under any regime. Flavigny's friends in Paris did their best to influence public opinion by appearing on horseback in the garden in front of the Tuileries Palace and distributing white cockades to an expectant crowd of royalists. They soon ran out of these emblems, but their wives were applauded when they began to make more by tearing pieces of white silk from their dresses.[4] The writer Chateaubriand rushed to a printer with a pamphlet which for a time had been hidden in his wife's bosom for safety. In it he scornfully attacked Buonaparte, using the Corsican form of Napoleon's name, and proclaimed that the return of the old royal family would bring peace and prosperity.

The true state of public opinion was revealed when a large crowd actually applauded the emperor of Russia and the king of Prussia as they paraded through the city at the head of fifty thousand men preceded by military bands. The allied forces were a splendid sight as they marched past with their artillery, cavalry of every description, and a forest of bayonets. That evening the Cossacks of the Imperial Guard lit their campfires in the gardens of Paris as the soldiers of Napoleon had done in Moscow. It was soon learned that Napoleon would be sent to the island of Elba, where he could cause no more trouble.

The monarch who now reigned over Marie de Flavigny was a large old man who took the title of Louis XVIII. The new king was an intelligent individual who had learned moderation and patience in his years of exile and humiliation, but many of his noble supporters were now eager to recover their confiscated estates and the privileges of former times. Unlike Marie's father, whose financial position was secure and who did not care for status, they expected to be given highly paid positions in the administration and in the army as a reward for their fidelity. The demands of this dispossessed class quickly aroused fear and resentment throughout the administration, and the scarred veterans of the army which had dominated Europe looked with particular contempt on these aristocrats with their antiquated titles and ceremonial manners.

Only a few months after the restoration of the monarchy, Louis XVIII made the crucial error of allowing discontent within the army to reach a level at which it began to threaten his regime. Soldiers and officers feared dismissal and openly expressed nostalgia for the empire, when the military had formed a rich and privileged caste; the working class also supported Napoleon because of the high employment during his regime. Soon a conspiracy for his return developed in military circles in every city, especially

Paris. During their stays in the capital Marie's family could hear the chanting of organized groups demanding food and jobs in front of the royal palace.

One center of protest was the Café Montansier, where glasses were raised to Napoleon and popular enthusiasm was encouraged by songs hinting at events to come. The disaffection of the working class was also shown by its animosity to the Catholic clergy, many of whom had been behaving provocatively since the change of regime. The intensity of anticlerical feeling was demonstrated during a violent incident sparked by the death of the actress Françoise Raucourt on 15 January 1815. Members of the acting profession were theoretically excommunicated because of the alleged immorality of the theater, but the rule had rarely been applied. When the priest in charge of the church of Saint Roch refused to provide a funeral service for this popular performer, an angry crowd broke down the doors and threatened to conduct its own ceremony. News of the commotion reached the royal palace, and Louis intervened at once by sending his own chaplain to say mass for the deceased actress. The harm had been done, however, and the incident was an ominous reminder of the power of the Paris mob.

Eventually a coup was planned for early 1815, the conspirators being known to one another by a violet worn in the buttonhole. Napoleon was given the code name Corporal Violet. Although he remained in Elba during these months, he was in touch with the conspiracy and awaited his chance. On the night of 25 February 1815 Napoleon decided to make his move. That evening, to prevent suspicion, his sister Pauline gave a ball in his small palace, and later that night his officers were summoned from their sleep and told to prepare for an instant departure. They sailed to France on a little brig called the *Inconstant* and landed in Cannes. It was the beginning of a remarkable episode in Napoleon's life which would forever be known as the Hundred Days, a period which would be Marie's earliest memory of a great political event.

One day in March of that year, nine-year-old Marie was with her family in Paris and noticed worried faces, unusual activity in the house, and urgent whispered conversations between her father and men she had never seen before. Their traveling coach was being prepared and its trunks brought into the house, where the maid quickly packed them full of clothes. Everything was done in a serious and secretive manner, and Marie did not dare ask for an explanation. Next day Flavigny was not present at dinner, and nobody would say where he had gone. His daughter went to hide in her room, where she anxiously cried.

After dark that evening there was a jingle of harness in the yard, and a man came to say that the horses were ready. The maid wrapped the child in a fur-lined coat and brought her down to the coach, where she was placed between her mother and her brother. The coachman cracked his whip and they set off into the night. Only then was she told that they were going to the home of her maternal grandmother in Frankfurt. What her mother did not explain was that they were escaping from a country which was apparently sliding toward civil war because Napoleon had gathered an army and was marching on Paris while royalist opposition was hurriedly being planned. In spite of this reticence Marie sensed the gravity of the situation from her father's disappearance and their own precipitate departure. On the evening of the seventh day they came to the end of their tiring journey, during which they had slept in an inn only three times. When she climbed the staircase of the old house in Frankfurt, she was embraced by a crowd of unknown aunts and cousins excitedly talking German, but she had tears in her eyes as she thought of her home in the French countryside and of her absent father.

When Napoleon landed at Cannes, he had found fewer than a thousand men awaiting him. Undeterred by the weakness of this meager battalion he began to march through the Alps toward Paris. In a mountain valley near Grenoble he found the road barred by a greatly superior force of soldiers under the white banner of the king. Halting his own column, Napoleon acted with his old daring and theatrical skill by advancing alone toward the rows of loaded muskets. He stopped and looked the soldiers in the eye. After a pause he said: "If any man among you wishes to kill his Emperor, let him do it now." The troops could not resist this dramatic appeal, and throwing down their arms they crowded around him. As he proceeded toward Paris other regiments mutinied and joined him, and soon he was back in the Tuileries Palace from which old Louis had fled in the middle of the night of 20 March 1815. To the delight of the soldiery the white flag of the king was promptly taken from the palace roof and replaced by the tricolor.

A renewal of hostilities was certain, and the allied monarchies of Europe now swore they would depose Napoleon permanently and reinstate Louis XVIII. A rising of French royalists in the western provinces was planned, involving Marie's father. While their supposedly secret preparations were taking place, Flavigny was astonished to be summoned by Joseph Fouché, Napoleon's powerful and unprincipled chief of police. Fouché revealed that he knew every detail of the planned rising. He claimed that he had not acted against it because he believed the newly installed regime of Napoleon was bound to fall once the allies resumed hostilities. He asked Flavigny to carry an important message to the conspirators, telling them to call off a rising which had no chance of success unless it coincided with an invasion. Flavigny accomplished his mission but failed to restrain more than a few of his courageous and imprudent companions. An insurrection therefore took place in the Vendée province in the middle of May. It was quickly put down by the imperial army, and many lives were lost, including that of the leader, Louis de La Rochejaquelein. The royalist cause might have benefited by waiting just one month, but the failed rising did have the effect of keeping an army of twenty-five thousand men in the region at a time when the emperor needed them on his frontier. Marie's father had now played his last role in historic events. In June 1815 the final scene of the drama was acted out with courage and desperation when Napoleon's legendary army was defeated on the low hills near a village called Waterloo.

CHAPTER 3

The Ways of the World

During the political and military events of the spring and summer of 1815, Marie and her brother were again making contact with their family in Frankfurt. Meanwhile their house in France became the temporary quarters of a company of Prussian soldiers. These uninvited guests, part of the army that occupied France after the battle of Waterloo, were sleeping in their beds, eating their food, drinking their wine, and playing on the piano brought from Vienna. Life in Frankfurt was more normal, and Marie, now an intelligent girl of ten, was observing the character of her German relatives. One member of the Bethmann family, Katharina Bethmann, Marie's maternal grandmother, impressed herself on Marie in a way she would never forget. A tall and heavily built lady in her seventies, she had the manner of a person who expected instant submission and obedience. A failed operation to remove cataracts had left her blind, and her eyes had the cold impassivity of an antique statue. She wore old lace and pearls, and from her neck hung a miniature portrait of her dead husband, Johann, in a medallion studded with large diamonds. She did not trouble to hide from her five daughters that her son was her favorite child. Only Möritz could bring a smile to her face; she could even recognize the sound of his feet on the thick Turkish carpet as he approached. Marie took an instant dislike to this cold matriarch who treated her offspring so unequally and in later life viewed her as an example of what a mother should not be.

It was easy to like Möritz Bethmann. Then in his forties, he was at the zenith of his personal and professional prestige throughout the German states. The wars in Europe had continued to serve him well, and many sovereigns had used his bank to raise the large sums of money needed for their armies. When peace came in 1815, the Austrian emperor had rewarded him with an aristocratic title. The czar of Russia had honored the banker by being godfather to one of his sons. Although Möritz remained in the family home in the Buchgasse, he lived like a prince. The luxuriously furnished interior of the old wooden house saw famous generals, high diplomats, and even reigning sovereigns. Möritz took pleasure in giving dinner parties and receptions at which the guests ate pheasants from his mother's estate in Bohemia and drank the finest wines of the Rhineland. These social events were graced by his beautiful Dutch wife, Louise Boode, whom he had married for love despite some opposition from his mother.

Möritz was a patron of the arts and enjoyed the company of writers, musicians and painters. In the gardens recently created on the former glacis of the city's fortifications he had erected a small museum in the form of a Greek temple to house his collection of antique statues. He gave literary evenings in which new books were read and discussed. Bettina Brentano, in a letter to Goethe, gives an amusing account of one of these soirées, complaining about a session devoted to the novel *Delphine,* by Madame de Staël.[1] The irreverent Bettina also recorded a memorable encounter between Madame de Staël and Goethe's mother. The former had made a theatrical entrance, holding a laurel branch and dressed in the orange silk costume of Corinne, the heroine of her Italian novel. Frau Goethe was costumed in an equally dramatic manner. On her head were three ostrich feathers; in one hand she held a large fan sparkling with diamonds, and in the other, a gold snuff box decorated with a portrait of Goethe in pensive mood.

Marie admired Möritz Bethmann for his patronage of the arts and took special pleasure in the concerts of the soprano Angelica Catalani. No talented musician, writer, or artist visited Frankfurt without being invited to the old house in the Buchgasse, and it was partly due to the example of Möritz that Marie would one day play a similar role in her Parisian home. From him she learned that wealth was not much in itself, but a means to an end. She also admired her uncle for his extroverted personality, which differed from her own quiet nature. He was vivacious and sociable, devoid of malice, at ease with people from every class, and popular among the people of Frankfurt as a generous provider of employment. With his charming manner and refined hedonism, Möritz Bethmann was a personification of the social ideal of the late eighteenth century.

Marie and her brother did not have such easy relations with the other members of the family, however, and felt themselves to be outsiders, despite the efforts of their aunts and cousins. Old Frau Bethmann had never forgiven her daughter for marrying Flavigny, though they had lived together happily for twenty years. Marie could speak German well, but her French accent was a source of amusement to her cousins. In addition, she did not know how to knit, a traditional female activity, and detested the obligatory sessions in her grandmother's drawing room after meals when the other girls were busy with their needles. During this ritual, she sat with empty hands and listened to the conversation. One day after dinner she was humiliated by her grandmother during a discussion about the price of game. They had just dined on hare, and the old lady asked Marie how much it would have cost in Paris. Marie knew more about hunting hares than about buying them, and when Frau Bethmann insisted on an answer, the preposterous price she suggested brought an outburst of laughter. Marie remembered the incident and vowed never to be sarcastic to her own children if she had any.

Religion was the most serious source of tension between her parents and her grandmother. Marie's mother had been brought up as a Lutheran but had been easygoing in her attitude to such matters. Her father was nominally a Catholic but shared the freethinking skepticism of much of the French aristocracy of his time. In their mixed marriage they had followed the usual Frankfurt compromise, which was to bring up boys in the religion of their father and girls in that of their mother. Marie had therefore been baptized in a Lutheran church, with Frau Bethmann herself as godmother. After their move to France the situation had been discussed with Flavigny's mother, Sophie, who had been widowed and remarried as Madame Lenoir. This practical lady, who had no interest in doctrine or theology and was concerned only with considerations of social advantage, pointed out that the future choice of a husband would be limited if Marie did not conform. It was simply not politic to be a Protestant in a country that was mostly Catholic. The change of religion was discussed with Möritz during one of his visits to Paris, and he had agreed that it seemed wise. Nothing was said to Frau Bethmann in the hope she would not find out.

The moment of truth could not be avoided now that fate had brought them back to Frankfurt. Frau Bethmann had waited until she found Marie alone one day and bluntly asked her if she had become a Catholic. When the young girl mumbled an evasive answer, the old lady sternly asserted that she hated Catholics. Sensing that this was an attack on her father, Marie felt even more dislike for the bigoted matriarch. The incident caused much friction between Marie's mother and grandmother, and all the diplomatic skill of Möritz was needed to make peace. Shortly after this event, Marie was placed in a boarding school in order to defuse the situation. This radical change in her life came as a welcome deliverance from persecution. At Christmas her grandmother gave her a peace offering in the form of a rich cloak of crimson velvet and fur, but she disliked the showy garment and wore it as little as possible. Although her relationship with Frau Bethmann had been ruined, the episode introduced her to the harsh reality of religious bigotry. Her future tolerance owes something to this early experience in the old house in Frankfurt.

The boarding-school experience was considered a useful stage in the process of growing up, and Marie's stay in Herr Engelmann's school was to last for most of the 1815–16 school year. It provided her first experience away from her mother and a taste of independence. Adaptation to her new life was made easy by the company of Catherine Boode, who was the younger sister of Möritz's wife. Catherine, a charming and flirtatious fourteen-year-old, was certainly not the most suitable companion for a girl as young as Marie. When they went for Sunday rides in an open coach, she noticed that Catherine not only attracted the attention of all the young men but gave them every encouragement. Marie was further intrigued by a minor drama in the school that had left one of the girls in tears and had led to the dismissal of a young male teacher. The older pupils were discussing the affair in excited whispers, and when Marie asked Catherine for an explanation, she talked mysteriously about a secret romance. This explanation did not fully clarify the situation, but it gave her a premonition of the power and the danger of love.

Marie's stay in Frankfurt was made even more memorable by a meeting with Goethe, who was then sixty-five and at the height of his fame as Germany's leading writer. He would be one of the great intellectual influences

of her life. She was already aware of his celebrity and his friendly contacts
with the Bethmann family. The encounter took place one Sunday afternoon
in September 1815 when she was in the garden of the Bethmann country
house with her cousins. Coming toward them was a distinguished man accompanied by all the adults of the family, much like an honor guard. "This
is my little Flavigny niece," said Möritz to Goethe. The writer smiled at her,
took her hand, and as they walked together said something to her that she
did not understand. He sat on a bench and kept her at his side while he continued talking to the adults. Eventually she looked up at his face. Goethe
then turned his large and fascinating eyes on her, leaving her spellbound.
When he was about to leave, he placed his hand on her head in a symbolic
gesture like a blessing. For the first time she felt herself in the presence of
greatness.

When Marie returned to France with Maurice and her mother in the
summer of 1816, the country was still feeling the shock waves of the recent change of regime. Only a minority of the French considered the battle
of Waterloo as a national defeat, and in some towns the invading Prussian army had been welcomed by a brass band and a parade of the National
Guard. Few were concerned about the fate of the emperor, who was on his
way to captivity on the distant island of Saint Helena, where he could stir
up no more trouble. The throne was once more occupied by the moderate
Louis XVIII, and the majority of the nation accepted his rule with relief,
although some groups of royalists were still determined to take vengeance
against the Bonapartists. Northern towns contented themselves with burning portraits of Napoleon and removing his supporters from the administration, but the south experienced an outburst of violence that history would
record as the White Terror. In the town of Avignon one of the emperor's
leading generals was murdered in the street — a scene in which the authorities dared not intervene. Not content with murder, the mob later broke
open the victim's coffin and threw his body into the Rhône.[2] An even more
sinister development took place in the region of Nîmes, where old hatreds
reappeared in the form of a massacre of Protestants. Marie would one day
meet a brave soldier called Auguste de Lagarde, who was one of the few
heroes in this dark episode in French history.

In Marie's own social milieu, this fanaticism caused no more than mild regret and was compared with what the aristocracy had suffered during the Revolution. Many members of her class, still believing that the restored monarchy owed them a privileged place in society, confidently expected to be offered high positions in the administration, the army, or the church as a reward for their loyalty to the king. Some, like Flavigny, had known the brilliant court life of Versailles before the Revolution, but years of exile had changed them and they now preferred life on the estate. Residency in other countries had enabled them to observe aristocrats who took an interest in agriculture without being considered unfashionable. Politically, it was believed that regular life in the local community would create closer links between the great landowners and the ordinary people and thereby prevent a recurrence of the dangerous resentments of the past. So it was that Marie's reunited family settled down again in their home near Monnaie, determined to enjoy the pleasures of château life after the upheavals of 1815.

The next two years were to be among the best in Marie's life, and she was glad to be far from the dark shadow of Frau Bethmann. At this stage, her education was being conducted by her father, and it was Maurice who was in boarding school. She worked contentedly by a window overlooking the garden and enjoyed these lessons given without pedantry or scolding. Like many other landowners of his class, Flavigny spent much time roaming his estate on horseback, accompanied by a favorite dog, and stopping to talk to the workers. His daughter's greatest wish was to win his praise when she had worked well and to be taken hunting as a reward. She relished setting off alone together in the misty woods on winter days. They took just two dogs, one to raise the bird and one to retrieve it from the bushes when Flavigny's aim was good. The second, a golden spaniel called My-lord, would first bring the partridge to his master and then place it gently in Marie's hands. On summer evenings they sometimes walked along the banks of a stream lined by alders and netted little crayfish, which Adelheid would serve up bright red at dinner. In autumn a young peddler wandered by with a great bag of treasures on his back, which were revealed as Marie watched excitedly. She eagerly bought ribbons and trinkets for herself and penknives for the children on the farm.

In the woods she had a touching encounter with a wild dog who a year earlier had been abandoned by its mother, named Diane. The departure of the handsome pointer had coincided with the occupation of the house by Prussian officers, which the family interpreted as a patriotic act of protest. It was known that Diane had had a litter of puppies somewhere in the thickets and eventually died of starvation. One day as Marie walked through the wood, she saw a thin dog emerge from the vegetation and watch her with hungry eyes. The unfortunate animal bore a distinct resemblance to Diane. Marie threw the dog some food, which it carried off with haste. Although she was forbidden to go into the woods alone, she returned the next day and quietly called the animal by its mother's name. Soon the dog appeared, and this time it came a little closer and ate the food in Marie's presence. Gradually she tamed the creature, and little by little it began to follow her home. One day she enticed it as far as the gate, though it would never enter the yard. Marie, who had grown attached to the animal, eventually told her parents about it. Having known only the wild, Diane could never be made into a pet. She was not much to look at, but she loved Marie and belonged to her alone. In later years she saw the episode as a sign of her need for an exclusive and perfect love.

By the age of ten, Marie was considered old enough to hear the conversations of her father's friends. These men who had been young before the Revolution had retained the charm and gaiety reminiscent of the old salons, and their years of exile all over Europe had provided them many an interesting story. In truth these old soldiers who met in the Flavigny home were more notable for their military courage and loyalty than for the sophistication of their political judgment. Remarkably, they had learned little from the Revolution and still believed that France needed a monarch with absolute power and an aristocracy respected by a devoted population. They considered the king himself to be a weak liberal. These grumbling sessions of old comrades were made even more agreeable by hunting parties in the woods followed by games of whist. Marie was thrilled by their accounts of battles in which loyal peasants had fought to the death for their religion and their king. When she met young Louis and Félicie de Suzannet, whose father had been killed, she was full of enthusiasm for these noble victims of fidelity. Ironically, her own political opinions in adult life would be very different from those inculcated by her father and his conservative friends. These happy evenings around the fire in the candlelit room often ended with a piano performance by Marie.

Although Flavigny was skeptical of religion and an admirer of Voltaire, he began to encourage his family to attend mass, at least in summer. The idea that the Catholic Church was a natural political ally had begun to penetrate the aristocracy. A newly forged alliance between nobles and priests might revive old attitudes of obedience and faith among the lower orders. Flavigny and his wife therefore started to show themselves regularly in the village church, though they sometimes complained audibly about the length of the service. Far from being bored, Marie enjoyed the music, the theatricality of ritual, and the play of sunlight through the biblically inspired stained glass windows. Since her brush with Frau Bethmann, she had felt herself to be a Catholic, though her only article of faith was a wish to be like her father and unlike her German grandmother. It was clear that the time had come for more-advanced theological instruction.

This task was assumed by her French grandmother, for whom she had much affection and admiration. Madame Lenoir had been born Sophie Hu-guenin, a middle-class girl who had made a love match with Flavigny's father and had been assimilated into the aristocracy. Family portraits showed her to have been beautiful, with the playfulness and easy grace characteristic of French women before the Revolution. In her old age she retained not only her vitality and quickness of mind but the tact and refined manners she had acquired in aristocratic circles. Although she had little formal educa-tion, her conversation sparkled with her native wit. Unlike Marie, she was not a dreamy idealist but a somewhat skeptical individual, though this did not prevent her from remarrying after the death of her husband and again finding happiness in love.

Madame Lenoir continued to be an enthusiastic supporter of the plan to have Marie confirmed as a Catholic. As a Parisian, she had not failed to observe that the royal family was setting a religious example and expect-ing the social elite to conform. To her mind, Marie's formal acceptance by the Church was not so much an end in itself as a necessary rite of passage before she could think of being introduced into the royal court, for this was the real ambition of Madame Lenoir. Marie therefore went to live with her in Paris in the winter of 1816–17, during which time preparations for her confirmation were set in motion. The episode began with an outburst from Madame Lenoir when a series of priests ruled that Marie's Lutheran baptism was not valid.

Now began an epic struggle between Madame Lenoir and the representatives of the archbishop of Paris. When she resolutely refused to have Marie baptized again, as if she were a heathen, the archbishop gave in, lest the Church alienate this determined member of a respectable family. The next stage, that of teaching the young girl the catechism, presented no theological or intellectual problems. In fact it proved to be the easiest part of the process, for the old priest had her do no more than learn it by heart, without any endeavor to arouse her interest or increase her understanding. The only part of the instruction she later recalled was a veiled allusion to sexual modesty, which he enigmatically declared to be like a mirror that can be sullied by hot breath. Marie was too innocent to know about hot breath but was intrigued by the metaphor. She did not dare ask for an explanation.

During the winter months in Paris she also received instruction in the social graces—an element of her education lacking as she roamed the estate with the country children. Dancing lessons, an essential for girls of her class, were to be given by the fashionable Monsieur Abraham. An austere and ceremonious little man, Abraham arrived at the homes of his pupils in a carriage as if dressed for a ball, and his every movement was performed elegantly, as if he were on stage. Much of his prestige was due to the fact that he had been employed by the court at the time of Marie-Antoinette. He regularly told his pupils how he had given the young queen lessons in order to correct the errors she had learned from her former instructors in Vienna. He claimed to be the only person in Paris who taught the minuet properly. As he played the tunes on a little violin, his fingers sparkled with large diamonds, each one of which had been the gift of some princess. From his powdered wig and lace ruffle to his black silk stockings and gold shoe buckles, everything about him reflected an elegant era long past. Despite his age he still danced with youthful ease. Marie felt an instinctive dislike for these artificial graces and sometimes invented a pain in her foot in order to miss the lesson.

One enjoyable part of her education was fencing, a martial art that was taught to some girls in the aristocracy because it was considered good for posture and therefore a suitable preparation for life at court. It is significant that Flavigny's daughter liked the combative element in fencing, and she expressed regret when it later fell out of fashion. In adult life she believed that the protective and sedentary education given to most girls tended to produce excessively delicate and emotional young women.

Marie was now attending a progressive day school run by an old priest named Edouard Gaultier, a cheerful and kindly man who spoke with a wavering voice. He had spent years of exile in England as a refugee from the Revolution and had brought back a new sort of teaching known as the Lancaster method.[3] Given its main principle — that learning was more effective if it was enjoyable — the teachers in his school were carefully chosen for their youth and charm. An unusual feature of the institution was that it was coeducational. Marie enjoyed the presence of both sexes, a system that was traditionally deemed inappropriate in France but that seemed to prevent the crudity found in boys' schools and the excessive competition found in those for girls. The pupils were taught Latin as if it were a living language, as well as French, history, geography, and mathematics. There was much use of rhyme to facilitate memory. Grammar was taught using a system of colored pencils, so that parts of a sentence could be coded: the subject in red, the verb in blue, and so on. Marie frequently won book prizes for her work and derived satisfaction from these symbolic trophies. She loved to be praised by Monsieur Gaultier, and her success in his school confirmed that Flavigny had not been wasting his time giving her lessons in the country.

An eccentric old man named Herr Vogel significantly influenced her intellectual development at this time through his history lessons, given in German. Like Monsieur Abraham, he wore the attire of the previous century, complete with powdered wig, knee breeches, and buckled shoes. From her window she could see him hopping over puddles in the street and sometimes reciting Latin verse by Virgil as he went along. Ancient history as taught by Herr Vogel gave a more sophisticated version of events than the traditional Catholic one offered by Monsieur Gaultier. It considered the birth and decline of civilizations and stressed the constant process of change, which she would one day acknowledge in her own historical writing. Although the lessons with Herr Vogel were dull, they improved her command of German, which she now wrote as well as she spoke.

Music was still her favorite activity, and she played daily on her mother's Stein piano, a distinctive instrument with a black keyboard. Madame de Flavigny loved to play pieces by Mozart, which she had learned in Vienna during her youth. Since her daughter had clearly inherited her musical gift, she received tuition from the very best teachers, one of whom was the celebrated Johann Hummel. The German composer and pianist, who had received his first keyboard lessons from Mozart himself, had come to Paris after an illustrious career in Vienna and Weimar. He encouraged Marie to compose her own music, and in the years which followed she was to write a number of pieces, including some inspired by the poems of Heinrich Heine, who like herself bridged the cultures of France and Germany. She later regretted the loss of these compositions, which she undervalued at the time and into which she poured the emotions and dreams of her early adolescence.

It was at this time that her mother made the astonishing revelation that Marie had a half-sister named Augusta who was an issue of her first marriage. This remarkable news must have created some unease in Marie as an example of parental deception and secrecy. By this time Augusta was twenty-seven and living in Paris; she and Marie soon began to meet regularly and grew close. Gradually the facts were revealed. The existence of her sister had been hidden because Augusta was considered a bad example. In her early years in Frankfurt, Augusta had been a passionate girl who was often in conflict with her mother, a trait that seemed to be a family specialty.

The first crisis had occurred in 1806 when Augusta, aged sixteen, imitated her mother by falling in love with a French officer stationed in Frankfurt. He was equerry to Hortense Bonaparte, whose husband was briefly enjoying his position as king of Holland. In the face of family opposition to an imprudent marriage, Augusta had thrown herself dramatically at the feet of Hortense in the vain hope of winning her support. When Hortense sensibly refused to get involved, the impulsive young woman did not take long to find another man. Once again it was someone unsuitable who appealed to her romantic imagination, namely, the poet Clemens Brentano.[4] As was to be expected, the Bethmann family found him no more acceptable than the soldier. He was not only a poet, which was bad enough, but a Catholic as well. Augusta had met him one evening in July 1807 at a reception in honor of Napoleon, and at first he had been favorably impressed by her quiet and thoughtful appearance. To his alarm Augusta decided that very evening that she loved him and publicly threw her arms around his neck in front of the high society of Frankfurt. It was particularly embarrassing for Brentano, because he had recently lost his wife and had been acting the part of a sadly bereaved husband.

Möritz Bethmann had felt that the best policy was to warn Brentano about the trouble Augusta had already caused. The poet at once wisely decided to put an end to the affair before things got out of hand, but he made the mistake of agreeing to one last meeting. The passionate Augusta turned up with a bag of clothes and somehow persuaded him to elope. They quickly got married, and regretted it for four stormy years before divorcing in 1811. During this time Flavigny himself had once intervened in a vain attempt to smooth things over. Augusta had twice threatened suicide, but the attempts were more theatrical than serious, as when she dramatically swallowed a concoction that turned out to be mostly tooth powder.

Augusta's next eccentricity was political. She had thrown herself into fanatical support of Napoleon and even tried to go into exile with him on Saint Helena. After this episode she at last followed the advice of Möritz Bethmann and married a suitable husband, by the name of Hermann. They settled in Paris, where they had four children and lived in apparent happiness. It was this change that persuaded her mother that Augusta was no longer a dangerous example for Marie. The Augusta story, with its passions and dark secrets, further introduced Marie to the ways of the world.

She was now thirteen, and puberty had aroused new curiosity about the ways of men and women. It was not the custom to instruct girls of her class about the facts of life, which were sometimes communicated the day before their marriage, if at all, and so she made some attempt to educate herself. In the room where she did her lessons was a bookcase full of leather-bound novels. Nobody had told her she should not read them, but she knew that novels were generally considered unsuitable for young readers, particularly girls, whose imagination they could stimulate in dangerous ways. Yet the books were there, the key was in the lock, and soon she was tasting forbidden fruit in a novel called *The Devil in Love,* by Jacques Cazotte. She went on to read the dark novels of Mrs. Radcliff and the love stories of Madame Cottin, Madame de Genlis, and Madame Riccoboni. Soon life itself seemed to be imitating fiction when she was courted by a fifteen-year-old boy named Louis, the son of a local squire.

One autumn day in the country Louis had called at the house with the present of a white partridge for her. He was asked to stay for dinner, and the whole family drank a toast to the young hunter. Louis began to call regularly, and a chance incident soon revealed his feelings: one day when he saw her looking for a glove, he claimed he had found it in the woods and would keep it forever. This turned out to be a lie, for the glove turned up, but Marie had read enough novels to recognize this as a declaration of love. She knew that her young admirer's family had little money, and looked forward to a great conflict in which she would equal the determination of the best fictional heroines. She was careful to say nothing to her school friends and felt superior to these uninitiated children, now that she had taken her first step into the charming world of love.

Maurice, who was nineteen, had a character very different from Marie's. Whereas she was reserved and a dreamer, he was a cheerful extrovert and realist. After several years in a college in Metz, he began studying law in Paris, once again living in the family apartment there. In 1817 he was sent to London to improve his English and to acquire some knowledge of the world. His letters show that the years of war had done little to alter the close relationship between the two nations. In one he made the surprising claim that Napoleon was so popular in England that many individuals kept a portrait of him in their pocket and spoke of him with enthusiasm. This may not say much about his reliability as an observer and cannot have pleased Flavigny. Marie envied her brother's freedom to travel abroad, while she was forced to live the sheltered life of a girl. At least she was free to continue her exploration of the world of fiction.

Two minor celebrities, Joseph Fiévée and Théodore Leclercq, provided an introduction into the world of literature. These amiable individuals had purchased a small estate near Le Mortier. Parisians who knew them described them as intimate friends, which was a euphemism for being homosexual. Because the newcomers were royalists, Flavigny and other nobles in the locality decided that their doors should be opened to these witty men from a lower class in the hope that they would provide entertainment. Leclercq was a lively man whose face was badly marked by smallpox. He had written a number of pleasantly satirical comedies, none of which had yet been published, and read some of them aloud in the home of his new friends, with great success.[5] He then persuaded Madame de Flavigny that they should continue the pleasure by staging the plays properly during the winter season in the capital. Their Paris home was therefore adapted as a small theater in which Leclercq was author, director, maker of scenery, and stage manager. He was an excellent actor and diplomatically took on unpopular roles such as that of rejected lover. The plays were staged with no more than a few candles and vases of flowers to separate the cast from the audience, and the convention was to act in a natural manner. No one showed more enthusiasm for these thespian activities than Maurice, who had fallen for Leclercq's pretty young sister, the bored wife of a rich notary. As she was eager to take advantage of this introduction to the prestigious aristocratic world, she did nothing to dissuade him.

These new activities brought excitement to the Flavigny home in the rue des Trois-Frères and even lent it a fashionable air. Marie was a little jealous because of Maurice's new friend but loved the amateur dramatics. They spent a whole winter season of 1818–19 acting a variety of plays. Their Parisian residence had never been so full of life. Some of the young men who attended paid her compliments, but Louis was still in her thoughts. At times she imagined the two of them sitting beside a distant sea while he held her hand and swore eternal love.

When they returned to Le Mortier the following summer, Marie, then thirteen, had the first cruel experience of her life. In October 1819, following an outing in the woods with some local children, she was dismounting from her donkey when she noticed their servant Marianne waiting at the door with a grave expression on her face. Many years later, in her memoirs, Marie recalled the details of that moment:

> I at once fell silent and ran to the door of my father's room and stopped there, not daring to knock or speak. My heart was beating. At last I took

courage and entered cautiously; I looked fearfully at the bed, which was near the door. My father was half asleep. He opened his eyes, saw me, beckoned me towards him and asked where I had been. When I told him, he looked at me in an alarming way and in a voice unlike his own he said: "I am glad you are having fun. As for me. I am in pain." He then turned his face to the wall and said nothing more. I too remained silent, holding my breath, motionless beside this deathbed. I do not know how long this moment lasted. I will never forget the solemnity of it. I had just heard the last words my father would say to me in this world.[6]

Flavigny's words had not been intended as a reproach to her, but for the rest of her life she would feel an irrational sense of guilt because she had been riding in the woods when her father fell ill.

It was all over in three days, during which she was not allowed to see him. A doctor came from Tours and held a whispered consultation with the village physician, but they could do little against an illness that was described as cerebral fever. On the third morning Marie went into her mother's bedroom, and Madame de Flavigny informed her that God alone could save her father. At first Marie was speechless with shock; then, while her mother was busy about the house, she slipped into her father's room: "My God! What a scene! My father had not long to go. His eyes were closed. His face had become dark. From his open mouth came the hoarse breathing of a man about to pass away and discover the secret of death. I do not know how long I remained there or how I left. Half an hour later my father had ceased to live." For days she tried to believe that it was a bad dream. When her brother arrived from Paris, they gave each other a long embrace. As she felt his arms around her, she secretly resolved to transfer to Maurice the loyalty and love she had felt for her father, but her happy childhood had come to a sudden and traumatic end.

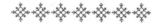

CHAPTER 4

Adolescence

MARIE's relationship with Maurice was good, and she appreciated his affection and easygoing character, which was so different from her own. In an apparent paradox, this proud and independent girl yearned for a guardian, a strong and protective male figure to whom she could show loyalty and deference. But there was a void in her emotions which her brother could not fill. Her puberty had begun, as if to confirm that her life had moved into a new phase. In later years Marie left no record of the effect of bereavement on her mother, but after many happy years of marriage it must have been considerable. Because Maria de Flavigny was a woman of mature years, she may have been more able to bear the blows of life. Whatever the truth may be, it seems that the death of Flavigny failed to bring Marie closer to a mother whom she apparently saw as a rival. Marie reminded herself dutifully of her mother's good points — her affection, her musical talent, her Germanic culture — but recognition of these qualities did not prevent the feeling that there was a distance between them. Madame de Flavigny was not fully aware of the problem, since perspicacity was not one of her virtues. Marie felt secretly guilty because she did not fully return her affection, and did her best to hide the fact. She had enjoyed her mother's company when she was little but increasingly found her conversation lacking in interest, though Madame de Flavigny was no more obtuse than her friends. During obligatory sessions with these women in the drawing room, Marie hid her impatience behind a polite smile.

With total injustice she was irritated by the careful way her mother managed financial matters in order to balance income and expenditure. The adolescent girl considered this to be bourgeois behavior compared to the aristocratic nonchalance of her father. Indeed nature seemed to have made her different from her mother in every way. Madame de Flavigny was short in stature, though shapely, whereas Marie was tall and slim like her father. She understood that her mother was generous and sensible but that she lacked Flavigny's indefinable charm and caustic wit, another characteristic Marie had inherited.

Since her father's death, Marie had become the focus of her mother's emotional life, and it seems that the attitude of Madame de Flavigny now crossed the line that divides normal parental affection from indulgence. Observing the persistent sadness of her quiet and reserved daughter, whose health even seemed affected, she looked for a way to soften the impact of bereavement. She concluded that they should return to Frankfurt and stay there for a considerable period, in the hope that a change of scene would help them both recover their spirits. The departure of Maurice on a diplomatic career was now imminent, and Madame de Flavigny instinctively felt the pull of the Bethmann clan at this difficult time. There was also a practical reason for the return, for her husband's aristocratic style of management at their country estate had left them with debts. Möritz would be the best person to consult about repairing the damage to the family fortune.

For these reasons Madame de Flavigny and her daughter again set off on the long road to Germany in November 1820, four years after their previous trip, accompanied by Maurice on his way to join the French Embassy in Berlin. They found Frankfurt changed since their last visit: it had spread progressively outside the former fortifications in search of space and light. The old city, with its wooden houses and narrow streets, remained the same, but the moats had been filled in and planted with trees and lawns. Beyond them were new villas constructed in the Italian style and set in attractive gardens. The contrast between the center and the suburbs was now striking. Around the town was a ring of meadows, cultivated fields, and orchards, framed by pine-covered hills in the background. It was a time of continuing prestige for Frankfurt, which had been chosen as the capital of a new federation of German states created by the Congress of Vienna, resulting in the opening of many new embassies. The political, commercial, and social scene of the city had also become more lively, with endless balls, concerts, and banquets attended by a cosmopolitan elite. As Madame de Flavigny

and Marie took up residence at the Vogelstrauss inn, the change must have
seemed a good antidote to the sadness which still gripped the girl. Marie
was now fourteen, though she looked older because of her height and serious manner. Her mother took her frequently to the Frankfurt opera, where
she discovered the magic of Glück, Spontini, and Mozart.

Marie also attended many balls with her mother but found the experience frustrating because she was not allowed to dance the waltz. Madame
de Flavigny imposed the ban because of French custom, which considered
this dance unsuitable for unmarried girls. It was believed that the waltz
provided too much contact between partners and might arouse imprudent
desires. German mothers were less cautious and thought the cheerful dance
to be without danger for their daughters, but Marie had the mortification
of waiting for quadrilles while other girls went whirling around the room
in their ballgowns. In reality her mother would have been wiser to let her
dance the waltz, in view of what was to happen.

One evening, as Marie watched the dancers, an elderly diplomat gallantly sat beside her and engaged her in conversation about Parisian society
life. Struck by the seriousness and precocious wit of the adolescent girl, he
introduced her to a group of his colleagues. Soon she had a regular court of
admirers as a compensation for the waltzes. For a girl of fourteen, it was
not good to be surrounded and flattered by a group of grown men, and the
attention began to go to her head. Always more affectionate than discern-
ing, and no doubt busy with her own social pleasures, Madame de Flavigny
did not react until Maurice commented on the situation while on a visit
from Berlin. In order not to antagonize her, they decided not to impose a
sudden ban on Marie's social activities, and she was allowed to complete
the season as a center of attraction. At least the situation had the advantage
of distracting her from the thought of her father.

It was in Frankfurt that Marie had the memorable experience of meeting Chateaubriand, who was still France's most famous writer. His works
had influenced a whole generation of readers, including herself. Chateaubriand was on his way to Berlin, where he had been appointed ambassador,
and had interrupted his journey in Frankfurt at the request of Madame de
Flavigny, who wished to recommend her son to him. Such initiatives were
considered normal at this time, when personal favor and protection were

openly sought and given, often to the detriment of important considerations such as competence. Marie was full of excitement at the thought
of meeting the author of *Atala*, a melancholy story of doomed love set in
America, and she happily recalled the lush descriptions of forests and the
mighty Mississippi. She had also been moved by *René*, a dark tale about an
emotionally troubled and weary young man who longs for some drama to
give interest to his life. This sinful wish is punished when his sister Amélie
falls incestuously in love with him, then enters a convent to expiate her
guilty passion. Marie had fallen under the spell and felt that she was like
René and Amélie, torn by passion and weary of the world.[1]

Madame de Flavigny had been invited to take tea with Chateaubriand
and had intended to go alone since she was unaware of the intensity of
Marie's desire to meet him. Seeing her daughter almost in tears, she relented and told her to get ready quickly. Marie ran to put on her best dress.
She had the impression she was about to see an exceptional individual, a
man above all others, a demigod. At their meeting in the French embassy,
Chateaubriand spoke politely to her mother but did not say a single word to
Marie. For a whole hour she contemplated him with admiration. She found
him handsome, though his head seemed too large for his body. In his fiery
eyes and abundant hair she saw genius. In his manner there was much grace,
and she could sense a certain weariness and solitude that linked him with
René. Many years would pass before Marie recovered from the intoxication
of Chateaubriand's fiction. She had now seen him with her own eyes—and
had not been disappointed.

Although Frankfurt was by then a modern European capital, a relic of a
somber past lay hidden in the maze of old wooden houses: the Jewish ghetto.
The gates were still closed every night, as in years past, despite efforts by
Möritz Bethmann and other enlightened citizens to put an end to the practice. Marie learned that her mother had played a small role in a significant
incident that had taken place four years earlier. Louise Bethmann had given
birth to a son and, according to tradition, was preparing to receive visits
in her bedroom, dressed in fine lace. Her husband happened to mention to
his mother that they could expect Amschel Rothschild, son of the founder
of the famous bank. The old lady had protested vigorously, and it took the

François de Chateaubriand, by Lordereau, ca. 1820.

(Photothèque des Musées de la Ville de Paris)

combined efforts of the family to silence her complaints at this symbolic gesture of friendship between Jew and Christian.

In the spring of 1821 Madame de Flavigny returned to Paris with the intention of once again placing Marie in a boarding school. Her plan was to return to the German city alone to complete her financial operations, having removed her daughter from the frivolities of high society. Marie quietly accepted the decision, knowing that it had been agreed between her mother and her brother. The school chosen was the highly fashionable Convent of the Sacred Heart in Paris, which was incongruously situated in a pleasure palace built by Marshall Biron in the sixteenth century. It was under the direction of the Jesuits, despite the fact that they were officially banned from France, and was soon to acquire fame as the symbol of aristocratic female education.

The nuns, who wore black habits and silver crosses, were almost all from noble families and had not found Christian humility an easy virtue to acquire. Madame de Flavigny had practically dictated her terms and demanded special privileges for her daughter. True to their reputation, the Jesuits had agreed to bend the rules, being eager to recruit a pupil who was likely to join the most exclusive circle of French society and who could help them in their ambitions. Madame de Flavigny's unprecedented conditions were accepted: her fourteen-year-old daughter would have her own room, instead of a bed in a dormitory, and a piano. She would be allowed out as often as she wished when invited by Madame Lenoir or by Augusta.

Marie first appeared at school during a recreation period and was at once surrounded by a group of girls eager to find out all about her. The revelation that she was to have her own room caused astonishment and respect. In spite of her reserve, she was quickly accepted and given the exotic nickname "Yngivalf" (Flavigny in reverse), which seemed to suit a tall, blonde girl who could have been the heroine of a Scandinavian novel. She was happy with this friendly reception and adapted with surpassing ease to the strange and artificially regulated life of a convent school. It had the advantage of putting her in daily contact with girls of her age, though their conversation was not equal to that of the diplomatic corps in Frankfurt.

She quickly made a new friend named Fanny de Larochefoucauld, who had had similar social experiences and who found it hard to adapt to convent life. Marie instinctively liked this pretty dark girl with large eyes and long eyelashes, though her coquettish nature was quite different from her own. Fanny did not hide her dislike of school discipline and her disinclination to go through the rituals of sentimental piety as they knelt in front of por-traits of Jesus. Unconcerned about her ignorance, she sat at the back of the class dreaming of elegant ballgowns and handsome partners. The nuns en-couraged their friendship in the hope that Marie's serious attitude toward religion and study might be infectious, but Fanny exhibited a strong re-sistance to the scholarly virus. This was confirmed in later years when she gained notoriety by leaving her husband to live with an actor.

Marie hoped to show herself to be educationally competent in her new environment, yet she felt inadequate and suffered agonies at the thought that in this prestigious establishment she might be placed in a class of juniors. She need not have worried, however, for she was put in the senior class with five pupils between the ages of fifteen and eighteen. (She was as-tonished that only two of them could spell correctly and that none seemed to know much.) To this reassuring fact was added her growing enjoyment of the new experience of communal life with friends her own age. In addi-tion, she liked her room, which overlooked the garden. On the other hand, the food was so bad that sometimes they ate only the bread. Nor were there proper provisions for cleanliness because of the convent attitude that the body was sinful and deserved little attention. Baths were taken only dur-ing illness, if ordered by a doctor. They washed themselves quickly using a tiny basin containing cold water and a small towel of rough material. The only mirror in the establishment was in the vestry, where the priest put on his robes before mass. Fanny and Marie already had breasts, so the nuns provided them with specially modified uniforms in case their young bodies should arouse impure thoughts in the visiting room, where the brothers of pupils were sometimes present. Whether it was because of the bad food, the prudish regime, or some unknown psychological factor, Marie's men-struation stopped for the whole duration of her stay in the convent school.

In addition to Fanny, she befriended a sixteen-year-old girl named Ade-lise who was ugly, dull, and devoid of charm. Not only did Adelise have unfashionable red hair, but she was slow-witted and backward, which was cause for the other pupils to bully her cruelly. One day Marie came to her aid during the recreation period when Adelise appealed to her for help. Marie rescued her by linking arms and talking to her until lessons began. Not content to leave matters there, she decided to stimulate the mind of her new friend, hoping to find glimmers of understanding in her eyes. Despite Adelise's intellectual shortcomings, she was affectionate and found many ways of thanking Marie. She knew that her protector liked flowers and broke the convent rules by secretly taking roses, carnations, and jasmine from the garden and placing them in her room. Between them grew a bond of friendship based on gratitude.

She also formed a friendship with a nun named Antonia, who taught the senior girls and was in charge of music in the chapel. Marie felt attracted to this sad and gentle person whose nature seemed to resemble her own. She had entered a phase of excessive religious piety now that she was no longer under the influence of a skeptical father who admired Voltaire and away from the healthy country life. After the evening service she began to linger in the chapel and would often hear the quiet footsteps of Antonia, who came to pray beside her in a silent act of intimacy.

The nuns were not allowed to have favorites, and this friendship between nun and pupil was to cause a major incident. For Antonia's birthday Marie had collected money from the students for a gift of flowers. The plan was to give an impressive present which would show their affection. Marie was entrusted with the mission, and from a fashionable florist in the Palais Royal she purchased a beautiful scented bouquet which she secretly placed in Antonia's room. There was consternation among the girls when the nun thanked them for the gift but revealed that she had not even seen it, as it had been confiscated. Marie was summoned to see the Mother Superior, accused of having broken the rules by introducing flowers, and scolded for setting an example of deceit and indiscipline. In addition, a bouquet containing red roses was an insult to the virginity of Antonia, so Marie must publicly ask for forgiveness in the next school assembly. She walked silently to her room and cried tears of rage. It was the first time she had come into conflict with authority and the injustice of the punishment filled her with anger.

The situation became a prolonged duel between the adolescent girl and the Mother Superior. Marie was determined to have revenge, and her first tactic was to make herself ill by refusing to eat or sleep for days. In the end the nuns sent for a doctor, who pronounced the ailment to be emotional, not physical. The struggle went on so long that the convent finally received a visit from the Mother General, a powerful figure who sat by Marie's bed, held her hand, and admitted that a mistake had been made. She accepted her explanation that she had not known about the ban on bouquets and the erotic symbolism of flowers, and took the opportunity to warn her of the danger of strong affections, even making her promise she would remember the advice. Marie had won her first battle, but as a consequence, the unfortunate Antonia was moved to another convent.

This episode had shown that Marie herself had little inclination for the virtue of humility, and the nuns began to find her general disposition wanting, despite her pious tendency. They had been disappointed by her refusal to become one of the Children of Mary, a group of pupils which was allowed certain privileges. For her part she disliked saying the rosary and praying in front of holy images and suspected the nuns of using the Children of Mary as a source of information about the girls' conversations. Much of the religious instruction was given by a Father Varin, a persuasive Jesuit who did his best to inspire an emotional and unquestioning faith. This was part of a strategy which sought to reverse the tide of freethinking that had gained prominence in France — and had influenced Marie when her father was alive. The aim was to enlist these daughters of the socially elite as docile allies who would in time influence their own children. The new method was to appeal to their young emotions with a mild and pleasant form of religion which relied on ritual, incense, candles, and music. The passionate writings of Saint Theresa were recommended as a suitable stimulus for the imagination; sermons spoke of love and of the pure joy which comes from perfect submission to Jesus. The effect of this on Marie's emotional nature was so great that she began to consider entering the religious life. The convent atmosphere already gave her certain pleasures. Her musical talent having been noted, she was allowed to play the organ in the chapel and directed the students' singing. She also sang solo cantatas and drew deep satisfaction from the combination of musical and religious feeling. As the young voices joined together in the candlelit chapel, the convent became a serene world full of charm.[2]

The religious idyll came to a sudden end when Madame Lenoir saw the danger of the adolescent wanting to become a nun and sent an urgent message to Madame de Flavigny in Frankfurt. One afternoon in the late summer of 1822 Marie was at the window of her room enjoying the scent of the lime trees in the garden when she heard a carriage enter the convent yard. The Mother Superior soon entered her room and told her that Madame de Flavigny had come to take her away for good. As they went silently down the stairs, the nun said: "Do not worry, my child, it is the will of God." Marie was on the verge of tears; Madame de Flavigny, herself moved, embraced her daughter affectionately. As if in a dream, Marie put on her cape, and they walked to the carriage. She felt sudden panic when the wheels began to turn and the great wooden doors of the convent slowly closed behind them. As they went through the busy streets of Paris, her mother talked of the balls and operas she would soon be attending. Marie fought to repress an irrational fear of this world of pleasure which was being offered to her. She wanted to be taken back to the convent but did not dare to speak the words. The memory of her father returned with intensity, and she felt afraid of life.

She was taken to their country home, where they spent the rest of the summer. In Paris Madame de Flavigny had rented the first floor of a large house overlooking the Place Vendôme, where the statue of Napoleon had been removed and melted down. Marie, now sixteen, was striking with her tall figure, blonde hair, and large blue eyes. To those who were aware of her beauty, intelligence, and wealth, she seemed the most enviable person in Paris. Marie, however, was already sensing that fortune brought dangers as well as privilege.

Her life became a round of pleasure as Madame de Flavigny devoted herself to the introduction of her daughter into society and to the selection of a suitable husband. In this new phase of her existence, she especially enjoyed concerts and the opera. The theater was banned by priests as a source of moral corruption for young females, but the opera was thought to be less dangerous because the words were in Italian. Among the French nobility, intellectual instruction was no longer deemed necessary when a girl reached sixteen. Indeed, Madame de Flavigny felt that her daughter's mind would be sufficiently filled by social and musical pleasures. Marie could expect to be married by the age of eighteen, and the few years between school and domesticity were seen as a pleasant apprenticeship to life in high society.

Marie was not satisfied by this existence, although she obediently did what was expected of her. She continued to feel the pull of the convent and sometimes returned to enjoy the sad charm of the music in the chapel. This tendency would have been restrained by Madame Lenoir or Augusta, but they had both left Paris. The departure of Augusta especially was a loss for Marie, who had frequently visited her home, where she experienced an intimacy not found in the salons of the aristocracy, with their lackeys in livery. The modest abode in the rue des Saints-Pères had a quiet courtyard and a pretty garden looked after by Augusta and her husband. It was like a country house surrounded by the city. Marie had enjoyed playing with her sister's children, especially a little boy named Léon. The family had returned to Frankfurt, however, where Augusta would one day come to a tragic end.

An event that occurred around this time made Marie increasingly aware of her situation as an heiress. It had become the custom to go daily to mass in the Madeleine, Marie for religious reasons and her mother mainly as chaperone; in the large church they often saw the same group of individuals, which included a priest, a middle-aged man, and three young men who could be seen praying in an ostentatious manner punctuated by sighs. As the weeks went by, it became clear that overtures of friendship were being made. The priest concentrated on Madame de Flavigny, while Marie found herself courted by a certain Monsieur de Bauterne. At home one day a servant informed Marie that the young priest had called and wished to talk to her. As prescribed by etiquette, she sent a reply that she could not do so in the absence of her mother. The visitor sent back his card with a penciled note saying that the matter was important, but she persisted in her refusal. Marie had in fact been warned by their vigilant parish priest who had noticed the episode in the church and had rightly suspected that it was part of a conspiracy to lay hands on the Flavigny wealth.

The leader of the plotters was François de Coessin, a man with an interesting record.[3] During the Revolution he had been a militant advocate of social reform and had planned an ideal republic in the French colony of Cayenne. When this failed, he turned to religion and founded his own sect. It was housed in an establishment known as the Maison Grise, where he preached with the fervor of a prophet and sought disciples, preferably rich ones. The Madeleine incident justified Marie's apprehension about the dangers of life in the city. One night at a ball in Paris she met the young hunter who had inspired her first romantic dreams. She had not seen Louis for two years, and when she danced with him she found his manners decidedly rustic. The girl of sixteen remembered her former thoughts of married bliss and looked back ironically on the child she had been.

CHAPTER 5

Marriage French Style

I N 1822 Marie began to participate more fully in social life, having become a marriageable young woman. The Parisian high society she was about to enter consisted of three groups which would soon be brilliantly portrayed in the novels of Honoré de Balzac: the old aristocracy, the new nobility created by Napoleon, and the increasingly important class of high finance. The old aristocracy itself was divided into two groups, those who were received in court and those who did not enjoy this high distinction. During the lifetime of Flavigny, who had become allergic to royal courts, Marie's social life had been based mostly on her father's circle of friends. This had included such families as the Suzannets and the Bourmonts, who preferred to spend much of their time on their country estates and to keep a low profile in Paris.

Now that Madame de Flavigny was a widow, with only herself to please, she decided on a new campaign. She would spend more time in the capital and would try to make their home into a place of social activity, a traditional Parisian salon with its own character and influence. Because of the Flavigny connections, her salon attracted a number of royalist members of Parliament, including Joseph Villèle, who became prime minister in 1822. Unimpressive at first sight, Villèle was short man with matchstick limbs and a somewhat nasal voice. He appeared diffident in manner and listened quietly and intently to whatever was being said. As soon as he spoke, however, his intellect seemed to light up his thin face and he was transformed. He expressed himself in a simple manner, with few gestures, but with such clarity and conviction that his words made a lasting impression on listeners. Villèle was the first of the five prime ministers of France who would be personally known to Marie, and he was one of the few in the royalist party to possess political ability.

Madame de Flavigny also cultivated the friendship of some top people in the diplomatic service in the hope of helping her son's career. The presence of Maurice's young colleagues added a touch of youth and vitality which was appreciated by Marie, whose intellectual interests did not prevent her from enjoying the usual pleasures of her age. Like other ladies with daughters to marry, her mother gave regular *soirées dansantes,* which were pleasantly informal, with only a piano, violin, and clarinet as an orchestra. The atmosphere was relaxed, and invitations to these parties were much prized by young members of the diplomatic service. The girls wore simple white muslin dresses with a colored sash and a flower in their hair. One of Marie's most frequent partners was a young officer named Alfred de Vigny, who would later win immortality as one of France's greatest poets. He was much attracted to her and would have liked to propose marriage but refrained from doing so because of his modest financial status. Marie liked him, but as yet he was just an ordinary mortal in her eyes, and not a good dancer in the quadrilles.

In March 1824 she had her first close look at a reigning monarch performing official duties, as Louis XVIII opened Parliament in the Louvre, in the presence of the court. The ceremony had political significance in that it was the intelligent old king's way of indicating the importance he attached to the parliamentary institutions which many royalists were plotting to destroy. Because Madame de Flavigny and Marie had not yet been presented at court, they were seated at the back, though they had a good view of the ceremony. It began when the invalid monarch was wheeled in by his pages. He wore a blue coat with gold epaulettes, and from his belt hung a ceremonial sword which looked incongruous on his large person. This was a sort of uniform, halfway between military and civilian clothes, which he had invented for himself. Like many of the older generation he still wore his hair powdered and tied in a pigtail. He looked ill, and Marie imagined she could see the pale figure of death behind his chair.

As the ailing king struggled to read his speech, she could see that he was making a courageous effort to uphold the royal dignity in his last major public appearance. Standing by him was the comte d'Artois, who was Louis's younger brother, and the duchess of Berry, who would briefly become Marie's friend a few years later. She noticed the young Italian woman's lack of solemnity as she fidgeted with her feathers and necklaces during a ceremony, which evidently bored her. Among the ministers, Marie observed the unremarkable Villèle and the striking figure of Chateaubriand, who wore his usual distant look. The great man was certainly unaware of the silent admiration of the girl he had briefly met in Frankfurt and whose mind was full of his novels.

When Louis XVIII died some months later, not many members of Marie's class had seen the wisdom of a man who had done his best to restrain the vengeful spirit of the Ultras, as the extreme royalists were called by their critics. He had understood that it was impossible for France to return to absolute monarchy, although this was still the common form of government in most European states. When he died, in 1824, official mourning was decreed for a whole year, the traditional period to mark the demise of a father. The comte d'Artois now became king, holding the title of Charles X. A man of little intelligence and no moderation, he nonetheless made himself popular in high society by expressing a wish that social life should not stop completely during the period of mourning. For this reason the usual balls took place in the winter season. though women made the concession of wearing black dresses and mantillas, a dark but stylish costume which was enlivened by bouquets of red flowers. In this way a new fashion was inspired, partly by the death of a king and partly by the costumes of the ladies of Spain, where the French army had just fought a campaign.

In addition to the usual balls and visits to the opera, Marie and her mother regularly went to concerts in private homes. At this time the musical scene in Paris was dominated by Rossini, who at the age of thirty was already a legendary figure; Stendhal's biography of the Italian composer appeared in 1823. Rossini had come to France after a series of musical triumphs in various Italian cities, and everyone had heard rumors of his early love affairs with the ladies of Venice, Milan, and Naples. It was said that a lawyer's wife in Bologna had eloped with him when he was only seventeen. His fame in Italy was so great that he was courted by popes and princes. By this time, however, he had settled down, having married the celebrated singer Madame Colbran. Rossini was not only a renowned composer but a

fervent royalist, and his political stance naturally contributed to his popularity in aristocratic Parisian circles. The creator of famous operas like *The
Barber of Seville* did not consider it beneath himself to play the part of impresario. A family wishing to give a concert would consult with Rossini, and
the maestro would provide a complete service, which included a choice of
music and the hiring of performers. Rossini and his musicians would enter
by a side door, as the nobility did not want too much familiarity with professional musicians. He would sit at the piano, from which he would direct
the whole performance. At the end it was usual for the musicians to receive
some words of thanks, after which they would all leave together. Madame
de Flavigny was more informal in these matters and invited them to stay
on; this gave Marie the pleasure of talking to the famous singer Madame
Malibran after she had charmed them with airs from *La gazza ladra* and
other operas by Rossini. The conversation of the diva had the same attractive vitality as her singing, and Marie wondered what her own life would
have been had she been born into the free and magic world of opera.

The world of literature was more accessible for a young woman of her
social class, and already Marie was secretly leaning in that direction, saying
nothing to her mother. The prestige of Madame de Staël was still great, and
Madame de Duras had shown again that a lady of the old French aristocracy
could produce novels without loss of reputation. And now a new female star
had entered the literary firmament: a young poetess named Delphine Gay.
She was the daughter of Sophie Gay, a former beauty who had been prominent in high society from the time of the Directory up through Napoleon's
era.[1] Since then Sophie had gained a reputation as a novelist and, with the fall
of the Empire in 1815, had come to rely on this source of income. Because
of the political change, she had encouraged Delphine to write poetry in a
royalist vein. The idea was a shrewd one in 1820, as the prestige of poetry
had been greatly increased by Lamartine, who had injected new life into
the old genre. The aristocracy quickly adopted this gifted and beautiful girl
of fifteen, with her dreamy look and sound political opinions. Madame Gay
had cleverly enhanced Delphine's reputation by arranging a meeting with
Lamartine himself. The encounter even inspired him to dedicate a poem to
Delphine, a meeting he later recounted like an episode in some Romantic
novel. It took place in the spring of 1825, at the Velino waterfall in Italy, a

Gioacchino Rossini, ca. 1820.

(Photothèque des Musées de la Ville de Paris)

beautiful setting which had inspired poets since Horace. Lamartine knew that Madame Gay and her daughter were in the vicinity and hoping to meet him. The poet found the plump young Muse sitting by the river, where her mother had arranged her in a careful pose, one shapely arm on the parapet, the other nonchalantly holding a bouquet of wild flowers while the wind caressed her light brown hair. Always a gentleman, Lamartine dutifully recorded the scene for posterity.[2]

Delphine's first official success had come in 1822, when the Académie Française awarded her a poetry prize. Under the skillful guidance of her mother, she then steadily increased her reputation in the salons of aristocratic ladies, to whom she addressed poems full of flattery and gratitude. Her greatest publicity coup came two years later, when she composed an allegorical piece about Joan of Arc and dedicated it to Charles X at the time of his coronation. This shrewd move led to an audience with the new king, who naturally found her charming. For some time the court was full of rumors that she would be elevated to the position of royal mistress, a desirable post which had been vacant since the reign of Madame du Cayla. It was said that one faction urged the king to offer Delphine a secret marriage. Nothing came of these schemes, as Charles wanted to keep a promise of fidelity made to his last love before her death. It seems that Delphine herself knew nothing of the plots, though one could not confidently say the same of her mother. Marie looked at the literary career of Delphine Gay with a touch of envy and noted with amusement the efficiency of Madame Sophie Gay in promoting it. Marie was suspicious of Madame Gay and saw her as a social climber addicted to celebrity. This assessment may have been unjust, given that her damp little apartment with shabby furniture received the spontaneous visits of some of the Parisian élite, including Chateaubriand and Madame Récamier. On the table they often saw the proofs of the novels and poems with which Sophie and her daughter courageously supplemented their income.

Marie first met Delphine in 1826, at a time when she had herself acquired a reputation in the salons as a pianist. Having been told that Sophie and Delphine Gay were eager to hear Marie play, Madame de Flavigny sent them an invitation to one of the musical evenings in her home. Marie was thrilled to think that she would perform before this young literary prodigy,

Delphine Gay (Madame Emile de Girardin), ca. 1825.

(Photothèque des Musées de la Ville de Paris)

talk to her, and possibly become her friend. For days she was full of enthusiasm and almost sleepless with excitement.

When the day came, she saw before her an unaffected girl with serene blue eyes. Marie at once liked Delphine because of her reserved and modest nature. She was simply dressed in white, and her long wavy hair framed her attractive face in a natural way. Delphine was tall and seemed to have a quiet grace which contrasted with the energetic and impulsive manner of her mother. When Marie sat at the piano that evening, she played the music of her former teacher, Johann Hummel, with new power. As applause filled the room, Madame Gay approached Marie and complimented her in a theatrical fashion. Delphine then went to the piano and silently held her hand in a long and affectionate grasp. Marie asked her to recite one of her poems, which she did in her pleasant and simple manner. The unspoken offer of friendship between the two became a reality, though many years would pass before they would see each other regularly. By that time, however, Delphine would no longer be an idealistic virgin, for she went on to marry the press tycoon Emile de Girardin and abandoned poetry for journalism. The friendship of the two women was destined to end in jealousy, when Delphine's husband made the mistake of falling in love with Marie.

The great concern for Madame de Flavigny was still the selection of a husband for her daughter, and there was clearly no shortage of suitors. Marriage customs in the aristocracy had not changed radically since the seventeenth century, when the young Saint-Simon went to see the duc de Beauvilliers and expressed a wish to marry one of his daughters, leaving the choice to him.[3] It was still generally accepted that parents should choose marriage partners, particularly for their daughters, who married younger and were less experienced than men. Girls were deemed ready for marriage at eighteen or younger, and everything was done to guard their virginity. This consideration also encouraged early marriage, since there seemed no point in increasing the risk of an undesirable love affair, which could only increase as time passed. It was also true that affectionate parents did not want to impose prolonged chastity on their daughters for fear of a fashionable condition called melancholia, which showed itself in symptoms of pallor and inertia.

Marie was ready to follow the usual course and accept a husband who would be proposed by her mother and approved by herself. There would of course be a few meetings of possible partners, but these first contacts were traditionally kept short lest some hasty objection should arise. The whole transaction was doubly important because it was usual for the parents to provide a wife with a capital sum which would remain her property, the interest from it being managed by the husband. Madame de Flavigny was to give her daughter three hundred thousand francs, a considerable fortune, and she could expect to inherit several times that amount from her mother's estate at some point in the future. In addition Madame de Flavigny was willing to house the new couple in her spacious Parisian home. When these financial advantages were added to the fact that Marie was a talented and good-looking girl with distinguished manners, they made an attractive marriage prospect.

Marie was worried about the influence of financial considerations and recalled that even in the convent school one of the nuns had tried to arrange a marriage between her and one of her own relatives, whom she described as being very rich. Madame de Flavigny had not rejected this possible husband out of hand, but had been told that the man was not sufficiently aristocratic by Madame de La Trémoille, a redoubtable dowager with an exclusive salon over which she reigned like a queen. As her husband had been a comrade of Flavigny's, she felt a duty to find a husband for Marie, whose mother thought her infallible in such matters. This faith was later shaken by the case of the marquis de Custine, whom she had strongly recommended for Marie, claiming that he had made his first wife very happy until her death. A few years later this pearl among husbands was disgraced by a major scandal in which he was accused of sodomy with a soldier in his regiment.

Maurice de Flavigny was a source of information about possible husbands in the diplomatic service; indeed, Marie's intelligence and social graces seemed to position her as the possible consort of some future ambassador. Many of Maurice's colleagues shared this opinion, and some did apply for her hand. Marie, for her part, had not yet shown any enthusiasm at the prospect of marriage, in spite of the status and freedom it would bring. The process seemed so abstract to her. She was told the names of men she did not know, followed by accounts of the deeds of ancestors she had never heard of and descriptions of châteaux she had never seen. She reacted to all this without interest, and negotiations never reached a stage where a meeting with a suitor could be arranged. All the wasted effort made her mother and Madame de La Trémoille feel some irritation at this intellectual daughter who would not do as other girls did. Friends such as Fanny chatted excitedly about their suitors even before they had met them, all of which reinforced Marie's feeling of difference and solitude.

Her first intense emotional experience with a man happened unexpectedly. Auguste de Lagarde, a diplomat in his forties, had been introduced to Madame de Flavigny because of a friendship with Möritz Bethmann in Frankfurt, though because of his age he had never been considered as a suitor. Hearing him talk about political matters, Marie was struck by his intelligence and charm. Lagarde, for his part, had been impressed by the attentive air of this girl of nineteen and became a frequent visitor. With each day she was more aware of a growing affection which drew him toward her. His prestige in her eyes was further enhanced by his reputation for bravery. As commander of the military division in the town of Nîmes, he had witnessed the violence which followed the change of regime in 1815 and had shown great courage by riding into a mob in a vain attempt to prevent a massacre of Protestants. He had received a pistol shot from close range, and in the eyes of Marie this wound inflicted by fanaticism was his greatest distinction. It seemed to say more about Lagarde's true merit than his aristocratic name and high position in the diplomatic service.

Her new admirer had another important quality: his interest in literature. He was not unknown as a writer of verse, and one of his pieces had been set to music by Charles Lafont, a reputable musician who composed hundreds of songs and seven concertos. Lagarde's intelligence, melancholy, and reserve made him into a superior man and even an attractively Romantic figure. Marie began to ponder the question of age and to consider the positive qualities which came with it: he had been ambassador in Spain and Bavaria; he knew the world; he was elegant, courageous, and interesting. For the first time in her life she had met a man who seemed the equal of her father.

A marriage between a man of Lagarde's age and a girl of nineteen would not have been considered exceptional, though it would have given rise to some comment. Needless to say, the secretive Marie had kept her affection hidden from everyone, including her mother. The love affair was at last detected by Maurice when he returned from an assignment to the French embassy in London. Marie felt a surge of happiness when she heard him tell their mother that Lagarde's frequent visits must have a serious motive and that the family needed to have an answer ready if he asked for her hand.

Weeks went by and the diplomat did not raise the subject of marriage. In years to come Marie learned that the reason for his continued silence was the fear of a refusal, which would have put an end to his visits. More than once on his way to their home he had decided to speak out, but never did so. Seeing her in her pretty dresses and hearing her speak of the future as if it would never end, he sometimes became saddened and left early. The next day he would apologize with a wistful smile and say that he had been troubled by his wound.

As more time passed, the possibility of a marriage between them became a great subject of debate in the family. Möritz had been consulted by letter, as had the inevitable Madame de La Trémoille. Their opinions were both favorable, though the female oracle did express some dissatisfaction with the liberal ideas of Lagarde. Madame de Flavigny and her son held the diplomat in high regard but were concerned about his age and health. For this reason they abstained from giving any positive advice to Marie, who was therefore free to make a choice. A whole winter passed and she grew increasingly impatient, but still he did not request her hand. She asked herself how he could not see that she loved him. She did not yet know that the situation had been complicated by the secret interference of a former mistress of Lagarde, who had done everything possible to delay matters and make him lose heart. Like some unscrupulous female in a Balzac novel, she wanted him as a husband for her own daughter.

Marie never forgot these events, of which she gave a detailed account in her memoirs. Matters came to a head one day in July 1825, just before Lagarde was to leave Paris to make his annual holiday visit to Gastein, Austria. He had still not made a proposal, and Marie was in a state of tension. He at last decided to risk it and act that very day. Unfortunately, he had been in the drawing room with Madame de Flavigny for an hour before Marie felt composed enough to show herself. When she entered, he was standing and ready to go. She went to him anxiously and said: "You are leaving?" He replied: "I am leaving," adding, with emotion, "I am going, unless you tell me to stay." Inside Marie a voice said "Stay!" but for some unexplained reason the word died on her lips. Lagarde then politely took his leave and left the room. She went back to her bedroom, from which she heard the door of his carriage close and the sound of wheels as it left. Realizing that her romance with the diplomat was over, she held her head and cried.

The events of that day showed that one word can change a life. In times of difficulty or solitude she asked herself why she had not said that single word to Lagarde. She imagined him as a perfect husband, friend, and guide. What joy it would have been to live with this kind, intelligent, and courageous man, and to give him happiness too! As she looked back, she blamed herself for not listening to the voice in her heart. What made it even harder to bear was that Lagarde soon married a cousin of his who had just left convent school. For Marie it was a crisis, and one made worse by the thought that it was all her own doing. For the first time she felt jealous, and in her imagination she made wild plans to prevent Lagarde's marriage. The situation was aggravated by the fact that she confided in nobody, preferring to seek consolation in literature. Perversely, she turned again to the works of fiction which had spread melancholy in a generation of young intellectuals and again found masochistic satisfaction in tales of failed love like *Werther,* *René,* and *Adolphe.*

A worried Madame de Flavigny consulted various medical experts, who naturally concluded that her daughter needed to have her mind taken off her troubles. She was therefore given new dresses and taken to even more balls. Maurice sent necklaces from Berlin, exotic feathers from Brazil, and a straw hat from Italy, which looked so well on the tall, beautiful girl that it was copied by milliners and launched a new fashion in Paris. Marie appreciated the gifts, but she continued to read gloomy fiction and to brood over Lagarde.

Apart from marriage, the standard cure for melancholia in a young woman was fresh air and exercise, remedies so rare in the life of young Parisian women that they were prescribed by doctors only in an emergency. Madame de Flavigny and her daughter began a course of this therapy in the Bois de Boulogne, situated well outside Paris. In her memoirs Marie recalled that this wood was still wild and lonely, unlike the modern-day park.

The rutted, dusty road leading to it — so unpopular with coachmen — made it seem even farther away. Because of the distance it was accessible only to those who owned horses and coaches, and visitors there saw mostly sick people or depressives who were trying to avoid human contact.

It was literature rather than the Bois de Boulogne that gave Marie some consolation from her first disappointment in love. She discovered the works of the sentimental Irish poet Thomas Moore and a whole new fictional world in the historical novels of Walter Scott, which were all the rage in France. Knowing that literature can be fully savored in the original language alone, and wanting also to feel the full force of the tragedies of Shakespeare, which she had read in German, she set herself the task of learning English. Her teacher was a Miss James from Ireland, who did not know how to make lessons interesting. After three months she had made little progress. When people now asked Marie if she could speak English, Miss James always intervened with solemnity and said: "She could if she would, but she won't." This ritual caused much hilarity and became a family joke. It seems that Marie spoke the language badly but wrote it with ease. This is apparent from the ingenious method which she suggested to her friend Lucile, who was also learning it. The plan was to write letters to each other in English so as to form a fictional correspondence in the form of an epistolary novel, the outline being provided by Marie. She later regretted not having kept this early experiment in creative writing. In the end she made significant progress in English, adding it to her perfect French and German.

Her sadness had not quite left her, however, despite these activities and the intellectual stimulus provided by the novels of Scott. Before the Lagarde fiasco she had considered discussions about marriage merely boring, but now she found them unbearable. It was while in this depressed state of mind that she made her first great mistake in life, that of adopting a policy of passive acceptance and fatalism about marriage. She told her mother she disliked the part she was expected to play in the search for a husband and wanted nothing to do with it. She conceded, however, that she should do her duty and get married and agreed to accept any husband approved by her mother and brother, requesting only that nobody mention the subject to her until all was agreed.

How could an intelligent young woman propose such an abdication in the most important decision of her life? Was she acting out the role of some fictional heroine who was a sublime and melancholic victim of fate? Part of the explanation was certainly her pride and the desire to be different. There was also the vivid memory of her hesitation and failure with Lagarde, an experience which caused her to doubt her ability to make a decision. In addition, this young intellectual had no knowledge of the power and intimacy of sex and could certainly not have obtained it through the works of Scott or the love songs of Thomas Moore. She still saw men as an abstraction — but trouble lay ahead.

The main responsibility for the disaster which followed can no doubt be attributed in equal parts to Madame de Flavigny, Maurice, and Marie herself. Her brother shared the common opinion that a girl should be wed by the age of twenty and that matrimony was the ideal prescription for paleness and melancholy. Besides, Marie herself was ready to try the remedy, and everything around her seemed to confirm that it was the normal course to take. Six months earlier, her friend Fanny had become the comtesse de Montault and seemed happy in her new life. Another friend, Esther Le Tissier, was about to get married and looking forward to it. Each time Marie went to confession, the parish priest said he hoped to see her at the altar before long.

The decisive move was made by Madame de La Trémoille and her husband. This couple, who rarely agreed about anything, claimed that they had the perfect suitor for Marie, a charming officer named Charles d'Agoult. He was a member of a noble family and had distinguished himself as a soldier. Unfortunately, it had been in the army of Napoleon, but this could not be held against him, as he had been too young to emigrate and join the royalist forces. He had volunteered to fight with Napoleon in 1807, when he was only seventeen, and had been lucky enough to survive the campaigns in Germany, Poland, and Spain. In the hopeless struggle against the invasion of France by the allies in 1814, the young officer had led his cavalry regiment against Russian infantry as they approached Paris, and in a battle near the small town of Nangis, he had received a bullet wound which left him with a permanent limp.

With this record there was a danger that d'Agoult would receive a cool reception from the royal family which had been restored to power by the very Russians against whom he had fought. However, he had an aunt who was a lady-in-waiting and a personal friend of the duchess of Angoulême, whose husband was the next heir to the throne. In addition Charles had an uncle, Viscount d'Agoult, who had been a favorite of Louis XVIII and who was entrusted with holding the royal snuff box on important occasions. In view of these important services to the nation by his close relatives, Charles d'Agoult's past was not held against him for long, and he duly received a sign of royal favor. A promise was made that the position of lady-in-waiting to the dauphine would go to his wife, when he acquired one. As for himself, he could count on some lucrative court position once he had left the royal army in which he now served. It was clear that d'Agoult was a very desirable husband in social terms. As for personal qualities, he was intelligent, honorable, good-natured, and liked by all. It is true that there was a significant age difference between him and Marie, as he was thirty-six in 1826, but at least he was younger than Lagarde and his health was good, apart from his limp.

The real problem lay unseen, in a difference of temperament which would later be the undoing of the couple. Whereas Lagarde's melancholy and reserve had been attractive to Marie, there was a gulf between her and this cheerful soldier. Even their physiques seemed to reflect their incompatibility: he was short and dark and did not walk with ease; she was tall, blonde, and graceful. How could a man of experience make the mistake of taking a wife who was so clearly unsuitable? He, too, would one day look back with perplexity and try to understand it.[4] No doubt it could be explained by her pretty face and his impulsive nature, and simply attributed to a form of folly called love. He met her on a Friday the thirteenth, which may have made him smile at first but which seemed less amusing as the years went by. Charles later recorded his first impression of Marie: "She had the magnificent blonde plaits, the pale skin and the tall figure of the daughters of Germania. She had an exceptional mind, a constant gentleness, an even temper which made life easy. In her conversation and her affections she remained calm."[5] He did not know it, but this deceptive calm hid a passionate inner nature.

Charles d'Agoult later claimed that he had been aware of an aspect of Marie's character which should have caused him to hesitate. He had noted a certain egocentricity, a certain complexity, and a tendency to prefer the world of ideas to the world of reality. As often happens when emotions are involved, he saw the evidence and chose to ignore it. After their first meeting, he told himself that a girl so attractive would want to make a mark in high society. Well then, he would put on silk stockings and take her to balls! He did not yet know the difficulty a man of his background and character would experience as the husband of a fashionable young woman. Some of his friends seem to have had a better understanding of the problems which lay ahead. One of them made a comment recorded by Charles: "My dear Monsieur d'Agoult, you must always do things differently. You will reflect for twenty-four hours and ask your friends for advice before accepting an invitation to dinner or making some futile decision. But when it is a matter which will affect your future life, you make up your mind suddenly without taking time to think and without consulting anybody." [6] It was to the credit of Madame de Flavigny that she appeared hesitant about the marriage, despite the social advantages. It was Charles himself who kept pressing ahead even when the negotiations broke down twice, whereas Madame de Flavigny seems to have prolonged them in order to give her daughter more time to reflect. The calendar for 1826 shows that there was a Friday the thirteenth in October, so if Marie first saw her future husband on that fateful day, a period of seven months must have elapsed before their wedding. According to the customs of the time, this would have seemed excessive.

Both Charles and Marie d'Agoult would one day bravely accept their share of responsibility for the error of their marriage. He realized too late that his simple pleasures and cheerful nature were not right for her, whereas she blamed herself for a lack of common sense and for accepting an arranged marriage in a wholly passive manner. The thought of having an older husband who might spoil her and do her bidding may have influenced her more than she knew. In addition, the prospect of an entry into the glittering world of the royal court may have appealed to her more than she would admit in years to come, after her political evolution toward the left.

The weeks before the wedding were a time of apprehension. This was a common experience in arranged marriages, and the usual remedy was to proceed as quickly as possible from the engagement to the ceremony. So many things could go wrong, such as the discovery of unpleasant characteristics in a fiancé whose visits were now more frequent. There was also the possibility of a scandal created by an angry mistress or the revelation that the future bride had written some love letters which had not been recovered, or even that she had lost her virginity.

For Marie there was no such hitch, and her wedding day approached inexorably. She and her mother were totally absorbed by the usual elaborate preparations. First, there were the endless purchases of elegant dresses and shawls of cashmere and lace, amid endless visits to fashionable boutiques. Then there were the formal dinners at which the two families met for the first time. About a week before the wedding the two parties signed the marriage contract, drawn up after detailed negotiations by the legal advisers of both families. This important document specified the ownership of property and money in every eventuality which could be imagined. After this crucial step, it was the duty of Madame de Flavigny to give a grand reception at which the presents received by the bride were put on show: diamond necklaces and bracelets; ostrich feathers; ermine furs; materials embroidered with gold and silver; shawls of lace and Indian silk. Also on display was her trousseau of dresses, petticoats, stockings, bonnets, handkerchiefs, and nightdresses.

This invasion of privacy was not to Marie's taste, as she knew that the older women would feel free to find fault in her trousseau. At last the wedding day came and the ceremony took place in the Church of the Assumption. That evening the Place Vendôme was full of splendid carriages bringing the nobility to their home. Marie resented the traditional sly jokes full of sexual innuendo to which the bride and groom were subjected during the celebrations. The long day then ended around midnight with the disappearance of the bride and her mother amid the knowing looks of all present. The moment for a crash course in sexual education had arrived at last. The date was 16 May 1826, and from this day her life would be forever changed. She had acquired social status as a wife and had become Countess Marie d'Agoult. It was a name which she would make famous in a manner not included in the marriage contract.

There is of course no account of Marie's sexual initiation, but she did provide some hint of possible problems in a story written years later. The custom of arranging marriages between partners who scarcely knew each other was not conducive to instant ecstasy, and contemporary literature suggests that sexual difficulties were common. Indeed Balzac's amusing *Physiology of Marriage,* published in 1828, was about to provide some frank discussion of the subject.[7] No man should get married without having dissected at least two women in order to acquire a knowledge of female anatomy, he asserted. Society is full of pale young wives who drag themselves around in constant pain and have attacks of nerves, all the fault of the husbands who commence their married life by an act of rape. The consummation of marriage could be particularly difficult for young women who were blonde and ethereal, said Balzac, and matters were even worse for the girl who made the mistake of marrying a soldier, as would the unfortunate Julie d'Aiglemont in his novel *The Woman of Thirty.* Marie too had married a soldier, and it does seem likely that she experienced the problem outlined by Balzac. There is nothing to suggest that she ever felt any physical attraction toward her husband, whereas it is probable that he did toward her.

Although Marie made no explicit revelations about her initiation, she protested in later years about the lack of sexual education for girls. Indeed her story *Valentia* treats the theme in a manner which suggests that it may have been inspired by a disturbing personal experience. The heroine of this fictional tale is a proud and sexually innocent girl who finds herself locked in an arranged marriage with a man she hardly knows. Her ignorance is so complete that on her wedding night she is surprised to see her husband enter her bedroom. He gives her a drink which sends her into a drugged sleep from which she awakes with a sensation of shame and humiliation. She remembers nothing but feels like killing either herself or her husband. Instinct tells her she has been violated in some way that she does not yet understand. Then Valentia recounts the first period of her marriage: "The next three months were what is called the honeymoon in high society. Count Ilse was drunk, one cannot say with love, so as not to profane that sacred word, but with the vanity of possessing a young and pretty wife. My passive submission to his desires, the complete silence which was my only response to the cynical expression of his passion, did not disturb him at all. When he thought fit to spare me from his caresses he would give me a conceited account of his past affairs, and go on about the passions he had inspired as if he wanted me to imitate him. My life was one long martyrdom."[8] It is fortunate that

Count d'Agoult's policy was never to read any of the works written by his wife in years to come, so it is improbable that he perused *Valentia*. He does not seem a likely candidate for the role of an erotic villain from a Gothic novel, but one never knows. How are we to take this lurid tale of conjugal rape and violation? What we know of the relationship between Charles and Marie does not seem to fit the story of Count Ilse and his fair victim, but Parisian readers of the time had read more than one confessional novel and were bound to see *Valentia* as a revelation of personal experience. We cannot hope to know the full facts, but this masochistic fantasy may reflect a real and traumatic experience in Marie's married life.

It is certain that Charles d'Agoult felt real affection for his young wife and tried to adapt to life with her. It is not so clear that the spoiled and inexperienced Marie saw the need to make an equal effort in order to meet him halfway. To judge by the letters of her husband, their married life seems to have started reasonably well with a trip to the seaside resort of Dieppe. Charles, who had a good relationship with Madame de Flavigny, whether because of a natural affinity or a similarity in the kind of affection they felt for Marie, sent her frequent letters, including this one written on 10 July 1827:

> Our apartment is one of the prettiest in Dieppe, and it is well furnished. Joseph, who always looks bad-tempered, serves us well nevertheless, and does his best to be a jack-of-all-trades. He makes quite a good stew, and we take other dishes from a nearby inn. In the morning, Joseph comes up to make chocolate or coffee for us, and with strawberries he buys or something left over from the previous supper we have a good breakfast; it all gives us a sort of life which is healthy and not too expensive. At Rouen we hired an excellent piano which arrived this morning. It will provide good entertainment for Marie. She has not yet taken any sea baths and does not seem to miss them and I think her health is very good; I think her appetite is better than in Paris. Every day we go for walks; in the evening we go to see M. and Mme de Castelbajac, or else they come and see us. There is also M. de Vigny and his family. His mother-in-law is about to give birth. How can a mother-in-law be so careless?

The author of this cheerful missive was evidently not a literary genius, but he does not much resemble the evil Count Ilse either. There is no sign of tension in this letter or in the one which relates how Marie persuaded him to go to London, where Maurice had been given a post as personal secretary to Prince Polignac, the French ambassador: "The rolling of the ship was so bad that one could hardly stand. The waves were reaching the deck and wetting the passengers. Mme d'Agoult was not seasick for an instant. She was steady on her feet and walked on the deck, wrapped in her cloak, admiring the conflict of the wind and the sea. She stood there, calm and inspired, like Corinne at the lake of Miseno."[9] Charles d'Agoult has got his geography slightly wrong in this reference to the Cape of Miseno. His letter refers to a scene in the novel *Corinne,* which had inspired a recent painting by François Gérard. There is some affectionate irony in this linking of Marie with the fictional heroine who poses so dramatically above the stormy sea at Naples.

They landed in Newhaven and set out to meet Marie's brother, who arrived with a group of friends. In Brighton they had a formal dinner, after which Maurice made a speech which Charles found rather long. Marie was enjoying her time in England. The couple went on to London, where they saw the usual sights and met people in the diplomatic corps. Marie also went shopping and bought a china tea set and material for dresses. Her husband was relieved to see this relative financial moderation and glad that she did not want to prolong their stay in a country where he had no friends and did not speak the language. On their return to France they remained for a time in Dieppe and then spent the rest of the summer in the Flavigny country home before going to Paris, where they settled in the rue de Beaune.

Charles d'Agoult soon began to reflect on the problems which lay ahead. He was aware of Marie's good qualities but could see that there was little chance of intimacy between him and this young intellectual who had entered marriage without knowing what it entailed. From the day of her wedding Marie asked herself how she could have let herself become the companion of a man she did not love. She had to endure the physical intimacy of marriage without the emotional bond which could make it pleasant. Although she was aware of her husband's decency and generosity of character, there was still a barrier between them which she could not cross. The situation was aggravated by the feeling that she could not communicate her problem to anyone. In her freely given marriage vows she had promised to love Charles but now felt a failure because she was unable to do so. The guilty secret had to be kept from family and friends. She did not even tell her confessor, to whom she told everything else, but did her best to keep up appearances and act the role of a happy young wife. Meanwhile sadness and tension grew within her.

The following year Marie gave birth to a daughter, whom she named Louise. Her new role provided some satisfaction but did not dampen her romantic ambitions. She still aspired to be a writer, and her husband noted with alarm that even when they traveled she surrounded herself with books and scribbled industriously on loose sheets of paper. There was some consolation for her in the thought that she would soon be in the Tuileries Palace, where she might play a significant role on a great new stage. Entry into the court of France had been part of the unwritten contract which went with her imprudent marriage. She had supplied her wealth, her youth, and her beauty. In exchange she would enter the corridors of power and enjoy the highest status which French society could give.

CHAPTER 6

The Wind of Revolution

THE regime which Charles and Marie d'Agoult now served was like a ship steaming toward an iceberg, with an incompetent navigator at its helm. Charles X had spent the first two years of his reign encouraging the demands of the Ultras, and in one of his first political acts he had alienated the army by the dismissal of most of the generals who had served under Napoleon. These men of experience and ability, many of them known to Charles d'Agoult, were replaced by inferior officers who were members of the old nobility. In a deliberate act of provocation the decision was published on the anniversary of Napoleon's victory at Austerlitz.

The king had also shown his skill at making enemies by supporting the more fanatical elements in the Catholic Church. One dramatic example was new legislation on sacrilege which came into force on 15 April 1825, bringing an automatic death penalty for the theft of silver or other valuables from a church. The worst aspect was the penalty prescribed for profanation of the sacred host. The criminal would be made to wear a black hood and walk barefoot to the guillotine, where his hand would be cut off by the executioner before his decapitation. This cruel punishment had not in fact been invented for the occasion, as it was simply a repetition of the old penalty for parricide, but the law caused furious controversy, and intelligent royalists like Chateaubriand vainly tried to prevent its adoption by the royalist majority in Parliament. In fact this punishment was never used during the six years of the reign of Charles X, as tends to happen with extreme legislation, and the law was repealed after his fall. Its main effect was to give the unintelligent monarch and his regime a reputation for cruelty and excess.

The reformed libertine who sat on the throne of France also sought to earn his place in heaven by acts of religious zeal intended to influence public opinion in a more attractive manner. In 1826 alone there were four processions attended by both houses of Parliament, the nobility, and the royal family. The king obviously enjoyed parading through the streets surrounded by priests and a cloud of incense; during one of these events he caused much interest by wearing a purple costume. The occasion was a ceremony commemorating the execution of Louis XVI, and the people of Paris, not knowing that purple was the color of royal mourning, began to believe a rumor that their king had become a bishop. As the power of the priests increased under this favorable influence, societies whose purposes were allegedly religious proliferated. The most notorious was called the Congrégation, a clandestine and powerful organization with tentacles in all parts of France. It had initiation rites as well as secret signals by which members could recognize one another, and it was whispered that the first indication of its power had been the abolition of divorce in 1816. The Congrégation's sphere of action included not only Parliament but also the press, the royal court, and the civil service; it reportedly had agents in every village as well. Into every significant French town came missions of eloquent priests determined to undo the work of the Revolution. The works of Voltaire and other rationalists were burned in symbolic fires.

It was easy to see the way to personal advancement under Charles X; ambitious members of the administration and army, for example, went in for religious ostentation. Marshal Nicholas Soult, a former general of Napoleon and notorious skeptic, could be seen going to mass with his whole family, while a member of his domestic staff carried his large missal on a silk cushion. The times had indeed changed, since Louis XVIII had made no such show of religious zeal. In fact the elderly monarch had continued the Versailles tradition by having a female favorite named Madame du Cayla as a sort of mistress. He had by this time become impotent, and it was whispered that the royal pleasure was to sprinkle snuff on her breasts and sniff it. His grandfather Louis XV would not have thought much of this performance, which inspired some witty songs by the satirist Jean de Béranger, but it seems that public opinion in France thought no less of the old king for his antics.

This was certainly not true of his brother Charles, who had the art of

Charles X, engraving of a portrait by François Gérard, 1825.

(Photothèque des Musées de la Ville de Paris)

attracting ridicule. At his coronation on 29 May 1825, he had decided to resurrect an ancient form of the ceremony which had last been performed over fifty years earlier. The traditional venue was the Cathedral of Rheims, which had been specially arranged for the occasion. The exterior of the fine Gothic edifice had been improved by stage scenery and in the nave had been erected a sort of stage and theater for the distinguished audience. At seven in the morning the new king had appeared in a tunic of crimson satin with seven apertures through which he would be anointed with oil from a Holy Phial. The sacred liquid was said to be the same used to anoint King Clovis of the Franks in the year 496, though everyone knew that in reality the glass bottle had been smashed on the base of a statue of Louis XVI by a revolutionary named Philippe Ruhl. The official version of events stated, however, that a few drops had been miraculously saved. The archbishop dipped a gold needle into the oil and anointed the last of the Bourbons, as prescribed by tradition. The king rose from his silk cushions and was handed his crown, sword, and scepter by Soult and other generals. At the end of the long ceremony, the curtain which separated the elite from the eyes of lesser mortals was drawn open. Great bells then rang out as a haze of incense rose under the high vaults, the organ played, and a flock of doves was released inside the cathedral, from which they escaped in some panic. Outside could be heard the boom of cannon and the crackle of muskets as a curious crowd awaited events.

The scenes were witnessed by the young Victor Hugo, who was there to record them for posterity. In an act of shameless careerism, he had written to the king to propose his services as official poet of the coronation. The offer was accepted, so the future champion of democracy donned a sort of fancy dress costume prescribed for the ceremony, which included a sword, shoes with silver buckles, and a feathered hat. Hugo duly produced a flattering ode full of platitudes in which Charles is compared to a beacon shining out in the darkness. That evening the king returned to the Tuileries Palace in Paris. Marie saw him arrive in a glittering carriage drawn by eight white horses whose heads were adorned with plumes. An unofficial version of the event was later provided by Béranger in a poem called "The Coronation of Charles the Simple," a piece of satire which earned him nine months in prison and provided some additional unpopularity for the king.

Those who had known Charles in his youth rubbed their eyes in amazement at this display of pomp and religion. In the prerevolutionary court, the young comte d'Artois had been famous for his frivolity and his addiction to every known pleasure, and his numerous love affairs had won him a reputation of sorts among the young rakes of the nobility. In those early days it was already clear that he was devoid of political sense: his lack of common prudence showed before the Revolution of 1789 when he loudly opposed all reforms. At the first sniff of danger he quickly left France and settled for a time in the court of Catherine II of Russia, a notorious nymphomaniac whom he charmed so effectively that she gave him a sword studded with magnificent diamonds. The ironical intention behind this gift of a warlike instrument was clear to all but Charles himself.

The low point of Charles's career occurred in 1795 when he moved to England and was given the command of an expeditionary force of French royalists who landed on the Quiberon peninsula in southern Brittany in an attempt to overthrow the Republic. Charles had deemed it appropriate to remain within the safety of his ship while the men under his command were cut down or captured by the opposing army. After this display of cowardice and incompetence, he returned to Britain, where he divided his time between his wife and his mistress, Madame de Polastron. As the latter lay on her deathbed she extracted a promise that he would remain faithful to her and devote the rest of his life to God. Charles X was determined to remain true to his word and to impose religion and obedience on the nation when his family so unexpectedly regained the throne. In his attempt to do this, he displayed that suicidal zeal characteristic of those whom nature has not designed for high office. Charles and Marie d'Agoult had tied their fate to this incompetent king as a tide of discontent began to rise around his throne.

Charles X was naturally surrounded by parasites and flatterers who did nothing to dispel his illusions, among them the beliefs that the nation felt esteem and affection for him and his family and that the unpopularity of Villèle and the other ministers did not affect him. In fact there was a small grain of truth in this, because public opinion still thought he was occupied almost exclusively with religion and hunting, and when he showed himself in Paris, the people reacted with indifference rather than hostility. In an attempt to improve the royal image he decided to review the National Guard in a spectacular parade which would equal anything produced by Napoleon. A good horseman, he felt he would cut a fine figure in front of his loyal troops.

The ceremony went ahead against the advice of both Villèle and Chateaubriand, and it was a political disaster. The National Guard was not a part of the disciplined regular army but a part-time militia drawn from the middle class. It had shown royalist sentiments at the time of the fall of Napoleon, whose constant wars had alienated it, but twelve years are a very long time in politics, and the bourgeoisie had been angered by the new power of the priests and the nobility. Here was an opportunity for some vocal members of the class to make themselves heard.

The traditional venue for military parades was the Champ-de-Mars on the Left Bank of the Seine and the date set by Charles was 29 April 1827, two weeks before the marriage of Marie and Charles d'Agoult. The king, accompanied by his minister of war, began to move on horseback along the ranks of guardsmen in their smart uniforms. The first incident took place when some voices from the ranks shouted "Down with the ministers!" The king smiled and said, "That is for you, Clermont-Tonnerre." The next event was less amusing for the king. It happened when a militiaman broke ranks, stood insolently in front of the royal horse and shouted "Down with Jesuits!" This brought an angry reply from the king, who was learning that royal authority was not what it had once been. There was further confirmation of this when the dauphine drove along the lines of troops in an open carriage and was greeted with a chorus of jeers and insults. Tears came into her eyes, and she must have remembered the fate of her mother, Marie-Antoinette, and asked herself if history was repeating itself. When she turned away to hide her tears, the gesture was interpreted by the militia as sure proof of aristocratic arrogance and contempt for commoners.

In the deliberation which followed these incidents the minister of war proposed a moderate reaction in the form of a selective disbanding of the unruly battalions. Villèle argued that a militia which saw fit to insult the royal person had become a revolutionary institution and should be wholly eradicated at once. The king shared this hawkish attitude, and the decree announcing the dissolution of the National Guard was signed the next day. The decision was resented by much of the Parisian middle class as an insult.

Charles X had taken one more small step along the road to his downfall. Anxiety reigned throughout the city as a vague fear of political catastrophe began to spread. The older people of Paris had not forgotten the chaotic and terrible events of the Revolution.

Shortly after the fiasco of the National Guard review, Marie d'Agoult was presented at court and came into contact with the royal family, which now sat so precariously on the throne of France. She had already had a close look at her husband's patron, the duchess of Angoulême, who liked to use the youthful title of dauphine, although she was approaching fifty. Marie-Thérèse had not inherited any of the wit and charm of Marie-Antoinette. Indeed she seemed almost to want to be the opposite of her unfortunate mother, as if her attractive qualities had somehow contributed to her downfall. Portraits painted in her youth show that Marie-Thérèse had once been good-looking, with blonde hair and gentle blue eyes like those of Marie-Antoinette, but as years went by she lost her waist and acquired the thick nose and hoarse voice of Louis XVI. It was during her time of exile in Austria that she married the duke of Angoulême, her first cousin, in a dynastic union which produced no children and little satisfaction. In her years of adversity she was generally admired for her courage and dignity. After a series of almost unbelievable events Marie-Thérèse was now expected to become the next queen of France. But she had not been prepared for the role and found it hard to acquire the necessary skills.

If the duchess of Angoulême was a sad and charmless person, her husband was not much better endowed. When Marie met him for the first time in 1828, she was not impressed by the appearance of the heir to the throne and quickly imagined the life of the woman joined to him in a loveless marriage. It was true that Antoine d'Angoulême had some good qualities, because he had recently showed competence as commander of a French military expedition in Spain. In official publications he was pompously called the Hero of the Trocadero because of his success in a battle in that part of Spain, but Marie could see that the great warrior was a puny little man with a facial tic.

Her introduction into court had followed a detailed procedure which the Bourbons had resurrected from the previous century. Each new wife was to be presented by two ladies of high status chosen from her family

circle and known as godmothers. The ceremony was complicated, so special lessons were taken from the familiar figure of M. Abraham. Despite a
quarter century of exile in various capitals of Europe, the old dancing master could recall every detail of the presentations at the court of Versailles.
The duchess of Angoulême therefore called him to the Tuileries Palace to
re-create the old ceremony in all its pomp and grace. The sprightly M. Abraham, with his lace cuffs and diamond rings, had scarcely aged since Marie
had last seen him. Three rehearsals were needed to teach her how to bow
to the king and how to deal with the long train on her court dress.

The first part of the presentation was relatively easy, as the ceremony
began with a slow movement forward, which was interrupted by three deep
bows. The first of these was made on entering a long gallery at the end of
which the king and his gentlemen stood. The second bow came when the
new wife and her godmothers moved in a stately manner to the middle
of the room. The third and final bow was made in proximity to the king,
who would advance and return the greeting. Then began the difficult part,
because the ladies had to depart from the royal presence without turning
their backs or tripping over their dresses. The trick was to move backward
and sideways in a crablike but elegant manner while giving discreet little
kicks to the heavy garment. There were stories about nervous new wives
becoming entangled in their finery and falling in a heap. Old members of
the court enjoyed telling newcomers these tales, which naturally increased
their anxiety on the big occasion.

Marie spent the day before the presentation in feverish activity with her
dressmaker and her seamstresses, while her godmothers watched closely.
Her gown was made of white tulle decorated with silver flowers, and her
cloak and train of velvet embroidered with silver. As decreed by the dauphine, Marie's hair was brushed into the stiff, high style of the previous
century and topped with ostrich feathers. On her head she wore a heavy
silver diadem set with diamonds, and around her neck was a rich confec-
tion of gems and emeralds. In her hands she held a handkerchief of old lace
and a fan inlaid with gold and mother-of-pearl. A thick layer of makeup
completed the costume.

As a special favor to her old friend the viscountess d'Agoult, the dauphine had expressed a wish to check Marie's appearance before the presen-

tation. Accordingly, Marie and the viscountess went to the palace and were taken to a room where they were told to wait. Suddenly the dauphine burst in and silently studied Marie from head to foot. After this unnerving examination she turned to the viscountess and curtly said, "She needs more rouge." Having made this peremptory statement, she turned on her heels and left as quickly as she had come, without saying a word to Marie. "How did I fail to see it?" said the viscountess in a tragic tone. She did not seem at all surprised by the strange manner of her friend. It was too late to rectify the error because the ceremony was about to begin and a king could not be made to wait while somebody looked for rouge.

Five minutes later Marie and her godmothers were making their bows in the splendid gallery of the Tuileries Palace as the nobility, in their richly decorated uniforms, stood around the king. Charles X was tall and slim and had a youthful air in spite of his years. He was obviously at ease with women, showing the charming manners of the old regime, and he made up for the rudeness of his niece by complimenting Marie on her appearance. After this he chatted affably with the three ladies before dismissing them with a gracious bow. From this time on, Charles X would always remember Marie's face when they met, an indication that he had at least one quality useful to a holder of high office.

Over the next two years she saw the king regularly during the course of the dauphine's dreary evenings, and he took pleasure in talking to the young woman who had been introduced into his inner circle. She always found him to have a polite and pleasant manner with ladies and to be devoid of royal pride in these small social gatherings. Indeed his personal attitude seemed to be the exact opposite of his political one, which showed an impatient desire to increase the royal power. Marie found the conversation of Charles X very limited, however. Was this the man whose witty quips were repeated in court circles? She concluded that he could not have invented them himself.

Because of the dauphine's lack of social skill, the royal soirées were not conducive to conversation, and for much of the time the duchess sat at the head of a group of ladies strictly placed according to status. As she worked with jerky movements on a piece of embroidery she would bark out a question to each one of the ladies in turn. The person thus honored would make

some banal reply amidst general silence. After this they all went on em-
broidering until the next question came. The duc d'Angoulême usually sat
apart and was often absorbed in a game of chess played with the viscountess
d'Agoult.

At the other end of the room the king would be playing whist, and
occasionally one could hear the royal voice raised in irritation after losing a
round or the sound of his partner offering an apology or some polite comment. When the king's game was over, he would rise to his feet, as would
everyone in the room. The dauphin would at once abandon his game of chess
to go and stand beside his father. The king would then say goodnight to the
company and retire. At once the gathering dispersed, and Marie would go
home reflecting on the intolerable dullness of these royal evenings, which
were considered to be a sign of the highest favor. She much preferred the
big receptions and concerts which took place in the public rooms of the
Tuileries Palace, though these social occasions were less to the taste of her
soldier husband, whom nature had not intended as a courtier.

After presentation to the king, all newly married couples had to make
a series of visits to certain noble ladies who had once played a role in court.
Failure to do so was a social crime of the greatest magnitude. Marie therefore dutifully showed herself to a number of dowagers who sat at their fireside with a cat or a box of sweets on their knees. The visit did not last longer
than ten minutes, which was long enough for them to assess the new wife by
looking her up and down and making comments on her eyes, teeth, bosom,
hands, and feet. After this visual dissection, there was fortunately no need
to see the dowagers again. Their traditional rights had been respected and
they were satisfied.

In her new status as married woman, Marie had regular contact with
other aristocratic females whose company she enjoyed. Her favorite was
Madame de Montcalm, whose older brother, Armand de Richelieu, had
been a prime minister of Louis XVIII. Her salon was frequented by a number
of eminent politicians, including Louis Molé, Guillaume Barante, Joseph
Lainé, and Claude Mounier, as well as by diplomats such as the Russian
ambassador Pozzo di Borgo and Marie's friend Lagarde. Armande de Montcalm was a slightly built lady who always reclined on a chair because of poor
health. She had grown up under the old regime and made no concession

to the current affectation of piety. She was a good listener who kept her
dark eyes fixed attentively on the person speaking. Marie had the impression that she had loved and suffered in her earlier life and wondered if her
role as society hostess was a compensation for a different form of happiness.
Madame de Montcalm did not try to be witty or to direct the conversation,
and discussions in her salon were informed and moderate. The usual subjects were politics, art, and literature, and she encouraged contributions
from everyone, including young persons like Marie. As a close friend of
Lagarde, she had a particular affection for the girl who had nearly married
him, and the evenings spent in her salon were the best part of Marie's new
life. In years to come she would recall them as an example of what was most
valuable in the social life of the aristocracy.

The salon of Madame de La Trémoille was less pleasing to Marie because
of the domineering personality of the hostess. She had never been good-
looking, and from an early age she had decided to cultivate her mind rather
than her appearance, deeming it a lost cause. Madame de La Trémoille had
gathered around her a group of distinguished Ultras, including the writers
Louis de Bonald and Joseph de Maistre, who were the principle propagan-
dists of the party. Her salon was also frequented by Jules de Polignac, who
was soon to become prime minister and precipitate a revolution. Despite
her total skepticism in matters of religion, she was cultivated by eminent
conservative clerics such as M. de Genoude and Cardinal de La Fare. Her
salon also attracted the usual crowd of minor flatterers and parasites.

Madame de La Trémoille could not bear the boredom of summer
months with her husband at their estate in Pezeau, in the province of Berry.
Politics were her obsession, and she was happy only in their Paris home in
the rue de Bourbon, where their garden overlooked the Seine. Her favorite room was an elegant library, where she held court in a green armchair.
There she entertained the elite of the royalist party with a string of sarcastic witticisms and vivid impersonations of her political opponents. The list
was a long one, since it included anyone who saw the need to make any
concession to modern times, and even Prime Minister Villèle, a staunch
royalist, did not always find favor in her eyes, as she suspected him of moderation. As for Louis XVIII, she had condemned him as being little better

than a revolutionary. She even had doubts about the desire of Charles X to bring back a proper system of absolute monarchy and used her infirmity as an excellent reason never to visit the Tuileries Palace, always preferring her personal court, where she used a mixture of flattery and authority to reign over her own subjects.

Within the royal court Marie felt drawn to Caroline de Berry because of her youth and spontaneity, though she did not see her often except in large gatherings. She recalled first noticing the young woman as she fidgeted during the king's speech in 1824. She now knew the details of her earlier life. In 1816 the princess had been sent from Naples to marry the duc de Berry, who was the younger son of the future Charles X and likely to become king in due course. She was only seventeen and had never met her husband, who was approaching forty. Both partners in this potential dynastic disaster were naturally anxious about the outcome. Arranged marriages did not always work out for the worst, however, and Caroline liked Charles de Berry, with whom she formed a happy union. He was a blunt, energetic man who had fought against the French Republic in Condé's army of exiles, as had Marie's father. When the force was disbanded, he settled in England, where he occupied himself with many mistresses. One of these was a singer named Amy Brown, who bore him several children and to whom he became very attached. After the restoration of the monarchy in France, he was given high rank in the army and became popular among the soldiers because of his frequent visits to their barracks and his concern for their welfare. He was also liked by the common people of Paris. They approved of this soldierly figure who made no affectation of piety and who did not act as if his royal blood placed him on a pedestal. Public opinion also looked favorably on the vivacious young Italian wife who lived with him in the Elysée Palace, the scene of summer balls in the gardens. They had artistic and musical tastes not shared by other members of the royal family.

Disaster struck the couple on the evening of 13 February 1820, as they were returning from the opera house in the rue de Richelieu. It was Mardi Gras, and the work performed that day was *The Carnival of Venice,* by Campa. About eleven Caroline began to feel tired and decided to go home before the end of the opera. As her husband was helping her into their carriage, a

Caroline de Berry, ca. 1820.

(Photothèque des Musées de la Ville de Paris)

man came up and stabbed him in the back with a long knife. The attacker ran for his life but was caught by an irate vendor of ice cream whose tray he had upset at the entrance to the Colbert Arcade.

The injured duke was laid on a couch in an upstairs room in the opera house, with the cheerful music in the background. Doctors were hurriedly summoned and pronounced the wound to be fatal. When this brought despairing cries from Caroline, her dying husband opened his eyes and said, "Be careful my dear for the sake of our child." In this way it became known that Caroline was pregnant, a piece of news which brought new hope to the childless Bourbons. Louis XVIII appeared and was laboriously carried up the stairs in order to say farewell to his nephew. Generous to the end, the dying soldier asked the king to promise that the life of his killer would be spared, but the monarch answered evasively. The assassin was Pierre Louvel, a saddle maker by trade and a fanatical Bonapartist. He was condemned and sent to the guillotine after coolly asserting at his trial that he had dedicated his life to the extermination of the royal family, starting with the only member who was capable of having children.

The boy born seven months later was called the Miracle Child by the jubilant royalists, and the event did much to change the status of Caroline de Berry in court. On her arrival from Naples, she had caused consternation in the straight-laced dauphine by her lack of regal qualities. The rigid etiquette of the Tuileries Palace conflicted with her nature, which was cheerful and vivacious, but also naive and ignorant. Her gaffes were an endless source of anecdotes. The dauphine and her ladies complained about her low-cut dresses, which were also too short for their liking. They also made acid remarks about her absent look in church and her careless way of holding a candle in a religious procession so that the wax fell on her dress. Her defenders pointed out that she had achieved the feat of winning the heart of her husband and stopping his roving eye. Because Charles de Berry was pleased with his young wife, her detractors had to keep their disapproval to themselves.

After his death Caroline won general admiration for her quiet courage as she brought up the royal child who would live in danger of assassination. The young widow continued to support musicians and the arts, as she had done in her husband's time. Gradually she began to appear in public again and to attend concerts and operas. One of her pleasures was sea bathing in the town of Dieppe, which she visited every summer. At this distance from the disapproving eyes of the dauphine, she could let her hair down and be herself. Remarkably, she was accompanied by two girls which Amy Brown had borne to her husband. He had made a dying request to Caroline to look after the welfare of these love children, and she had loyally carried out her promise to do so in spite of disdainful comments in court. Caroline's attitude added to her popularity with the public, which showed a true appreciation of her generosity. Nowhere was she more popular than Dieppe, which was quickly made fashionable by her patronage and her liking for the local jewelry carved from ivory.

It was in Dieppe that Marie met Caroline for the first time. The year was 1826, the summer before Marie's marriage. There she observed a ludicrous piece of etiquette invented to give solemnity to the duchess's first sea bath of the season. It involved the participation of a fully dressed doctor wearing white gloves and a top hat who would walk slowly into the sea with the duchess, holding her hand as if they were about to dance a minuet. Once the royal immersion had taken place, the event was marked by the firing of a cannon.

After this dramatic initiation, Caroline and other bathers could revert to the usual procedure for ladies at the seaside: one disrobed in a tent erected on the sand and emerged wearing a tunic of black wool over long pants of the same material, cloth slippers, and a scarf around the head. It was fashionable to take the first dip with the help of a professional bather — strapping men who carried the ladies into the water and plunged them in, head and all. They were then placed upright with their feet on the sandy bottom and left to themselves. Marie met Caroline because they had the same bath attendant. Forgetting all protocol and dignity, the Neapolitan princess would splash water over anyone who came near her and insist on retaliation by the injured party. Marie enjoyed these boisterous games and was amused to see the young widow as happy as a schoolgirl on holiday.

The final part of the sea bath was the return to the tent, which was sometimes a considerable distance from the sea because of the tides. As female bathers emerged from the water, their shapeless woolen costumes clung to their bodies, and they did not much resemble the sea nymphs portrayed by classical painters. In addition, as they made their way to the tents, they were aware of being watched by numerous gentlemen with opera glasses. Such conduct was considered highly improper, but Caroline did nothing to avoid this common fate, either because she did not want to become unpopular or because she enjoyed it.

Marie's acquaintance with her was mostly restricted to these summer encounters, because the court did not approve of Caroline's regular attendance at the home of Philippe d'Orléans, a cousin of the king who was suspected of having designs on the throne. Politically, he showed progressive tendencies, and his home in the Palais Royal, unlike the Tuileries Palace, was open to a mixture of classes. When Marie received an invitation to attend a concert there, she felt that she had to consult Madame d'Agoult before accepting. The viscountess reacted warily and expressed her distrust of the duke and his faction. "I do not like that lot," she said with a frown. However, an invitation from the cousin of the king could not be lightly refused, and Marie was advised to accept. It was customary in court to speak critically of the low company kept by the duke of Orléans, but when Marie went to his home she was impressed by the quality of the politicians, financiers, and intellectuals of the liberal opposition, whom she was meeting for the first time. It was true that the royalists had such distinguished literary figures as Chateaubriand, Lamartine, Hugo, and Vigny on their side, but this upcoming group might be the new elite of the nation.

For Marie, who was more interested in culture than in politics at this time, the poetic works of Lamartine and Hugo provided more emotional than intellectual stimulation. Her interest in poetry once caused a fiasco which she would always remember with amusement and some mortification. Wanting to have a literary salon, she persuaded her friend Alfred de Vigny to read one of his new compositions before an audience in her home on 20 April 1829. The cream of Parisian society was invited for the occasion. Vigny's narrative poem was an anglophobic account of the sinking of a French naval frigate called La Sérieuse by Nelson's fleet some decades earlier. When he finished the reading, there was an awful silence among her guests. My frigate has been shipwrecked in your salon, said the poet to Marie when

Alfred de Vigny.

(Photothèque des Musées de la Ville de Paris)

he later took his leave. The Austrian ambassador had politely asked Marie whether the young gentleman wrote much verse.[1]

She was beginning to take note of the contemporary debate about the future of society. On one side there were the new theories of Saint-Simon concerning the eradication of poverty and the improvement of society by science and industry. Opposing them were reactionary writers like Joseph de Maistre protesting the very notion of individual rights and the idea of social progress. Suffering and war were an integral part of life, he argued, and the salvation of society would come from a return to obedience and religion. In the world of art, too, there was controversy, as the audacious paintings of Delacroix and Géricault drew sharp reactions from the critics. Marie continued to enjoy the traditional pleasures of Italian opera and to listen to the works of Rossini, Bellini, and Donizetti, magnificently sung by outstanding artists such as Madame Pasta and Madame Malibran. More daring sounds were heard in concerts featuring the works of Berlioz, and a new musical star had appeared on the Paris scene. His name was Franz Liszt, and his impact on Marie's life would be profound.

While this intellectual and artistic ferment was taking place in Paris, she continued to ask herself if she really wanted the high honor of her position in court. The favor of the dauphine should ensure a lucrative position for Charles d'Agoult when he left the army, and this could not be forgotten. Neither Charles nor Marie had sufficient understanding of the political situation to know that the regime was seriously threatened. The king was obstinately refusing to make concessions to a Parliament in which the opposition achieved a majority in late 1827. As is the way with political leaders, he had convinced himself that he enjoyed considerable personal popularity. This illusion was based on a visit to Alsace, where he had been applauded by the peasantry. Since he was dealing with a hostile Parliament, the king resolved that the situation was ripe for a final confrontation in which he would curb its power and establish himself as the master of France. To succeed in this secret plan, he knew he could call on a faithful accomplice who had been kept waiting in the wings. The stage was prepared, and the new protagonist, Jules de Polignac, emerged. At the time, he was still the French ambassador to London, where he was in daily contact with Marie's brother, Maurice.

Jules de Polignac had good personal reasons to support the French monarchy, since the family fortune had been made by Marie-Antoinette, an intimate friend of his mother's. The queen had noticed the witty and charming Gabrielle de Polignac at a ball in Versailles and had taken a passionate liking to her. On inquiring why the young woman came so rarely to court, she learned that the modest income of the Polignac estate did not make this possible. Marie-Antoinette quickly set this right by showering Gabrielle and her husband with money and favor, causing a considerable scandal; the tongues of courtiers began to wag as they speculated about the nature of this friendship between the two young women. As a consequence of this royal favor, the Polignacs became extremely unpopular in Paris and quickly fled the city when the trouble began in 1789. Jules then served in the exiled royalist army and became famous for an unusual act of generosity. He had been captured in Paris in 1803 and sentenced to prison for his part in a plot by Georges Cadoudal to assassinate Bonaparte. As his older brother had also participated in the undercover operation and had been condemned to death, Jules had asked to take his place. In the end neither brother was executed, but his courage won him a reputation in the royalist party. With the restoration of the monarchy, he had received his reward in the form of high office in the diplomatic service. In this new career he became known as an inflexible and opinionated man who made no concessions to changing times. He was unwilling to take advice from anyone and claimed to receive instructions directly from the Virgin Mary during her regular apparitions to him.

Marie had often heard her brother talk about Polignac, but she had been busy with her first experience of motherhood and unaware of the political drama in which he was about to play a part. In her social milieu there had been little serious discussion of the symptoms of political and intellectual opposition to the regime, and she was scarcely conscious of the role played by men such as François Guizot, Victor Cousin, and François Villemain. If her friends happened to mention Constant and his newspaper, La Minerve, it would be with a disdainful smile. She was therefore ill prepared for what was about to happen.

Her first real intimation of trouble came on an evening in August 1829, when she had gone to the opera to see Rossini's William Tell. As she sat in

Jules de Polignac, ca. 1825.

(Photothèque des Musées de la Ville de Paris)

the court box, she was joined by Madame du Cayla, who was dressed in her usual ornate manner. The former royal favorite seemed anxious and during the interval revealed the cause of her concern: it was rumored that Polignac had been recalled to Paris and was about to become prime minister. Marie did not understand why this was a cause for anxiety. Her brother, who had worked under Polignac for the past year, described him as a kind and charming man. How could his promotion be a calamity? When Madame du Cayla rose to leave, she said, "Madame d'Agoult, I am afraid." Marie noted that her face was pale beneath its thick layer of makeup and that her breathing was agitated. She would always remember the prophetic words of Madame du Cayla, whose apprehension she now shared.

Before the week was out, the king made Polignac prime minister and started a train of events which would lead to the downfall of his monarchy. The appointment of Polignac was seen in Paris as a sign that a collision between king and Parliament was coming, a confrontation loudly welcomed in royalist newspapers like *La Quotidienne*. In the eyes of the majority of the nation the move was seen as a provocation; even the dauphine had doubts, which she vainly expressed to the king.

The year 1830 began with extreme cold. Ice was so thick on the Seine that it was feared the bridges would be destroyed. There was much hardship in Paris, but *La Quotidienne* reported that the royal family had made a large donation to the poor. Meanwhile the opposition in Parliament was preparing for the coming battle. The first confrontation took place on 2 March 1830, when the king, in an address to Parliament, threatened to curb its power. Parliament answered by sending a delegation to the palace to assert its constitutional rights and to demand the dismissal of Polignac. Charles X abandoned his usual courtesy by remaining seated and showing signs of impatience while the delegates delivered their address. He then put his hand under his posterior and pulled out a prepared statement, which he proceeded to read. It curtly informed them that he had made his decisions, which would soon be communicated to them.

Reports of this confrontation were soon in the press, and *La Quotidienne* exultantly proclaimed that at last France had a king who knew the meaning of firm government. It was clear from the terms of the royal address that he was preparing to assume special powers and to suspend the normal workings of the Constitution. It was a dangerous and provocative move, but Polignac continued to exude calm. It was at this crucial moment in French history that Marie met Polignac, for the first and only time. The reason for the encounter was her brother's marriage, at which the prime minister had agreed to be a witness. The date was 8 July 1830, just three weeks before the coup which had already been secretly planned by Polignac. Marie saw before her a handsome man who had evidently inherited the good looks of his mother. He was tall and slim and had a pleasant smile, a graceful manner, and a certain nobility in his expression. She noted that he resembled Charles X physically and remembered the rumor that he was his natural son. He was also like the king in his relaxed and easy manner.

At the wedding lunch Polignac was in excellent humor and showed no sign of preoccupation with the serious political matters on his mind. After the meal he even remained for some time to play with Marie's daughter, Louise, now aged two. The child had been given a Noah's ark and a set of animals by Maurice's new wife, Mathilde, and the prime minister explained the difference between a camel and a dromedary and helped her arrange the animals on the table. When he mentioned the political situation, he spoke with complete nonchalance, which surprised and reassured Marie. A man who was capable of such calm and who showed kindness to a child was surely a good leader.

On 25 July 1830 Polignac brought the details of his political plan to the palace of Saint-Cloud, where the royal family was spending the hot summer days. The king would simply make emergency decrees which suspended the freedom of the press and dissolved Parliament, all of which was allowed by the Constitution. Charles X breathed heavily as he read the text of the decrees and seemed to hesitate. Then he took his pen and signed the document. When the news spread through the palace, there was jubilation, and the duchess of Berry impulsively came to kiss his hand and congratulate him for having made the throne secure for her young son. Well pleased with his decision, the king then went hunting in the forest of Rambouillet. Polignac had told him that the army regiments in Paris were perfectly adequate to deal with any possible trouble. The prefect of police had given him a similar assurance about the municipal forces under his control.

When the manuscript of the decrees was delivered to the editor of Le

Moniteur that same evening, he turned pale with apprehension. The fateful text was given to the printers and was published the next morning. At this time Marie and her mother were in their new home in the rue de Beaune where it joined the part of the Quai Malaquais that is now the Quai Voltaire. A large house known as the Hôtel de Mailly, it was pleasantly situated on the Left Bank of the Seine, its rows of chestnut trees overlooking the river. Marie was heavily pregnant with her second child, and on these hot days she liked to sit and muse among the flowers and birds. Across the river could be seen the Tuileries Palace, framed by the tranquil gardens which would soon be a battleground.

She was sitting outside with her mother when news of the royal decrees was brought by friends. The two women felt that violent protests were to be feared and were worried about Maurice and his bride, who had not yet returned from their honeymoon. When the young couple reached Paris the next morning, Maurice expressed astonishment at the events and quickly set off for the Ministry of Foreign Affairs, where he waited for his superior to appear. When Polignac reached his office later that morning, he was quietly exultant and quite unconcerned by the stones and insults which had been hurled at his coach as it progressed through the streets of Paris. He received Maurice with his usual smile and a jaunty look which showed his satisfaction at having been so secretive and profound. He told him to inform his relatives that the situation was completely under control. When Maurice politely expressed some doubts, Polignac smiled in an enigmatic manner, as if to imply that he had some superior source of information which could not be revealed.

As Maurice returned with news of his meeting with the prime minister, he was far from reassured. In the streets he had seen excited crowds shouting "Down with Polignac!" and columns of soldiers advancing to take up position around the Tuileries Palace, amidst provocative jeers. In Madame de Flavigny's drawing room, however, their royalist friends were noisily expressing their satisfaction and welcoming the prospect of the good hiding which was about to be given to the rabble in the streets. After some discussion of the situation, they dispersed and went out to observe events.

On the afternoon of 27 July, as the city sweltered under a prolonged heatwave, Marie went into the garden to feel the coolness of the Seine as it flowed quietly past. Some family friends arrived and joined her under the trees. Their voices were now subdued, however, and a new note of anxiety could be sensed. During the morning the situation had become serious as opposition papers appeared, in spite of the ban, and called for civil disobedience. The authorities had answered by having the presses of the dissident newspapers smashed with hammers. This at once precipitated street demonstrations by print workers and students. There were reports that in parts of the city bands men had broken into gunshops and taken arms and ammunition. Meanwhile the army was still grouped around the ministries and palaces in central Paris. About five in the afternoon Marie heard a loud detonation and was informed that it was a volley of musket fire. A frisson of fear ran down her spine as she imagined the dead and wounded lying in some nearby street.

Maurice returned shortly after this with the news that a crowd in the rue des Pyramides had refused an order to disperse and had been fired upon by a company of infantry. Those not killed or injured had taken to their heels with cries of anger and vengeance. Madame de Flavigny, now beside herself with worry, made the irrational suggestion that Marie be sent to Brussels because of her advanced state of pregnancy. Charles d'Agoult could not be consulted, as he was with his regiment, but Maurice argued that his sister would be safer in Paris than traveling the roads at a time of unrest.

While this anxious deliberation was taking place, more regiments were pouring into the center of the city. There were detachments of cavalry and infantry on the Place de la Concorde, and the rumble of cannon wheels could be heard echoing in the narrow streets. As the hours went by, Marie's servants brought back ever more ominous news. Barricades of cobblestones and overturned vehicles were being constructed in the working-class areas of Paris, and the insurgents were trying to fraternize with the soldiers. That night all seemed quiet, but Marie could not sleep. She rose very early on July 28 and went into the garden to listen to the sounds of the city. She found her mother already dressed and talking to the royalist friend who had been so pleased at the thought of what would befall the rebels. He was now pale with worry and told her that during the night the royal insignia on every post office and public building in their area had been broken. The insurrection was taking an ominous direction.

About ten that morning Maurice went through the cordon of troops surrounding his ministry and returned in an hour without having seen Polignac, who was at Saint-Cloud reporting to the king. He brought the news that everyone in the ministry expected the imminent declaration of a state of siege. This would give General Auguste de Marmont supreme power in Paris until the rising was under control. But the insurgents were quickly gaining ground: it was learned that they had captured the Hôtel de Ville and replaced the royal flag on the roof with the tricolor. In addition they had seized the stores of guns and ammunition kept there by the municipal authorities to be used in times of unrest. The chanting of the rebels was no longer directed against Polignac and the ministers alone, Maurice reported, but against the royal family itself. The rebellion which had appeared to start spontaneously now seemed to be orchestrated and controlled by persons unknown.

As Maurice reached this point in his account there was a sinister sound they had never heard before. It was the *tocsin,* the ringing of all the church bells of Paris to warn people off the streets. Not even in the dark days of 1814, when the Prussian and Russian armies were outside the walls, had this alarm been given. Marie would never forget the deep resonance of the bells as their sound mingled with the beating of drums and the crackle of gunfire. She shivered with apprehension as she felt the wind of revolution rise around them.

In the early afternoon friends eagerly brought the news that the insurrection would soon be crushed because a state of siege had at last been declared and that leading opponents of the regime were to be arrested. The army was to use its artillery to demolish the barricades and sweep the rebels from the streets once and for all. During the rest of the day they remained inside their house, listening to the thunder of the cannon and the sound of musket fire in the streets across the Seine. The army seemed to be making little progress as the well-organized insurgents made tactical retreats from barricade to barricade while snipers kept firing on the troops from windows and rooftops. All day the blazing sun beat down on the soldiers, who had received neither food nor drink and were nearing exhaustion. Soon the insurrection had control over much of the city, except for the heavily protected central area around the ministries and palaces, where the royal flags could still be seen from Marie's house. Despite these events Polignac continued to send reassuring notes to Saint-Cloud, where Charles X expressed the opinion that the population of Paris would soon tire of anarchy and return to obedience. He revealed his intention to give a generous pardon to all except the most dangerous elements. He affected the usual routine during the emergency, and consequently the royal family had its usual game of whist that afternoon. The king was occasionally seen to twitch as the sound of cannon came through the open window.

At eleven that night the tocsin stopped and there was no more firing. Fortunately there had not been any fighting in the Saint-Germain area where Marie lived. During the day they had heard contradictory rumors. Where was the king? Where was Polignac? Nobody seemed to know. Some said that the Marquis de Vitrolles was trying to achieve an agreement between the rebels and the cabinet, but events had surely gone too far for compromise. From her upstairs window Marie could see the summer night lit by the flames of burning buildings. In the city there was a pregnant silence as the insurgents melted lead from the roofs to make bullets for a final push.

On the morning of 29 July the area around her home was filled with agitation as a column of students and workers came from the Latin Quarter along the rue du Bac. They were a motley crew, some in uniform, some in overalls, some in smart suits, some in rags. Their weapons were a mixture of sporting rifles and heavy army muskets; some army veterans carried old sabers which had seen service in the Napoleonic wars. They attempted to erect a barricade on the Pont Royal despite being fired on by the troops defending the palace. Meanwhile another group of insurgents was making a parallel advance across the Pont des Arts toward the Louvre palace. Volleys of bullets were coming from the windows of the royal building, and Marie left the garden for the relative safety of an upstairs window from which she could see something of the scene.

It was a dramatic sight. After hours of resistance from the soldiers within the two palaces a group of attackers climbed scaffolding and suddenly appeared inside the buildings. The defenders suddenly panicked and abandoned the fight. They could be seen jumping from the lower windows and escaping through the Tuileries gardens in the direction of Saint-Cloud. At once the royal buildings were filled with insurgents and from across the river came wild cheers followed by the sound of breaking glass as pieces of furniture were hurled through the windows. The firing soon stopped and Marie saw the tricolor flag being raised over the palaces.

Although Paris was in the hands of the rebels, the regime of Charles X could probably still have been saved by energetic action, and Marie's royalist friends were repeating rumors about an immediate counteroffensive. The duke of Angoulême was about to march on Paris with a new army, said some. There would be a siege of Paris and Madame de Flavigny should lay in food at once. Others claimed that Polignac had been dismissed to placate the opposition and that a new cabinet would make the necessary concessions and get things back to normal. The next day brought a truer indication of the situation when they learned that during the night the walls of Paris had been covered with posters urging the population to give power to the duke of Orléans. Meanwhile Charles X tried to save his succession by abdicating in favor of Caroline de Berry's young son, Henri, now ten. Seeing that the time had come to give the king a fright, the leaders of the insurrection shrewdly sent a column of insurgents armed with muskets, sabers, and pikes towards Rambouillet. It was preceded by delegates who warned him of the approaching mob and offered him safe conduct if he wanted to withdraw. Charles X quickly decided to offer no resistance and set off for Cherbourg in unmarked coaches which had been provided as an incentive.

Marie saw the column of rebels that evening as it rushed back to Paris with the news of their final victory. They had helped themselves to the royal coaches and had whipped the king's fine horses into a frenzied gallop through clouds of dust on their way back to the capital. The men, after much drinking, were shouting and singing at the top of their voices. Some of the insurgents had clambered on top of the richly decorated vehicles, while others could be seen inside as they reclined on the white satin cushions and enjoyed their moment of glory. Peace returned to the city, and Parisians could begin to take stock of the astonishing events of a week during which an urban insurrection had defeated a professional army. The royal family that the great powers of Europe had restored to the throne of France after many years of war had been swept away in just three days.

When Marie's friends returned from an inspection of Paris, they reported that the center of the city was a sorry sight. A gloomy silence reigned, the shops were shuttered, and the streets were filled with the remains of barricades. The streetlights were broken, and at night the only light came from the flickering lanterns and campfires of the insurgents. These signs of the defeat of their king filled them with gloom, and they wondered what lay ahead. The answer came on 9 August, when Parliament proclaimed the duke of Orléans king, with the title Louis-Philippe. As Marie sat in her garden that day she saw the new monarch and his wife drive past in an open coach. It had all happened so quickly that it seemed more like fiction than reality. She turned to a friend and said, "Once upon a time there was a king and a queen." Marie saw the new ruler as a traitor to his family and remembered the prophetic words of the viscountess d'Agoult.

The viscountess herself was in exile with the grieving duchess of Angoulême, who had tried to dissuade her loyal friend from leaving France again. From Cherbourg the royal party had sailed toward England on an American ship which happened to belong to the Bonaparte family. As Charles X looked on the receding shore of France for the last time, he attributed his misfortune to the inscrutable working of providence.

Marie received many expressions of sympathy for her loss of position in the royal court, but she felt no real regret. Her daughter, Claire, was born on 10 August, and she once again busied herself with the activities of motherhood. As a sign of fidelity to Charles X she decided that she would never enter the court of Louis-Philippe. Charles d'Agoult, too, remained faithful to the fallen monarch and retired from the army rather than serve the new king. The life of Paris would slowly begin to return to a relatively normal state, whereas that of Charles and Marie d'Agoult was about to enter its own phase of turbulence and revolution.[2]

CHAPTER 7

Elopement

MARIE'S assessment of the new French king as a traitor to his family was harsh in that Charles X had lost his position owing to his own political errors. His cousin had not actively conspired against him but had simply accepted the crown when it was offered, and this after the spineless Charles had capitulated. Philippe of Orléans, for his part, had showed himself to be a man of courage and energy. In his early years he had experienced poverty in exile and had at one time survived by giving drawing lessons in the town of Reichenau, Austria. He had acquired knowledge of the world by traveling widely in Europe and America. He had returned to France as soon as it became possible and risen to the rank of general in the army of the Republic. Despite his recovery of the family fortune after the restoration of the monarchy and his installation in the Palais Royal, he had continued to get up early and light his own fire. Unlike Charles X, who had rarely appeared without a hat adorned with white feathers, he dressed like an ordinary mortal.

Louis-Philippe soon proved to be a moderate and intelligent ruler of France, but for some time the kings of Europe shared Marie's opinion of him as a usurper and a product of revolution. The danger of anarchy remained, and one evening at a diplomatic dinner in the palace the noise of a riot in the street outside grew so loud that the ambassadors stopped talking and looked at their plates in embarrassment. Then came the sound of a cavalry charge, followed by silence. After this interruption the polite conversation resumed, but with some effort.[1] Long after the installation of the new regime the streets of Paris were regularly occupied by unruly crowds with radical demands. One recurrent theme was a call for the execution of Polignac and the ministers of Charles X who had sent the army to fire on the people of Paris. Some of the ministers had managed to escape, but Polignac had been seized in the little seaport of Grandville, from which he had hoped to sail to the nearby island of Jersey. He protested with dignity at what he called the arbitrary nature of his arrest but was locked up in the castle of Vincennes, in eastern Paris, to await trial on a charge of treason. A large crowd soon appeared with the intention of lynching him, but the military commander informed them that he would blow up the castle before he would hand over his prisoner. The mob then returned to central Paris, where it managed to burst into the royal palace and get halfway up the stairs before it was stopped by force.[2]

The trial of Polignac and his colleagues was held in the Luxembourg Palace, which was continuously surrounded by a hostile crowd whose shouts could be heard inside the building. In the nearby area of Saint-Germain, where most of the aristocracy had their homes, there were fears of pillage and riot, and those who had not already done so took the precaution of going to the country with their portable valuables. When Polignac was not sentenced to death, the mob began to direct some of its anger against the aristocracy. A new political term had been invented for supporters of the traditional monarchy, who were now known as Legitimists. On 14 February 1831 the intense resentment of a segment of the population toward this conservative faction was revealed. To mark the anniversary of the killing of the duc de Berry, a group of Legitimists had gathered in the church of Saint-Germain-l'Auxerrois for a service. A silent but hostile crowd waited outside. There was no incident until a young man in the uniform of the Saint-Cyr military cadets went to the catafalque with a portrait of the young Henri de Bourbon, whom the Legitimists saw as the rightful monarch. At once the church was invaded by a mob, which spent several hours wrecking the interior until nothing was left but a pile of debris.

Since the collapse of the regime in July 1830, most members of the aristocracy had withdrawn from public life and were spending more time at their country estates. It was said of them that they were sulking in their châteaux. Marie's social life suffered also from the closing of the salons of Madame de Duras, Madame de Montcalm, and Madame de La Trémoille for reasons of death or old age. She still attended soirées in the Austrian embassy, where Madame Apponyi, the ambassador's wife, had a special welcome for the Legitimist aristocracy. In the winter she gave splendid balls, and in the summer there were lunchtime parties, with dancing under the trees in the embassy garden. Despite this, the social life of the nobility had lost much of its former air of confidence and gaiety, and the class began a decline which was to prove terminal. Some aristocrats who had lost lucrative positions in 1830 now wore old clothes and affected an appearance of poverty. In their eyes Louis-Philippe was a bastard king, an unprincipled opportunist who had risen on the barricades, and they spoke of him with sarcasm.

In reality the Legitimists had not given up hope that the regime which had risen so quickly could be swept away with similar rapidity. Rumors of a possible rising soon began to spread, with whispers that a leading role might be played by Caroline de Berry. The Italian princess had quickly tired of life in the fogs of Scotland, where the exiled Charles X had attempted to continue a sort of court life in Holyrood Palace. The chronic state of disorder in Paris convinced her that the time had come for a royalist counterrevolution which she would lead herself in order to take advantage of her personal popularity. The undertaking would not be an easy one, but that had not deterred Joan of Arc, she reasoned. Charles X was naturally doubtful about Caroline's ability to recover the throne, but in early 1832 he gave his consent to the attempt, after much hesitation. The necessary agents were therefore sent to France to make preparations. He agreed that her twelve-year-old son would take the title as Henri V, with herself as regent.

The unlikely escapade began when Caroline assumed a false name and set sail for Holland. From there she took another ship to Italy and landed near Massa, in the duchy of Modena, whose reactionary ruler was hostile to Louis-Philippe. On 24 April 1832, under the cover of darkness, she sailed from Massa on the *Carlo Alberto* and headed toward France. Four days later, after evading French warships with some difficulty, the ship landed near Marseilles, and Caroline confidently awaited news of the promised insurrection. Instead she received a message saying that the rising had failed to materialize and that she should leave France at once. On the horizon the *Carlo Alberto* could be seen fleeing from a fast French frigate, so another escape route had to be found.

Undaunted by the lack of support in Marseille, Caroline made her way undetected across all of France to Brittany and Vendée, where the main royalist support was still to be found. By then all of France knew that something was afoot because of press reports, and in the western provinces an army of thirty thousand men was put on alert. Disguised as a young farmer, she entered the region dressed in the local costume of blue trousers, green jacket, and yellow waistcoat. She wore a brown wig over her blonde hair and had darkened her eyebrows with shoe polish. To complete this theatrical disguise the diminutive duchess had adopted the name Petit-Pierre. Some of the local royalists courageously agreed to attempt a rising, but it was soon crushed by powerful government forces. The main incident was the siege of a village called La Pénissière, where two army trumpets played night and day while a force of five hundred struggled to defeat a company of sixty insurgents. This pathetic event was the Waterloo of the Legitimists, whose cause was now dead.

In a stubborn refusal to accept defeat Caroline retreated to the town of Nantes, where a safe house was ready. To avoid detection this time she masqueraded as a peasant woman carrying a basket under her arm and coolly munching an apple as she walked through the city gates. Soon the whole nation knew that she was sought throughout Brittany by a large army. Weeks and months went by, and still the fugitive could not be detected despite the determined efforts of Adolphe Thiers, the minister of the interior. The government had resigned itself to searching every house in Brittany, but an easier method of detection was found when Thiers received a letter from an unknown individual who promised interesting information if Thiers went for a walk after dark in the rue des Veuves near the Champs-Elysées. He took the risk and did as requested. His contact turned out to be a renegade royalist agent named Deutz, who offered to reveal Caroline's hiding place in exchange for a large sum of money. A deal was quickly struck, and Thiers was informed that the fugitive was in Nantes in the home of two apparently inoffensive sisters by the name of Duguiny. A coded message was at once sent from Paris, and the house was surrounded while the police searched it from top to bottom, fruitlessly looking for hollow walls and secret cellars. At the end of the day the searchers gave up in frustration but left two men in each room as a precaution. At dawn next morning one of these guards

felt cold and began to burn some old newspapers in a large fireplace. A little
later he was amazed to hear the sound of coughing and a voice from behind
the wall saying, "We give up. You can arrest us." The metal plaque in the
fireplace was pulled aside, and out came Caroline de Berry and three male
companions who had been concealed in the hollow wall for sixteen hours.
The hiding place had been constructed for royalists and aristocrats during
the Terror in 1793 and had proved useful once again.

Caroline was put in a military fortress at the town of Blaye while Louis-
Philippe decided what to do with her. It was an embarrassing situation,
because she was a woman and his relative by marriage, but she was clearly
guilty of treason, having led an armed insurrection in which lives had been
lost. Public opinion and logic demanded a proper punishment. Polignac had
received a life sentence for less serious actions when he was prime minister, which was very different from starting an armed rebellion. The king's
personal preference would have been to have Caroline taken to the nearest
frontier and expelled, but this would have seemed too lenient.

Naturally, Caroline de Berry was a heroine in the eyes of the Legitimists, who put on mourning and organized petitions for her release. When
the government asked for a volunteer to be her prison companion in Blaye,
it was inundated by offers from aristocratic ladies, but the situation suddenly became slightly comic in January 1833, when Caroline could no longer
hide the fact that she was pregnant. Three months can be a very long time
in politics, and the revelation seriously dented her image as a selfless young
widow entirely devoted to her son and to the royal cause. It transpired that
the impulsive Caroline had taken advantage of her escape from the royal
court by secretly marrying a minor Italian nobleman named Lucchesi-Palli.
As she was now discredited among the Legitimists, she was no longer a
danger to Louis-Philippe, who promptly had her shipped back to her original home in Sicily. After these tragicomic events Caroline caused no more
trouble and lived quietly with her new husband and family.[3]

Marie d'Agoult shared the royalists' admiration for Caroline's courage.
It was true that the conspiracy had been a spectacular failure, but the young
Italian woman had shown determination and energy and had entered the
world of action. In addition the episode of her personal emancipation and

pursuit of emotional satisfaction provided an interesting model. Its significance was certainly not lost on Marie, who knew the dull and puritanical
court atmosphere in which Caroline had been living. At this time Marie was
in deep emotional crisis as she sadly considered a situation which to others
seemed enviable. She was married to a decent and honorable man and was
the mother of two charming daughters. She was rich and could purchase
anything she wanted. She enjoyed the usual freedom of women of her class,
had an active social life, was able to explore intellectual and musical interests, and lived in a beautiful home in Paris. She had youth and beauty and
intelligence. In fact she had everything except happiness.

Again she asked herself how she could have let herself be married to
a man she did not love; the passing of the years had, unfortunately, done
nothing to reduce their difference of temperament, mind, and character.
Although Charles must have been partly aware of the distance between
them, he was able to live with it, believing that mutual adoration was not
essential to marriage. Marie's emotional problem was aggravated by the fact
that she hid it from everyone. To do otherwise would have seemed an act
of treachery to the man whom she had freely taken as her husband. She still
kept the secret from her mother, from her closest friends, and even from
her confessor, Father Gaspard Deguerry, to whom she still dutifully bared
her soul in other matters. She was proudly playing the role of a contented
woman, but this deception was a constant contamination of her inner life.
Her emotions were a mixture of guilt, anxiety, and frustration, as she recalled her hopes and aspirations as a girl. The error of her marriage seemed
so immense as to be almost incredible. Was the life of some individuals controlled by an unkind fate? It seemed that a cruel and capricious force had
condemned her to unhappiness.

She tried to fill her emptiness with social activities, but her character
was too serious for this to be successful. The pleasures of motherhood did
provide some satisfaction, but at times she could not help feeling regret
that her daughters on her knee were not the progeny of a happy marriage in
which the parents were close and loving. To make matters worse there had
been serious friction between her husband and Madame de Flavigny as well
as between Maurice's wife and herself. The result was that she saw little of

her mother and her brother, which only increased her feeling of isolation. She no longer went to her former country home, which was so full of happy memories.

Marie tried the standard remedy by looking for consolation in religion. From an early age she had been taught that suffering brought one closer to God, and she now did her best to persuade herself that it was true, meditating about the pains of Jesus until she began to shed tears. This brought her some relief, but the respite did not last. She then applied herself to acquire a better understanding of the Bible and began to study the writings of the great theologians approved by the Church. This was surely the road to salvation, she reasoned. She had been brought up to respect the Bible, and she now turned to the fathers of the Church for enlightenment and a consolidation of her faith.

What happened was the very opposite of what she expected. From her attentive study of the writings of Augustine and Bossuet came her first religious doubts. In her mind there appeared suddenly a great gulf between dogma and reason, between miracles and common sense, between faith and observation. She was taken aback and alarmed by this unexpected consequence of her studies and decided that she should return to a simple acceptance of the articles of faith. The kindly Father Deguerry exhorted her to take communion frequently, to hope for divine grace, to beware of pride. For a while Marie did her best to comply, but within time her conscience no longer allowed her to do so. She had lost her simple faith and it would never return. She now felt the anguish that comes with freedom, and her situation seemed worse than before.

Charles was aware that all was not well and decided that some radical form of distraction was needed. The couple therefore set off in the direction of Switzerland in the spring of 1832, accompanied by four-year-old Louise (Claire had been left in the care of Madame de Flavigny). Marie's depression was not helped by tragic news sent from Frankfurt by her half-sister, Augusta, who reported that one of their female cousins had put a pistol in her mouth and blown her brains out while her husband was at church. The young woman had been pregnant and had seemed calm and contented. When her husband had left the house that morning, she had shown no signs of her inner anguish or intention to take her life. The news of the sad event apparently had an impact on Marie, and one day as she and Charles stood on an Alpine peak, she turned to him and asked if she should throw herself off. Her husband replied with defensive humor by asking her not to do it because he might be accused of having pushed her.[4] More bad news came on 22 May, when Maurice's wife, Mathilde de Flavigny, wrote to say that Augusta herself had taken her life.[5] A few hours after one of her periodic quarrels with her husband, the impulsive woman had walked to the Main and thrown herself in the water. The row had been a minor one by their standards, so the real cause of her suicide must have been an accumulation of some irrational depression or despair. The condition was clearly common among the females of the Bethmann family, and Marie knew it well. When they reached Geneva, her own crisis was so intense that she entered the Saint-Antoine hospital, where she was treated by a Dr. Coindet, a specialist in mental illness. While she was recovering under his care, her husband and child went back to Paris without her.

On her own return to the capital she felt much better and busied herself with a new project which combined intellectual and social activity. As women of the aristocracy were no longer obliged to live under the disapproving eyes of the duchess d'Angoulême, now safely exiled in Scotland, they felt that they could make contact with the exciting new generation of writers, artists, and musicians who were making Paris the intellectual center of Europe. Madame de Rauzan had been the first to open her doors to writers such as Sainte-Beuve and the novelist Eugène Sue. Soon she was imitated by Madame de La Bourdonnaye and Madame de La Grange. Marie followed suit, and her life began to acquire new purpose as she continued to recover from her depression. The more conservative part of the aristocracy still smiled ironically at these bluestockings on whose tables they saw the works of Senancour, Dumas, Vigny, Balzac, and Sand, but Marie was now determined she, too, would have a leading salon and play a role in the literary and artistic life of the period.

To succeed in this plan she decided to purchase a country estate near Paris, which would make up for the virtual loss of Le Mortier and allow her salon to function during the summer season, when it was fashionable to leave the city. Good fortune seemed to favor the project when M. de La Trémoille revealed that he wanted to sell his property at Croissy, a magnificent château surrounded by a moat and extensive grounds. The interior was richly decorated, and from the upstairs windows one could see endless lawns sloping down to a large fishpond, beyond which stood the village of Croissy. Pleasant excursions could be made to the banks of the Marne and to the nearby forest of Armainvilliers.

In this fine setting Marie's guests devoted summer evenings to literary and artistic activities. They listened to readings of verse by Madame de Lau, Alexandre Guiraud, Alexandre Soumet, and Emile Deschamps and even busied themselves with amateur dramatics by staging the comedies of Eugène Scribe and other popular writers. The real speciality of her salon, however, was music, and her own talent as a pianist was still well known. Indeed Charles d'Agoult recalled an evening during which Rossini heard her perform the overture of his opera *Semiramis* with such virtuosity that he declared it the best performance since its writing. In his enthusiasm he went at once to sit at the piano vacated by Marie and accompanied himself in an aria from the *Barber of Seville*. In her Paris home and in Croissy she put on concerts in which the new music of Berlioz, Chopin, and Schubert was played. An increasingly frequent participant in these performances was the brilliant and handsome young Franz Liszt, whose extraordinary talent and person were already arousing in Marie a passion which would transform her life and stir the deepest part of her being.

The story of their first meeting was told by Marie herself in pages which were written many years later and intended to be published after her death.[6] Her account of events has a literary and often a dramatic character as she relates the most important encounter in her life. It tells how she first met Liszt in December 1832, after her recovery from her mental crisis and her return from Geneva. At this time he was twenty-one, six years younger than Marie. She knew that since the age of thirteen he had been known as a child prodigy in Paris, where his concerts had been received with rapture. After a series of piano improvisations performed in the Paris opera house in 1824, the handsome boy had been taken to the boxes of ladies who stroked his silky fair hair and gave him sweets. Everyone was speaking of a new Mozart, but one surrounded by mystery and strangeness. The newspaper *Le Corsaire* had even announced his death on 23 October 1828, but then he reappeared. Liszt had stopped giving concerts, for unknown reasons. There

An Evening at the Opéra, by Gavarni, 1832.

(Bibliothèque nationale de France)

were rumors of disappointed love, and some claimed that the young virtuoso was going to give up his musical career to become a priest. It became
known that he was supporting himself and his mother by giving piano lessons and that he had deliberately abandoned the salons where he had been
adulated by the ladies of the aristocracy.

One of the few pupils whom Liszt still taught was the niece of Madame
Le Vayer, an elderly friend of Marie. On rare occasions he agreed to participate in a small concert in her home, having received her assurance that
it would be for the family only. The promise had proved too difficult to
keep, and the hostess had gradually opened her doors until she was inviting
everyone she knew. Marie did not feel inclined to hear yet another virtuoso and had declined several invitations. In the end she thought her refusals
might offend her friend, and she agreed to attend a concert which Liszt had
announced as his last. When she arrived, she found an expectant audience,
but Liszt was not to be seen. Madame Le Vayer explained that some choral
music by Weber was to be sung and a part of the music had been lost. Liszt
was in the next room writing it out from memory.

The door then opened and through it came the most extraordinary individual Marie had ever observed. She saw a tall, slim figure, green eyes full
of light, a face full of strength and suffering. When he walked he seemed to
float, and she thought he had the anxious and distracted air of a ghost waiting
for the chime of the clock to recall it into darkness. After being introduced,
he sat beside Marie and spoke with ease, as if they had known each other
for years. Beneath his unusual appearance she quickly detected the force of
his intellect. His conversation did not have the polite restraint which was
usual in her social circle, as he communicated in an impetuous and abrupt
manner, expressing thoughts and ideas which were new and strange in her
ears. Marie noted the power of his eyes and the way in which his smile was
alternately caustic and then gentle. She listened almost silently as he spoke,
surprised by his lack of reserve with a person he did not know.

The hostess arrived and put an end to their conversation as the piano
was opened and the lamps were lit beside it. Liszt at once rose from his
chair beside her, and his manner betrayed a hint of irritation which showed
that he had not mastered the art of courtesy as practiced in high society.

Marie d'Agoult, by Chassériau, 1841.

(Réunion des Musées nationaux)

Franz Liszt, by Achille Devéria, 1832.

(Photothèque des Musées de la Ville de Paris)

Following a sudden impulse Marie also rose and walked behind him to the piano, where the young female choir was waiting. Reading from the sheet held by one of the girls she joined in the singing with considerable emotion. At the end of the performance Franz turned to look and saw that she too had sung the music. At first he seemed pleased, but then his face darkened and during the rest of the evening he made no move toward her. After his solo performance on the piano, she joined those who were complimenting him and added her own words of admiration, to which he replied with a silent bow. She went home late that night, and some time elapsed before she fell into a sleep troubled by strange dreams.

The next day she received a visit from Madame Le Vayer, who spoke with enthusiasm of Liszt's musical genius. His character was just as admirable as his musical talent, she added. He was charitable and gave freely to the poor in spite of his own modest financial situation. It was impossible to know him without liking him. She then asked why Marie had not invited him to her home, as this would certainly be agreeable to the virtuoso. As soon as she was alone Marie took up a pen to invite him to the next soirée in her Paris apartment. Three times she started the invitation and three times she tore it up because it seemed either to express too much pleasure at the idea of seeing him or to sound too formal. During the previous evening she had noticed that the artist seemed aware of his inferior social position in spite of his immense talent, which in her opinion placed him among the social elite. Franz did not reply to her carefully worded invitation, but he did attend the reception, and her reputation as a lover of music made his presence there natural. When Liszt sat at the piano that evening, he appeared to abandon himself to music and rise above the petty concerns of ordinary life. She observed his lips move as if he were speaking and his handsome face become transformed by power and dominance.

Not only was she was transported by his music, but she was attracted by his personality. Their conversation was never banal, as they always discussed great and serious themes which interested them both. They spoke about the human condition, with its doubts and lack of certainty. They spoke about God and the soul and the question of a future life. Although they did not say it openly, it was clear that both had experienced unhappiness and had known disappointment. With every day that passed their intimate discussions acquired more charm; in music, too, they expressed their emotions. One day after Marie had played the music of *Erlkönig* for him, he wrote to express his rapture at her talent, thereby forming another bond between them: "You were *sublime* on Saturday morning, yes really sublime. . . . Goethe and Schubert have never been performed like that. . . . Never before did such a deep emotion seize my inner self and burn my forehead. Oh! one would like to die after such hours of enthusiasm and delirium." [7] Her mind and emotions were enlivened as they had never been before. She was also learning more about Liszt and hearing details of a childhood made difficult by constant pressure to develop his talent. Six rich Hungarians had joined together to give financial support to the young prodigy, who had received lessons from famous musicians such as Czerny and Salieri. He had known times as the darling of queens and princesses as well as times of obscurity and uncertainty. Although he was reputed to be a good Catholic, he also admired the social theories of Saint-Simon and Lamennais, a dissident priest who agitated on behalf of the lower classes. Liszt's own political stance was republican and radical. His literary heroes were Werther, Obermann, and Childe Harold, the proud and melancholy protagonists of the Romantics. Their passionate discussions were now full of their most personal thoughts and emotions. Marie was completely under the charm of the fervent and handsome Hungarian. His radiant personality was like a sudden light shining in the darkness of her life.

The change of season put an end to this first phase in their friendship, as Marie left Paris to spend the summer of 1833 at Croissy. The routine of château life was hard to bear after the excitement of conversations with Liszt. The best part of the day was the time she devoted to the education of her daughters, but that could only fill a few hours because they were so young. Each day she sat at the piano and poured out her emotions in wistful pieces by Schubert. In this way six long weeks went by before she had an opportunity to invite Liszt to her country estate. When he arrived he entered the drawing room and saw her with her children. This was the first time he had seen her daughters, as his visits in Paris had always happened after their bedtime. Noticing a change in his expression when he looked at them, Marie wondered what was in his thoughts. For a moment they could find no words. It was as if they had been simultaneously invaded by a feeling of guilt. Liszt remained standing in the doorway, and she nervously went toward him to offer her hand.

This experience affected their friendship for a time. She did not see him as frequently, and there were often others present when they met. Their relationship was now so different that their encounters left her in a state of anxiety. They still talked about the same subjects, but the tone had changed. Liszt was moody and strange, and she no longer felt at ease. Sometimes there were silences, and at other times Liszt spoke in a feverish and excited way, with affected gaiety. The man who had spoken to her so eloquently about his high ideals, who had revealed his wish to devote his life to art and virtue, was full of dismissive irony. He now proclaimed that one might as well enjoy life's easy pleasures and not try to raise oneself above the common herd. At times he congratulated her with apparent sincerity on the enviable life she led in rich and elegant surroundings. Marie was alarmed by the mysterious and moody nature of this man, who was already playing an important role in her life, but her letters show that she had passed the point of no return:

> One day you told me that you loved me so much that you did not even need to see me! This idea struck me; today I feel how true it is. . . . You are here, still here and I find you even in the smallest details of my life. When Adèle does my hair, I look at my forehead because you like it, at breakfast I drink coffee, amused by the idea it was the only thing lacking for me to become Mme de Staël; even chicken with rice is linked to a memory . . . and when I sit on a tree-trunk or a stone bench talking to my country folk I take pleasure in their naive replies, convinced that you too can hear them. . . . And then the piano where tears come to me again. *The Captive Woman, The Withered Limetree,* and then in the evening before bed your notebook in which I write things which struck me when reading. . . . What I cannot explain is the astonishing invasion (I cannot find a better word) of religious feeling in me. . . . My life is a prayer, a perpetual adoration. If it were not so long I would write out for you the music of *The Blessing of God in Solitude.* There is no better expression of my feelings. Nevertheless I have had some awful days to which I alluded in my remark about the possibility of something happening (which you may have misunderstood), days of the sort of anguish which sometimes ends in madness or suicide; but God took pity on me. I wanted to tell you that, whatever my present or future sufferings, you should shed no

tears, because you have done me more good than you can ever do me
harm. You completed the breaking of all the bonds which still tied me
to the world and in my soul you awoke universal charity, that love of all
people which was smothered in me by a feeling of my personal sufferings
which I was offering to God as a sacrifice, believing that resignation was
the only virtue possible for me and that it would have to serve for all the
others.[8]

On the night of 20 May 1833 she revealed more anguish in another letter
to the man she now loved: "Today we are giving a dance for the country
people and I am alone in my room writing to the sound of the violin and the
clarinet. They are happy people, and probably envy me. I can give them joy,
but cannot myself expect it from any thing or any person. Oh how your letter made me cry! So short, so curt, so little for my heart! But you are right.
The air is so good here, the fields are so green, what more do I need?"[9] A
change in Liszt's mood was evident when he improvised on the piano. When
she had first heard him play, he had produced soft and gentle harmonies
which seemed to transport her to heaven. Now his powerful fingers were
producing harsh and discordant notes which resounded angrily through the
château. He said nothing, but acted resentful toward her. When she made
attempts to revive the intimacy of their former conversations, they foun-
dered on the rock of his reserve. Withdrawing within herself, she wondered
what had caused the transformation.

One day after he had spoken harshly to her, she reproached him bitterly
and burst into tears. He was taken aback and seemed torn by conflicting
emotions. Then, with a sad look which she would always remember, he
asked her forgiveness. For the first time they passionately held hands and
swore that they would love each other until the end of time. When he had
returned to Paris she poured out her happiness and adoration in a letter to
him: "Gulliver in his travels meets a man who explains that one of the main
cause of sadness and unhappiness in this life is the disappearance of the sun
for a large part of the year, causing winter, cold dark days and bad harvests,
but he has found a great remedy: it is a crystal bottle in which he gathers
the sun's rays and lets them out when he needs them! I too have my crystal
bottle which I have filled with the rays from your soul. My days had become
dark because I no longer had your eyes and your smile to bring life to them,

now they are with me, deep inside my heart, all around me in everything I see and breath."[10] The unfinished memoirs of Marie recount the idyll of their platonic love in the months which followed. Liszt stayed frequently at Croissy and the summer days seemed enchanted. They learned more about each other, and Liszt revealed details of his joyless early years.

Liszt was born in a little town in Hungary in 1811 but never experienced a normal childhood because of his extraordinary musical talent. He began giving concerts at the age of nine and was performing in Vienna by the time he was twelve. One concert had been attended by Beethoven, who was so impressed that he went backstage and planted a kiss on the brow of the young performer. Later Franz visited the deaf old composer in his home, where he saw the sad sight of a piano with its strings torn out. For the next three years, Liszt's ambitious father exhibited him in the major cities of France, Germany, England, and Switzerland, a tour that exhausted Franz and affected his health. He had become rootless and friendless and began to experience periods of depression alternating with periods of mystical fervor, which would become one of the dominant elements in his personality.

When his father died, his mother had joined him in Paris, where he earned his living mostly by giving piano lessons to the daughters of rich clients. He had been in love with the aristocratic Caroline de Saint Cricq, the daughter of a government minister, but when her father refused to contemplate the possibility of letting her marry a pianist, Liszt fell into a depression so deep that it was rumored he had died. Thereafter his life was marked by phases of ambition followed by times when he wanted to hide himself in a monastery. In his love for Marie he alternated between days full of wild hopes and suicidal periods. As the two lovers spoke, they saw the similarity of their natures, which oscillated wildly between joy and despair. They recalled their first impressions of each other and relived the encounters again and again. It was impossible that they could not have fallen in love, they agreed. Liszt was discovering new sounds and sensations as they walked arm in arm among the sunlit meadows, where he listened with rapt attention to the song of nature. Marie too heard the music of summer and wished that time could stop.

All too soon he had to return to Paris because of his career, though their courtship continued by letter. As Marie roamed the countryside she felt his continued presence and shed tears of joy as she played on the piano which the fingers of Franz had touched. Each day she recorded her thoughts and emotions in a notebook to be shown to him on his return. Knowing her eagerness to enjoy the artistic life of Paris, Liszt wrote to invite her to a performance of the *Symphonie fantastique,* by his friend Hector Berlioz, and to see the drama *Antony,* by Alexandre Dumas, a celebration of passionate love. One day she sent him a dejected message expressing guilt because of their relationship and a wish to end it. Liszt sent a dramatic reply in which he manipulated her emotions without scruple: "I know that I no longer have the right to ask for anything, my existence (what I do and think) apart from the memory of me which you will have for a few days, a few hours more, is entirely indifferent to me and replaced by you. . . . If however just once (either tomorrow, this winter, or later, no matter!) you were to consent from pity, from *curiosity* perhaps to grant me a few minutes . . . I would bless you—I would thank God."[11] Marie's good intentions did not last, however, and they became lovers around December 1833, after knowing each other for one year. Marie had been a faithful wife for six years, and the decision to take a lover was not easy. Among her papers she religiously preserved a note from Liszt in late 1833 saying that he was looking for a small apartment where they could meet secretly in Paris. She was about to experience fully the guilt of adultery as well as the sensation of pleasure with a man she loved. Her sexual experience had been limited to the satisfaction of her husband's needs, and as an innocent compensation she had allowed herself the platonic indulgences of being courted by hopeful and respectful young men like Alfred de Vigny and Théophile de Ferrière. Her passionate relationship with Liszt was certainly a new and profound experience for this wife and mother.

The following months were filled with the intense and stormy emotions which were to punctuate their future years together. On days when he was full of self-belief, Liszt was buoyant with the joys of love and musical creativity. At other times he expressed feelings of failure and solitude and begged her for more frequent replies to his messages. They had their first quarrel when she found old love letters he had written to Euphémie Didier, a former pupil. The young woman had returned the missives, which he had carelessly left in the bottom of a box in which he had sent Marie some music.

She reproached him for his past affairs, in which he had sworn eternal love to Caroline and Euphémie. To make matters worse, she learned from friends that there had also been an affair between Franz and Adèle de La Prunarède, a woman fifteen years older than he, with whom he had spent some months in the Alps! In addition there was talk about a Charlotte, a Maria, and a Hortense! In her wounded pride Marie sent sarcastic letters asking for an explanation of these past episodes. This was a new and bitter experience in her emotional life. She reflected that Liszt might be an unreliable lover and recalled all the rumors which had been repeated in her presence. Liszt's reply to questions about his past was an angry riposte of a type she had never experienced: "Have I not already requested you to stop reminding me in any way of my theatrical declarations and the women to whom I may have made them? In case you have forgotten I ask you again." [12] After some weeks of mutual reproach she wrote to make peace, upon which Liszt joyfully celebrated the end of the quarrel: "The cloud is torn and ended. I am reading and reading again your recent words. My strength is returning. Once more I believe in this life, in you, in God. I thank you for this. You may find some bitterness in my last two notes, that is now past. As you know, I am extreme in my emotions. Farewell. A thousand joys and blessings. We have both been petty. Let us aim higher!" [13] In a lyrical letter written after one of their meetings he expressed religious and mystical thoughts: "I felt as if we had not yet left each other. Your look still seemed to be magically radiant in the sky. Your breath was still on my lips and my eyelids; your heartbeats were still mingled with mine and were infinitely prolonging this intense double life which we have revealed to each other; all day long I felt as if I were among countless choirs of Angels and celestial figures . . . taking part in some mysterious festival which was both new and eternal." [14]

Having agreed to spend some time in the country home of Madame de Haineville, near the village of Bernay, while Marie remained in her château, Liszt suffered feelings of solitude. At one point his emotional state became so intense that he regularly intercepted the woman on a donkey who delivered mail to the house, with the hope of finding a letter from Marie: "I cannot become accustomed to receiving your letters. Every morning when I expect one I feel a thousand anxieties, a thousand vague and painful irritations, then I start to walk, I prepare myself for some *real* and *heavy* disappointment, my old sadness takes me over, in the end, when I hold it in my hands I can hardly dare open it, then I break the seal and the words 'I am going to live' almost always escape from my lips before I have read a syllable."[15] From the beginning of their relationship Liszt and Marie had spoken about artistic, literary, philosophical, and social matters. This enthusiastic intellectual exchange now continued as they read and discussed the works of Senancour, Chateaubriand, Saint-Simon, Ballanche, Quinet, Sand, Hugo, and Lamennais. Liszt recounted meetings with his friend Sainte-Beuve, whose novel *Volupté* had deeply impressed Marie, and also told her of his discussions with Victor Hugo and other famous names of the day: "I was so happy to see V. H., Chopin and Berlioz again. When I have spent some hours with V. H. there is a surge of ambition within me. Yesterday he said something very interesting to me: 'We are at a point in civilisation where the defects are ugly, very ugly.' Next Sunday the *Revue de Paris* will publish a piece by him about a worker. Its conclusions are religious, highly religious. It is pleasant and consoling to see that all superior individuals now agree on the few truths on which the salvation of the world depends. Chopin is looking forward to spending some days at Croissy when you wish to invite him."[16] Liszt also regularly met with Lamartine, Lamennais, Balzac, Sand, Musset, Chateaubriand, Nodier, and Heine. It appeared to Marie that the man she loved was not only a genius but walked in the company of the gods.

At this time Liszt was becoming increasingly influenced by the progressive social ideas of Lamennais, who was soon to be condemned by Rome for his work *Paroles d'un croyant*. Over the months he did his best to communicate to Marie his own fervent belief in the need for radical measures to end poverty and injustice, and she was receptive to his enthusiasm for political freedom and social progress. In this way the rich aristocrat was taking the first major step along the road which would lead to a rejection of the conservative ideas of her upbringing. The time for moderation is past, he told her, and it was not enough for those privileged like herself to provide soup kitchens for the poor. Replying to Marie's anxiety about the danger of radical politics in an unstable society, and her ironic comments on some aspects of the ideas of Lamennais, Liszt expressed his own beliefs with eloquence: "To speak frankly (and it is to you alone I can do so) I do not think the work of Lamennais is at all *definitive* and *dogmatic;* it is a protest, a burst of fierce indignation against those who are big and powerful in the world, the words which a priest who understood and felt all the pains and all the anguish of common people was *obliged* to speak. But I expect that liberation will come from God alone, and the day has not yet come. I do not have many convictions; I have some belief in my work, and much faith in God and in Liberty. Do you know that sometimes your ironical remarks irritate me. . . . Why contradict me like an old woman when I am not saying anything with which you really disagree?"[17] The day of violent revolution might come, he warned her, if the brutal governments of Europe continued to crush the common people in order to maintain the privileges of a rich and powerful minority.

The letters exchanged by Liszt and Marie during the summer months of 1834 continued to reflect the agitated nature of their relationship. Marie felt unable to invite him to stay at Croissy, because she had learned, to her horror, that the rumor that she was the musician's mistress was now circulating—in fact, everyone except her husband seemed to know about it. She worried about her reputation and its effect on her daughters in years to come. When she complained to Liszt, he was in favor of a dramatic response, and in his anger he was sufficiently reckless to create the scandal of a duel, which would only make matters worse. Although he at times shared her moments of despair, he also did his best to combat them: "Sometimes also I have a painful feeling that I have placed on you a weight which is too heavy for you. Then I weep and my heart overflows with anguish and despair. . . . I have pity on you. . . . I am penetrated by cold remorse which enters the marrow of my bones . . . and yet I do not weaken. I accept with joy not only my pains and sufferings but yours too. . . . Except when I read your letters. . . . Oh! your letters, they kill me."[18]

In accepting the invitation to the country home of Madame de Haineville, Liszt had been motivated partly by the wish to reduce the gossip about Marie and himself. He spent time reading, playing the piano, and taking walks in the countryside, all the while longing for her. His letters give an account of his love and angst, which is at times barely coherent: "At times I would forget everything when beside you. . . . It is true that later you often reminded me cruelly of the situation. . . . But no! . . . besides it is my fault. I am so moody, so bitter, so extreme. You tell me you are already absorbed by the thought of our next meeting! Oh! that was what I too used to feel, night and morning, the first days. Why did you destroy that hope in me?"[19] What was to become of her love for this exceptional and demanding individual whose swings of mood were so similar to her own? Not long after this somber message she received a letter in which Liszt was again full of hope and energy: "My soul seems almost calm and my mind is pretty strong. I have never felt such fullness of confidence in God, and, let me say it, such overflowing love for Mariotte. I ask no more questions, I have no more doubts, I have no more anger; now there is neither mockery, nor vanity, nor disenchantment, nor sad regret, nor fear of the future, nor hungry despair in my heart. No, nothing of that. . . . I am abandoning myself to the torrent which bears me along and which will engulf me one day, I feel it. I accept my life and bless God."[20] Yet when she sent him a carefully written letter asking him to help her protect her reputation by being more careful in his behavior, he replied by sending her a sarcastic compliment regarding her self-control. You will have no more cause to complain, he told her with resignation. He had hoped for too much, and if death should come and take him now, he was ready and willing.

Marie felt obliged to take stock of the situation after a year of torment and emotional drama. Not having the strength to choose between love and duty, she went to consult a fortune teller named Marie-Anne Lenormand. This individual had achieved lasting fame many years earlier with an astonishing prediction made to Josephine de Beauharnais that one day she would wear a crown. Remarkably the prophecy had been made even before the marriage of Josephine to an unknown soldier named Bonaparte. After this success the sibyl had been consulted by a series of highly placed persons, including the duke of Wellington and the emperor of Russia.

She found the elderly woman sitting in a dark room with a large black cat dozing at her feet. The soothsayer sat with her back to the window and looked shrewdly at her client while she shuffled the tarot cards and slowly laid them on the table. She then pronounced dramatic words which Marie never forgot:

> In two or three years there will be a total change in your life. What now seems impossible will happen. Your way of living will be altered com-

pletely. Even your name will be different, and your new one will become known throughout not only France but Europe. You will leave your country for a long time. Italy will be your country of adoption, and you will be loved and honored there. You will love a man who will create a sensation in the world and whose name will be very famous. You will be hated by two women who will try to harm you by every means. But have no fear; you will overcome all obstacles. You will live to be old, you will be surrounded by true friends, and you will have a good influence on many people.[21]

If Marie's account is accurate, a remarkable amount of the prediction, which took place in June 1834, came true. Indeed she would look back in years to come and ask herself whether the whole course of her life had been decided by destiny rather than by the logic of character and circumstance.

Not many months would pass before her life was affected by dramatic events. The first occurred in the winter of 1834, when her daughter Louise fell seriously ill. She recognized the symptoms only too well as the malady that had killed her father. The little girl had periods of high fever, which made her nearly delirious, followed by phases of immobility in which she seemed almost dead. She did not respond to any treatment, and as Marie spent the night by her bed she saw no sign of recognition in her child's eyes. The sound of her hoarse and uncertain breathing was hard to bear. During the third night of the illness Louise seemed to move her hand toward her mother. At once Marie ran to the window and opened the curtains in order to see better. With a surge of hope she noted that the child appeared to be breathing more easily. For a short time Louise opened her eyes, smiled, and spoke to her mother, after which she fell asleep. Intoxicated with joy, Marie said a silent prayer of thanks. At once the good news spread throughout the house. While preparations were being made for breakfast, she returned to her daughter's bedside and was shocked to find the little girl sitting up and staring emptily. Louise threw her arms around her mother's neck as if to seek protection from some invisible hand which was pulling her away. As Marie held her child, she felt her young body gradually go limp as life withdrew.

In the first days which followed the loss of Louise, Marie wanted to throw herself in the Seine and put an end to everything. This shared sorrow between husband and wife did little to bring them closer together, and there was now a tragic silence in their home. She even felt irrational anger against Claire, because this child of four could not understand death. Her husband and mother therefore decided to place the little girl in a boarding school until her mother recovered. Her departure naturally increased Marie's sense of isolation, and things were made worse by the fact that Claire soon grew accustomed to her temporary home. For some months Marie cursed the pitiless God to whom she had prayed in vain for her daughter's life. Then came a period of inertia and depression during which her only hope in life was her love for Liszt. During the illness he had called daily for news of the child's progress, and after the death of Louise he had sent Marie an almost mad letter in which he urged her to be strong:

> Blessings unto God, blessings for ever.
> Here is what she wrote me this evening, perhaps after leaving her daughter. Oh! thank you, thank you. My heart is opening again! I too was in despair. I suffered everything it was possible to suffer! Now my heart is full of joy and pride.
> Oh! I cannot write to you. I do not even know if I will be able to see you, as my poor heart is so struck down with sorrow and love!
> You thought constantly of me during these two days, you say. You thought of me at the bedside of Louise, yesterday, today.
> Forgive me, Marie, if in this moment I forget all your sorrows and all our problems and speak only of me and of these words: "I always thought of you." Forgive, poor bereaved mother, this appeal to that which is most lively, intimate and powerful in our souls and our bodies beside the deathbed of your daughter. Forgive me, Marie, and allow me now to bless you, as I have just blessed God.
> Thank you and bless you always, Marie, Marie!
> Oh! you understand me, do you not? you feel me living inside you in your flesh and bones? Today you understand this inner need to seek and experience sorrow in all things, . . . you understand perhaps also how hard I have tried for some time to shape and accustom your soul to misfortune. No, do not listen to me, do not read me. I think I am becoming mad, but I love you so much, in such a high and elevated way.[22]

In her distress Marie stopped speaking of separation and desperately turned to Franz for consolation.

The next major shock came in May 1834 when she discovered that she was pregnant. As a woman whose love affair was about to produce an illegitimate child, she faced a radical decision. Adultery was classed as a crime, and in theory she could be sent to prison for two years, though in reality the law was rarely invoked. It was certain that Charles was not the sort of man who would want to inflict painful publicity on his wife and child. A woman in her position could choose among three courses of action. One was to resume sexual relations with one's husband in order to persuade him that the new child was his, but Marie was too honest to consider this. The second was to make a clean breast of the situation and ask for tolerance, a solution which had certainly been adopted in more than one family in order to preserve the peace. Appearances could be maintained, and the love child need not suffer as shown by successful bastards like the painter Delacroix and the press baron Girardin.[23] More than one woman of Marie's class had had a known liaison with a man who was not her husband — for example, Madame Récamier with Chateaubriand and the duchess de Dino with Talleyrand. Charles could be expected to show understanding provided there was no scandal. She would be able to continue her official roles as wife and mother while furtively visiting the secret apartment across the river. As she was too proud to ask Charles for his complicity, Marie chose the rarely used third solution. She would make a public stance, turning her back on conjugal duty and deception. She would start a new life of freedom. Like Adèle in the play *Antony* she would be condemned by many, but she would be understood by some. Like Elvire in the poems of Lamartine she would be the inspiration of a great artist. Like Indiana in the novel by George Sand she would escape from an unhappy marriage and assert her right to know happiness and love.[24]

Liszt reacted with joy to the news that Marie was expecting his child and was prepared to live openly with him. More than once he had urged her to abandon their life of illicit meetings and deception. Their consciences were pure, he had always argued, and their love had been willed by God himself. Now was the time to escape. They would need to forgive each other for things in their past relationship which were incomplete, imperfect, even wretched. For his part Liszt would show himself to be capable of sacrifice, virtue, and moderation. Marie d'Agoult and Franz Liszt were about to spread their wings and begin a new life which would bring joys as well as troubles.

Marie took up her pen to inform Charles d'Agoult that their ways were to part forever. It was the hardest letter she had ever written:

> I am going to leave, after eight years of marriage, we are going to sepa-rate forever. Whatever you may think, it was not without cruel anguish and bitter tears that I have been able to make a decision like this. I have no reproach to make you, you have always been full of affection and loy-alty, you have always thought of me, never yourself, and despite this I was very unhappy. I do not say that it was your fault; you may think (and I cannot complain if you do) that it was my fault, all mine; I do not think so; when fate has brought together two persons who do not know each other and who have characters and minds as unlike each other as ours are, then their most constant efforts and greatest sacrifices only serve to deepen the gulf between them. However, I do not deny any of my short-comings and on the grave of Louise I ask for forgiveness; she is asking God to show us forgiveness and pity, and in her name this is what I request from you. I will always speak of you with the respect and esteem which you deserve; as for myself, society will heap abuse on me and I ask you only to say nothing.
>
> Adieu. There can be no more happiness for either of us, but I fer-vently hope that you will at least find peace and quiet.
>
> M.
>
> 26 May
>
> P.S. I do not need to tell you that we shall never have the slightest dis-agreement about money; whatever you think fair will be acceptable to me.[25]

To the end of her life Marie kept the promise made in this sad letter. After writing it she spent her last moments in her garden, which was now in flower. She then set off toward Switzerland, where Liszt was to join her a few days later. She knew that she would be censured and mocked by the ladies of Paris, and possibly envied by some. Her burden of guilt would be a heavy one because she was leaving a little daughter whom she might never see again. What sort of vagrant life would she lead with Liszt? She instinc-tively knew it would not be an easy one, but the day of emancipation had come.

CHAPTER 8

Life with Liszt

S HE left Paris on the first day of June 1835 in the company of her mother, who thought the purpose of the journey was to give Marie a holiday. Five days later they arrived in the town of Basel, Switzerland, where Liszt was already waiting. She dreaded telling her mother about her planned elopement and postponed the revelation for a few days. When it came, Madame de Flavigny took the news badly, and there followed tearful scenes in which she begged her daughter to reconsider a decision which would have such a profound effect on the whole family. She capitulated when she saw that Marie's resolution was not to be shaken—and may have recalled her own determination many years earlier to spend her life with Flavigny in spite of family opposition. Her daughter's intention was more radical than her own, however, as she was about to forfeit a high and enviable position in society by living in open adultery. Did Marie really want to throw it all away for the love of a pianist?

After the departure of Madame de Flavigny, Marie and Liszt left the medieval gates of Basel behind them and began a journey through Switzerland which he would later immortalize in a series of compositions called *The Years of Pilgrimage*.[1] They had no precise plan except to spend time together and enjoy the beauty of nature, leaving all their worries behind them. Liszt was weary of his celebrity as a pianist and painfully aware that his fame would be as ephemeral as his performances. He increasingly felt the need to devote himself to the production of musical works which would live forever, while also encouraging Marie's literary ambitions, which were well known to him. For five weeks they blissfully roamed around Switzerland, enjoying the spectacular scenery and engaging in discussions about literature and music. Did art have the power to bring social progress? This was his fervent belief, and Marie now shared it. For the first time the lovers were living together, and every little incident in their pilgrimage seemed full of charm. No letters reached them in the village inns where they stopped, and nobody knew their real names. Given the similarity of their eyes, voice, and appearance, they were often taken to be brother and sister, a mistake that filled them with happiness. What better proof of the deep affinity between them, what better confirmation of the fact that they could not have failed to fall in love?

They began their journey by heading up the valley of the Rhine toward Lake Constance, where they took the steamboat to Rorschach. During a stay at the village of Walenstadt, Liszt composed for her a sad and beautiful piece which reflected the lapping of the lake waters. In the wild and deserted Saint Gotthard region, they followed winding paths up the mountain until they could overlook the glacier from which the great Rhône began its course. Eventually they ended their travels by taking a steamboat from Villeneuve to Geneva.

When they landed on the quayside, Marie feared they had reached the end of their idyll, now that they were back in a city and surrounded by touts from hotels and other parasites who lived from tourism. A temporary home was provided by Pierre Wolff, a young musician who had known Liszt since childhood and who now lived in Geneva with his wife and children. This precious contact would provide them with necessary information about the libraries and music publishers in the city, but Marie did not feel at ease in these busy streets, fearing she might run into someone she knew among the French visitors to Geneva. She was concerned that Liszt might notice her anxiety, but he was too busy with practical arrangements for a long stay. He had gone to the post office and returned with two letters for her which had been waiting for some weeks. One was from her mother, the other from her brother.

She was moved to see that the letter from Madame de Flavigny did not contain a single word of criticism of the daughter in whom she had invested so much affection and hope. Her mother did express some astonishment that Liszt, whose decency and religious principles were well known, could have caused a break between Marie and her family. Madame de Flavigny, who did not know that Marie was pregnant, seemed to hope that the passing of a few weeks would have allowed the lovers to look at the situation coolly and change course while there was still time. If so, she would help to smooth things over by meeting Marie in Basel and taking her back to Paris, as if nothing untoward had happened. After all, the rumors of her elopement had not yet been confirmed. If Marie wanted a lasting separation from her husband she could live with her mother, as she had in the old days.

Maurice too was ignorant of the fact that she was carrying Liszt's child, and his letter was helpful and diplomatic. The situation was not yet out of hand, he said, and Charles himself would agree to her having a totally independent life. In his letter he inserted a note from her little daughter asking if she would soon come home. Marie felt a surge of guilt and of nostalgia for her home and the garden where Claire used to play. The affectionate support of her family was impressive, and it was true that public opinion would be satisfied by a respect for appearances. It was also possible that she would outlive Charles and be able to marry Liszt one day. In the meantime, her lover would certainly not try to prevent her from doing what she wanted, she reasoned, and might even be relieved to be free from the responsibility of living with a fallen woman.

She could hear the voice of conscience, but it was overcome by that of passion, the recent weeks having increased her feelings for Franz. More than ever she saw in him an exceptional man who was superior to any other she had met. In moments of mystical intensity she felt that God had intended her to be the Beatrice of this Dante, the protector of this young genius who could not be expected to live an ordinary life. She would therefore devote herself to him and his art and accept the social consequences. It was in one of these moments of ascetic fervor that she found the courage to tell her mother and brother that her decision was to remain in Geneva.

While Marie was brooding on these matters, Liszt was busy with practical things and unaware of her thoughts. When he asked her what news she had received from Paris, she did her best to hide her worries, and he did not drag them out of her. Unreasonably, she felt that he should have penetrated her reserve and blamed him for not doing so. There was now a barrier between them, for Marie did not want to keep secrets from the man she loved. It was a time of learning for both of them. Marie was accustomed to a polite and distant relationship with her husband, but life with Liszt was different. He was more sensual than she and desired her body with the ardor of a young man. Marie was idealistic, sentimental, and reserved.

They rented an apartment in the rue Tabazan in the upper part of the town. From the windows they could see much of Geneva, with its narrow streets, and the Rhône; from the balcony Marie contemplated the Jura Mountains. She liked the simplicity of this new home and the bouquets of Alpine flowers she bought daily from a peasant woman. She had recruited a pleasant village girl as a maid and reflected on the difference between her present existence and the life of privilege she had led in the château of Croissy.

Her life with Liszt in Geneva now had a pattern, with much time devoted to reading and talking. He had begun to compose new music on their Erard piano and liked having her with him when he did so, saying that her presence helped him to concentrate. Pretending to read, she watched his shining eyes, noted every movement of his pen and lips, and felt deeply moved to see his musical genius at work. Yet it was not his music which she loved but the man himself, and her instinct must have told her that his art might create a barrier between them. The days were passing happily as Liszt remained in an excellent mood and continued to compose.

The first cloud in their sky came in a letter which she saw him read twice with rapt attention before passing it to her without a word of comment. It was from a gifted but weak-willed young pianist, a fifteen-year-old boy named Hermann Cohen, who had been Liszt's pupil in Paris. Since Liszt's departure, Hermann had been unable to work and had become totally discouraged. In his letter he begged Liszt to let him live nearby just so that he could see him from time to time, leaving out any mention of lessons. "He must come," said Liszt, taking the letter from her hands. "I will write to him." Marie had been touched by Hermann's letter, but she felt that Liszt should have asked her opinion. She had given up everything in order to be alone with him, and already he was going to open their door to an intruder. She sensed that if Hermann came to Geneva, he would invade their life, but she did not want to impede the typically generous impulse of her lover.

Some days later there was a loud knock on the street door, followed by the sound of someone running up the stairs; in burst Hermann, who threw his arms around Liszt's neck. That evening they naturally invited him to dinner, and the next day he returned for his first lesson, after which the two went out together. Soon it was agreed that he would come every day; as part of the daily assignments, Liszt made him read books and do written comments of the contents. Marie took an interest in the rapid progress shown by Hermann, who was known to Liszt by the nickname Puzzi, but the situation also served to remind her poignantly that she was neglecting the education of her own daughter in Paris. Although she hid her growing resentment, she asked herself how Franz could fail to understand her feelings.

There was no longer any city in Europe in which Franz Liszt could avoid the consequences of celebrity. This was true even of Geneva, a town notorious for its interest in money rather than art. It was also a puritanical city that frowned on his immoral situation. Marie was now visibly pregnant and wanted to turn her back on society for a time. Society, however, was seeking her out. Already in July she had received a letter from Adèle de La Prunarède, Liszt's former mistress, who had seen him in Geneva and expressed a wish to meet Marie. The offer could be seen as an act of generous condescension from a woman of virtue to an erring sister, and Marie's proud rebuff was a masterpiece of sarcasm:

> As you said to Franz yesterday, you are much respected in society. This same society which respects you does not respect me at all and, what is even more terrible, I could not care less. The respect which you have acquired is the result of a sort of prudence which must be protected from contact with my unusual sincerity! It is very remarkable! It is said that you convert sinners, that you keep to the straight and narrow path, leading your disciples behind you. Perhaps I too would feel the irresistible power of your lovely blue eyes. But I think not. My sole mission has been the humble task of finding out what suited my nature and character; having found it, I need nothing more, and no power could separate me from it. All this does not mean, dear beautiful Countess, that I do not take the greatest interest in your life. Our starting point was the same and it is always with pleasure that I recall the circumstances which brought us together for a moment. As chance has once more brought us to the same place, you should write again to Franz. You know that he *returns letters* when asked to do so.[2]

After her love affair with Liszt, Adèle had adopted a policy of piety and virtue to repair the damage to her reputation, hence the scorn of Marie and this display of touchy pride. Marie did not doubt the sincerity of Liszt's attachment to her, but she had difficulty in accepting his spontaneous and friendly attitude toward all, including past mistresses. It was ever more clear that their intimacy was progressively threatened by the outside world.

There was worse to come. One day Pierre Wolff came to speak to Marie about the offers being made to Liszt. A musically gifted and aristocratic Russian lady had an intense desire to have piano lessons from him and would pay handsomely. What was more, the ladies of Geneva were planning a charity concert and would like Liszt to perform. The cause was worthy, the proceeds of the concert to be distributed among refugees living precariously in Geneva. This strange community of deposed monarchs, dismissed ministers, and failed generals had asked Wolff to contact Liszt, and he had begun by mentioning it to Marie so that she could overcome any possible resistance on his part. Public performance was exactly contrary to the plan agreed upon for their stay in Geneva, and she showed no enthusiasm for the proposal. They had vowed to live quietly and to devote themselves to art and love! She let herself be persuaded, however, by the argument that the concert would be attended by influential people who had never heard Liszt play and would thus be very useful to his career.

When she broached the subject, she discovered that her lover knew all about the proposal. She had no persuading to do, as he was already disposed to perform. It is a bit of bother, he said, but I understand from Wolff that you think I should accept. He had, however, imposed the condition that Marie would accompany him. She could hardly believe her ears. Not only had he committed himself without telling her, he had also brought her into it. His intentions were of course excellent, since he wanted to conquer the high society of Geneva by forcing it to accept the woman he loved. But what about her feelings? It was so soon after the scandal of their elopement, and the product of their adultery was becoming ever more visible. What would her husband and family think if the concert was reported in the French newspapers? She realized that Liszt did not for a moment doubt that she would agree to accompany him, and she did not have the heart to speak out and disappoint him.

When she was alone, she weighed her predicament and asked herself how she might have avoided it. No doubt she should have spoken sooner and communicated her real feelings. The question now was how to escape from the situation, but instead she waited and hoped that some chance event might help her. Thankfully Wolff had taken Hermann to Lausanne for a while, and the weeks before the concert were a time of renewed intimacy with Liszt. As she did not want to spoil this time of serenity, she simply abandoned herself once more to the enjoyment of her love. When the day of the concert arrived, Liszt told her that Wolff would call for her that evening and accompany her. Marie replied that she was not feeling well and did not want to go. Liszt was so worried at this news that he questioned her until she finally told him the truth. Inevitably there was an implicit reproach in her explanation, and he reacted in his usual impulsive manner by getting to his feet and announcing that he was going to withdraw from the concert.

At once she regretted what she had said. To go back on his word on the very day of the performance would greatly damage his professional reputation. At all costs she wanted to prevent this and begged him to go. She had had a moment's weakness, she said, and felt better now. Besides, people would blame her as much as him if he did not perform. Liszt was maintaining his refusal to play, and she could see the hands of the clock moving toward the time when he would have to leave. In a last effort she persuaded him to change his mind, managing even to convince herself that she had been in the wrong.

The concert took place in the home of Prince and Princess Belgiojoso on 1 October 1835. Marie made her entrance in the company of Wolff and sat discreetly at the back of the splendidly illuminated room. From the ceiling hung a great cluster of lamps which were dripping oil on the hats of the elegant ladies below. The stage was pleasantly decorated with white draperies and flowers, and at the back of it sat a small orchestra on raised tiers. In the audience could be seen Jérôme Bonaparte, once king of Westphalia, and a beautiful blonde daughter with a sad and gentle look. Among other representatives of fallen greatness were generals who had served under Napoleon and a minister of Charles X who thought it safer not to live in France. It had been some time since Marie had been in a gathering of this sort, and the sight of the densely packed audience made her strangely apprehensive. The concert began with an expert rendering of airs by Bellini and Schubert by Prince Belgiojoso himself, who could have been a professional singer had he not been born rich. Beside him at the piano was the very different figure of young Puzzi, whose dark hair, pale face, and melancholic look caused a stir among the young females in the audience. After the interval the hubbub of voices gave way to a prolonged storm of applause as Liszt appeared for his solo performance. Marie's breathing seemed to stop while the noise grew and faded and grew again as if it would never end. Then came a deep silence after which she heard the first chords ring out. At once she had a strange new impression. She could see Franz, but it was not Franz. It was as if she were seeing an actor playing his part with much skill but remaining on the surface of things. In front of her was Franz Liszt the performer who belonged not to Marie d'Agoult but to the world. While she admired the prodigious skill and incomparable emotion of his playing she realized it was a force Franz could not control.

After the concert they were submerged by written congratulations, invitations, and expressions of admiration. Every prominent person wanted to be introduced to Liszt, whose intelligence and talent were the talk of the town. It seemed that every woman in Geneva was fascinated by his handsome looks, his passionate character, and the romance of his life. Wolff was beside himself with pleasure. He had become the intermediary who dealt with all these solicitations and as such had acquired sudden importance. Each day he subjected Liszt to more pressure because of the number of people who wanted to meet him, and there were always excellent reasons for doing as he said. Some were travelers who were about to leave Geneva, so there would be no further commitments. Others were prestigious individuals whom one could simply not refuse. One was a rich admirer of Beethoven who had funded performances of his music; another had a greater interest in literature than in music, which would be a pleasant change for Franz.

At first Liszt tried to resist this invasion, but with decreasing determination. Their doors were opened to a small number of new acquaintances, some of whom were to become good friends. He no longer had the peace and time he needed to devote himself to serious composition. His savings were running out, and he was receiving tempting offers from music publishers asking for light and easy pieces which amateur pianists could play in their homes. Liszt was irritated by these marketing considerations, which could not be avoided, and during the time devoted to lesser compositions he completely ceased work on serious music in order to avoid possible corruption. It was a frustrating situation, and Marie saw his dissatisfaction grow as the weeks went by.

On Friday, 18 December 1835, their life was marked by the birth of a daughter, whom they named Blandine. The child was registered as the natural daughter of François Liszt, twenty-four, a music teacher, and Catherine Méran, twenty-four, a lady of private means, both unmarried and living in Geneva. They were extremely economical with the truth, since Marie was two weeks from her thirtieth birthday and still married to Charles d'Agoult. The episode is useful as a reminder to the historian that official documents cannot always be trusted. Marie had good reason not to use her real name on the birth registry, as French law wisely specified that any child must be officially considered the offspring of the woman's husband.

The situation of the lovers in Geneva was strange. The city contained a tolerant cosmopolitan community alongside a native society composed of rich Calvinists who were embarrassed in their attitude toward Liszt and Marie. Wolff kept the lovers informed about public opinion. The elite of Geneva were dying of curiosity to meet Liszt and to hear him perform, but the bohemian artist was openly living in adultery, with no sign of shame or remorse. No doubt he was a basically decent young man whose head had been turned by fame and women. During his time in Paris, his principles had apparently been contaminated by immoral writers like Alexandre Dumas and George Sand, who wrote subversive nonsense about marriage and the rights of individuals. What else could one expect of Paris? It would not have been so bad if he had had the sense to keep his delinquent countess out of sight, but he expected decent women to receive her in their homes.

The ladies of Geneva were naturally more severe on Marie than on the man for whom she had given up everything. Gossip abounded, some of it true. She was older than he and therefore less deserving of pardon. She was an insipid blonde who had been a good wife and the mother of five or six children, the story went, until her mad passion for Liszt. She had disguised herself as a man in order to be with him once when he played the organ in the cathedral of Notre-Dame at midnight. To cap it all she had left Paris with a couple of children and persuaded Liszt to elope with her, to the detriment of his promising career.

While her female censors were busy with such speculation, Marie was occupying herself with the serious business of writing. In April 1835 an article by Liszt on the position of musicians in society had appeared in the Parisian periodical *La Gazette Musicale*. Marie's first publication in collaboration with her lover was an article called "Lettre d'un voyageur à M. George Sand," which appeared in the same revue on 6 December under Liszt's name. The piece expressed gratitude for an earlier article in which Sand had paid homage to the talent and character of Liszt and had spoken of Marie as his inspiration. Then followed more articles signed by Liszt, though in these one can detect Marie's more disciplined style, starting with a complimentary review of Hugo's new volume of poetry, *Les chants du crépuscule*. This piece appeared in *L'Europe Centrale* on 19 December 1836 and was followed on 16 April 1836 by an unsigned article in which Marie sternly castigated the high society of Geneva for its failure to appreciate music. The specific case involved a concert given by Puzzi, with a contribution by Liszt. This had led to the event being boycotted by the prudes of the city as a protest against his immorality.

The article is a bitterly satirical account of a fictional concert which the ladies of Geneva decide to sabotage for a variety of reasons: the pianist has a bad reputation, his hair is untidy, he plays too many sharps and flats, he wastes time on transcendental ornithology instead of practicing scales. They therefore decide to form an Association for the Prevention of Concerts in Geneva and agree that no member will attend a musical performance unless there is some exceptional reason, such as free entry. They also pledge to make at least two silly statements about music every week and twelve similar comments about musicians every month. In this way the inhabitants of Geneva will be protected from the influence of art and can continue to devote themselves exclusively to money and puritanism, she sneered. The bitter note in this attack reflects Marie's frustration upon finding herself, however predictably, a social outcast. The ladies of Geneva might express their disapproval, but she would hit back.

In reality certain relations between the lovers and one section of the population were good, since the intelligentsia at least visited them. Some went with their wives, and some without, but they went. Among them were the specialist in linguistics Adolphe Pictet, the historian Jean de Sismondi, and the botanist Pyrame de Candolle. They found in Marie a witty hostess whose wide interests ranged from literature, history, and philosophy to science. Men reported to their wives that she seemed so much at ease that one soon forgot her delinquent status. In fact she was again showing her old ability to charm certain young men to the point where they were prepared to serve her like the troubadours of old. In Paris she had enjoyed the faithful services of Théophile de Ferrière, who was now replaced by Louis de Ronchaud, a shy and intelligent young man with vague literary ambitions. Remarkably, this new admirer would devote the rest of his life to her, asking no more than to be her companion and run errands to shops and libraries for her, harmlessly filling the void during the absences of Liszt. She was the sun, and he lived by her light. For her part she undertook a methodical reading of Fichte, Schelling, Spinoza, and Kant, serious studies she viewed as the necessary basis of a career as a writer.

About the middle of April 1836 Liszt and Marie experienced their first significant separation, when he went to Lyon for more than two months to organize a series of concerts. After traveling on top of the stagecoach in order to enjoy the scenery, he sent her a letter full of idealistic love, which also makes a rare allusion to their sex life: "From Bellegarde to Nantua I enjoyed intense pleasure (as much as I can without you). I am sure you would like this countryside which is serious, soft, calm, even a little monotonous. There is a little lake which reminded me of our dear Walenstadt! Oh! for me it is an intense happiness to think that soon we will travel together! I think I am now more worthy of it; little by little I will be purified by the resignation and by the higher life which you have taught me to appreciate." [3] In a series of affectionate letters he wisely advised her to maintain her spirits by doing some riding and urged her to resume playing the piano as it was a joy for him to hear her. From Franz Liszt, this was praise of a high order. His letters are full of entertaining details of his stay in Lyon, where he was receiving the full celebrity treatment. He was having his portrait done by a female painter, and a woman was overcome by emotion one evening when he played after a private dinner party. In a moment of imprudent sincerity he revealed to Marie that their separation might be extended so that he could return to Paris to attend a concert by the Austrian pianist Sigismund Thalberg. This new rival was currently acclaimed as the leading performer in the capital, but it would be enough for Liszt to appear suddenly, like Napoleon back from exile, to win back his crown.

This idea drew a stern response from Marie, who did not want him to prolong his absence. Had they not agreed that he would forget celebrity and devote himself to lasting works? The reproach hurt him, and he poured out his heart in a fervent protest of his devotion: "Do not listen to me when I speak to you of anything other than love and happiness; tear and burn the pages of my letters which may contain a name which is not yours, a thought unworthy of you; throw into the dust of the road and the mud of the gutter all memories, all affections, all imperfections of my life which was so empty, unhealthy, and unfortunate before you."[4] Why did he absent himself at all, he asked himself? Two weeks would pass before he returned to Geneva, and he was dying of impatience to talk to her, work with her, and sleep with her. If she should change her mind and travel to Lyon she would find him on the fifth floor of the Hôtel de Milan, and above all she should come without Puzzi.

In the end Liszt did go to Paris, and at the request of Marie herself, who wanted him to meet her brother and discuss such matters as her possible return to the city. During his stay Liszt renewed contact with a number of friends, including Chopin, Delacroix, Lamartine, Meyerbeer, Vigny, Musset, and Lamennais. He also took professional advantage of the situation by giving a concert which drew a generous homage from Berlioz in *La Gazette Musicale* of 12 June 1836. Meanwhile he continued to write anxious letters expressing his loneliness and impatience and was understandably worried by the reproachful tone in some of her letters. In a missive written on 2 June 1836 Marie attempted to reassure him, despite ominous overtones:

> I think I sent you a very bad letter this morning. I am tormented by this thought and feel I must send this one at once to make up for it. I was very sad, I had spent a whole day in bed just because I could see no reason to get dressed, and as my mind was obsessed by some vague demons, it showed in my letter. Do not worry about it, and put yourself in my position. For three weeks I have been excluded from your life. All your words

Franz Liszt, by Henri Lehmann, 1839.

(Photothèque des Musées de la Ville de Paris)

and thoughts are lost for me. I drag myself from hope to hope, and your letters burn my heart like a hot iron. Yesterday I ran out of courage, I am not even capable of wanting anything. I know that I shall be sad when I see you again, and yet what you tell me of your stay in Paris makes me so happy. Why do you think I do not approve of everything you have said and done? Have we not one heart?[5]

The separation of more than two months had been too much, and the demons of her depression returned, possibly triggered by her recent maternity. One part of her knew that his absences in Lyon and Paris were useful to his career, and she felt the sincerity of his love even from afar, but still she had dark, irrational days. When Liszt returned to Geneva, the two devoted time exclusively to themselves, clutching at a happiness which already appeared fragile. Liszt understood her all the better because he too had moments of lassitude and doubt.

During Marie's long stay in Geneva, she was to develop a new and passionate friendship with George Sand, who had for some time maintained a cordial relationship with Liszt. Marie was excited at the thought of meeting the creator of the character Indiana, this fictional sister in whom she saw so much of herself. She must also have considered the risk of losing Liszt to George, who was well known for her love affairs and had just broken off a relationship with Musset. When Liszt told her of Marie's literary ambitions, George sent her an effusive and flattering letter: "Beautiful, blonde Countess, I do not know you personally but I have heard Franz speak about you and I have seen you. For this reason I think I am not doing something foolish and forward if I tell you my affection for you, and say that you are the only fine, valuable and truly noble thing which I have seen shining in the patrician sphere."[6] Marie responded with an invitation to Geneva, and George replied with another flattering letter expressing the hope that Marie's social class would not be an obstacle between them: "Your rank is a high one, and I salute and recognise it. It is that you are kind, intelligent and beautiful. Let me have your noble coronet and I will break it, giving you a coronet of stars which will suit you better."[7] Their correspondence continued in the same complimentary mode as George repeatedly admired Marie's intelligence, beauty, and happiness in love. George also warned Marie of her bluff manners. She was playful, capricious, and rude and could be as prickly as a

George Sand, by Auguste Charpentier, 1839.

(Photothèque des Musées de la Ville de Paris)

porcupine, she explained. Would she be acceptable to a lady with the refined manners of the aristocracy? Marie replied in the same jocular mode, saying that she was willing to risk the encounter and would let her know if she found her intolerable. One notes that her cleverly written letter contains a warning concealed as a joke: they must indeed become intimate friends, but Marie would put poison in George's coffee if Franz asked her to do it.

The strange friendship between these women who had not yet met was handsomely sealed when George dedicated her novel *Simon* to Marie, who wrote at once to express her appreciation. She greatly admired this fictional evocation of a childhood like her own in the Loire Valley. The picture of provincial life was full of truth and charm, and she envied George's narrative ease, she said. George replied by urging Marie to trust in her own literary talent and follow the path traced by the writer Hortense Allart: "Write about the position and the rights of women; write with daring and modesty, as you are capable of this. Mme Allart has just produced a brochure in which there are really some excellent arguments and true remarks. But she is pedantic and has no charm. I am too ignorant to write anything other than stories, and do not have the application to learn."[8] George in fact was writing a modified version of her novel *Lélia* to expound a new morality, no less. It was not a philosophy fit for grocers, she explained, but one which would suit free spirits like Marie. A long and affectionate letter written in July gave intimate details of George's life and showed a character very different from that of her correspondent:

> I leave the house on foot at three in the morning with the firm intention to return by eight. But I get lost in the tracks, I linger beside the streams, I run after insects and get home by midday completely roasted. The other day I was so overcome by the heat that I got into the river fully dressed. I had not intended to do so and had brought no suitable garment. A little farther along the bank, as my clothes were dry and I was again covered with sweat I jumped into the Indre again. My only precaution was to hang my dress on a bush and to bathe in my shift. I put my dress back on top of it, and the few people I met did not notice anything strange in my clothes. Taking three or four dips every time I go out I can still cover three or four leagues on foot, in a temperature of thirty degrees, and what leagues! I run after every moth. Sometimes when my clothes are completely soaked

I lie in a meadow beside the river and have a siesta. What a wonderful season which enables one to enjoy the pleasure of primitive life.[9]

One imagines Marie's reaction to these revelations by the nymph of No-hant, who could also write serious novels. She admired this buoyancy of character which kept her afloat in the sea of conjugal, financial, and emotional troubles. George evidently enjoyed a form of happiness which was more physical and less sublime than her own love of Liszt. Perhaps she could learn something from her new friend.

Replying to an anxious letter from George, who was involved in a lawsuit with her husband, Marie assured her that she and Franz would postpone a trip to Italy and wait for her. What were the ruins of Rome compared to a noble heart and a loyal friend? Liszt had returned from Paris and was in Lausanne for a concert, and she was writing from a little house in the mountains where she was escaping from the city heat. From the window of her simple whitewashed bedroom she could see the Lake of Geneva and the snowy summit of Mont Blanc. Accompanied by the farmer's dog, she was enjoying walks among the fields of summer wheat. Like George, she was now determined to savor the pleasures of the earth and for once turn her back on her old introspection and reverie. She eagerly anticipated the time when the two women would discuss literature, society, and morality while enjoying the peaceful harmony of nature in the Swiss mountains. Having lost her old religious beliefs forever, she envied George her confident faith in human nature and social progress. She exulted at the news that her friend had won custody of her children and possession of the house at Nohant. Marriage was like a chain around the neck of women, Marie commented bitterly, and they even had to pretend to be grateful to society when the noose was momentarily loosened.

Their first meeting took place in the Hôtel de l'Union in the village of Chamonix, which George charmingly recounted later in one of her travel articles.[10] Her arrival in male attire had caused a stir in this country inn, and Liszt had attracted attention by registering as a philosopher-musician born on Mount Parnassus. The party included Puzzi and George's two children, as well as the intellectual Adolphe Pictet. The plan was to set off on mules to explore the mountains for a week. They were a strange-looking cohort,

a mixture of the elegant and the bohemian, Marie's veil and parasol contrasting with Franz's old straw hat. Puzzi looked for all the world like a girl
in male clothes, whereas George's daughter Solange was already a fearless
rider like her mother. George herself wore a huge blue smock which made
her look like a bell. As they proceeded on their journey Liszt was cheerfully
making pronouncements about the future of humanity and the inevitability
of progress. George could not refrain from teasing Pictet, who was reading an abstruse work of philosophy instead of admiring the scenery. What
is the use of abstract theory, she argued, when the world needs democracy
and humanitarian action? Pictet answered by accusing her of being a public
danger and a revolutionary. At the moment he was pondering a profound
statement by Schelling that the absolute is identical to itself. This unwise
revelation caused much hilarity, and the obscure maxim became an end-
lessly repeated joke as they proceeded. At one point the argument between
George and Pictet became so heated that Marie intervened with tact and
said that both of the combatants were right. Puzzi had frivolously avoided
the whole philosophical debate by chasing butterflies in the bushes.

Boisterous activities occurred in the inns where they stayed along the
way. On one occasion George threw water from an upstairs window over
some English tourists; on another, the group drank so much wine that Pictet
began to talk to the ceiling in Sanskrit, George danced around the room,
and Liszt sang at the top of his voice while conducting an imaginary concert and admonishing the chairs for being out of tune. Their antics got so
bad that Marie thought they had all gone mad and withdrew to bed. For all
George's childlike playfulness, she had been observing Marie with interest.
Her account contains some perceptive comments on her new friend: she
had been disappointed by the glaciers, which had not been white, and by
the mountain streams, which had not been dramatic. George lacked Marie's
sensitivity and high aesthetic aspirations and was more easily satisfied, as
was shown by her repeated attempts to find a suitable lover.

Even Marie was thrilled by a visit to the cathedral of Freiburg, renowned for its organ. After introducing himself to the organist, a plump
and eager young man, Liszt began by playing a simple air with single notes
in order to savor the purity of the sound. Soon he was asked to move aside by
the organist, who proudly produced sounds emulating rumbles of thunder,

howling winds, human voices, cowbells, and a noise like that of trees being split by lightning. Then came an unforgettable moment, as rain began to beat against the high windows and Liszt played Mozart's *Dies irae*. George looked at Marie and saw an expression of deep emotion on her face as the sublime sound of the music reverberated within the cathedral. Suddenly the magic ended in a dying wheeze. The bell for the evening service had started to ring, and the man at the bellows had stopped pumping air into the lungs of the great instrument. George felt like hitting the culprit, but prosaic reality had returned.

After a happy week together, they reached Geneva and George was invited to prolong her stay. In the daytime she explored the city, where her presence caused much interest, and in the evenings they stayed up late having long conversations about the state of the world. George departed for France in early October, having become impatient to return to Michel de Bourges, her current lover. She was well pleased with the time spent with Franz and his fair companion. Marie, however, was concerned that she might have disappointed her ebullient new friend who had so flatteringly courted her by letter before meeting her. George had proved to be unlike anyone Marie had ever met, and she had not known how to react to her playful and exuberant behavior. Before their meeting, Marie had adored George as a literary genius, and George had idealized Marie as a woman, so some rectification was inevitable.

Despite this necessity the two women were determined to develop their friendship, and Marie took practical steps to do so when she and Liszt returned to Paris in October 1836. A new stage in their life was about to begin after sixteen months of living together. During this time their relationship had not been free from conflict and had required concessions from two proud individuals. There had also been times when Marie, absorbed in her sad thoughts, was unresponsive to the desires of her young lover. The birth of Blandine had forged a new bond between them, but when they quit Geneva they left the baby in the care of a paid foster family in a village near the city. By doing so Marie was simply conforming to a practice common among women of her class, who found it perfectly natural to employ another woman to nurse and care for their child during the first years of its life. In their eyes the physical role of motherhood was less important than other social duties. Marie would not see her ten-month-old child again until the following August, and then briefly, but this was not a source of guilt. It would not be until the little girl reached the age of four that she would finally live with her mother.

The months in Geneva had allowed the scandal of Marie's elopement to recede into the past and had enabled her to complete her extracurricular pregnancy in a city where she would have fewer embarrassing encounters. The stay had served its purpose, and the lovers were eager to end their exile for both personal and professional reasons. After three years of intense joy and sorrow, she felt able to build a new life in the city she had left so dramatically. Paris would be more welcoming than Geneva to a couple openly living in adultery, though it would of course be necessary to avoid Saint-Germain and to live in the bohemian world of writers and musicians. Paris was also a leading city of culture, unlike Geneva, and in a era when musical performances could not be recorded, Liszt's absence caused his reputation to slip. This loss of favor was partly explained by a sort of conspiracy by the Austrian ambassador and his wife to promote Thalberg and portray Liszt as a musical charlatan, a subversive, and a seducer. Thalberg, by contrast, was the official pianist of the Austrian emperor and his political ideas were wholly sound. Aristocratic circles had found it fashionable to find his playing superior to that of Liszt. A new campaign in Paris was therefore essential.

Marie and Franz took up residence in the Hôtel de France, and Marie's first visit was to her daughter Claire, now six, in her convent school. She then prepared to contribute actively to the creation of a support network for Liszt. Her new social circle contained some remnants of her previous life, mainly the writers Custine, Sainte-Beuve, and Sue. Their group included Liszt's musical friends, such as Berlioz, Chopin, Meyerbeer, and the singer Nourrit, but also such exiled writers as Adam Michiewiez, Bernard Potocki, and Heinrich Heine. Other visitors included the radicals Pierre Leroux and of course Lamennais, both of whom also knew George Sand.

It was an impressive constellation of gifted individuals, and Marie at once acted to recruit George Sand herself by inviting her to settle under the same roof. It was a decisive move, and not without risk: "Come and live with me in the Hôtel de France, rue Neuve Lafitte. It is comfortable and not too expensive: I have a bedroom and a rather fine sitting-room. If you like I will reserve a room for you and you can use my sitting-room during the day to see your friends. In this way we will be certain to see a lot of each other. I feel that I now need this." [11] George accepted with enthusiasm, and for three months the arrangement worked well. Marie now had a small salon where she sometimes dressed in a Spanish costume — a black gown, pink shoes, and a black lace mantilla on her blonde hair. In this new milieu she soon won a reputation as a hostess with gracious manners and high intellect.

These first months back in Paris were also a time of work, with Liszt making efforts to continue his ambitious compositions despite days of distraction and discouragement. On 18 December he played in a concert organized by Berlioz and was at first coolly received. The audience was soon won over, however, and rose to acclaim his rendering of a cavatina by Pacini. During this time Marie had continued her intellectual support of Liszt's career by writing an influential article which would appear in La Gazette Musicale on 12 February 1837. The young Liszt had been exploited by aristocratic Parisian society and distracted from his true vocation, she explained. He was not an entertainer but a serious composer and an innovator who was destined to cause controversy. Music could be a total expression of the human condition, she asserted in eloquent defense of Liszt's artistic aspiration. It had the capacity to contribute to social progress and to civilization itself. Even in a prosaic modern world the myth of Orpheus had not lost its essential truth.

In early January 1837, George Sand returned to her large country home at Nohant, well pleased with the time spent close to her talented and idealistic friends. The months of proximity had not diminished her enthusiasm for Marie. She had long wanted Marie to visit Nohant and the time had come, now that Franz's career was back on track. Sand's concern, which was not without foundation, was that Marie might find her local friends a little rustic and her house reminiscent of a Cossack camp. Marie accepted the invitation at once, explaining that God had just saved her from a serious gastric infection so that she could visit George in her home: "He did the right thing: I want to see Nohant; I want to live your life, to become the friend of your dogs, to feed your hens; I want to sit at your fire, to eat your partridges and revive my poor thin body by breathing the same air as you. Without you knowing it and without me knowing it you have freed my mind from a languor which I thought incurable. You will do the same for my body and then I will thank you for that which nobody has ever been able to give me, the ability to enjoy my good fortune." [12] The sincerity of this attraction to George is confirmed by a letter from Marie to her childhood friend Louis de Suzannet shortly after her arrival. George was the only deeply kind woman she had ever met, she explained. Marie was happily reading by her fireside and sitting up late for long conversations about everything under the sun. [13]

Other letters, however, show some recurrence of her fits of depression during which she wondered whether George or even Liszt himself, with all his love, could save her. George was having emotional difficulties of a different sort, because Michel de Bourges had grown tired of her. Her problem seemed relatively simple, since it could be solved by her finding a more suitable lover. Marie was afraid that her own unstable moods might endanger her relationship with Liszt. Writing from Paris, where he was absorbed by his plan to displace Thalberg, he urged her to join him. She replied that she feared she might disturb his work, even bring him bad luck, but finally she did return to Paris to be with him during the crucial weeks.

The rivalry between the two musicians had become a source of considerable excitement in the capital. The Thalberg camp was encouraged by one section of the press, such as *La Quotidienne,* and Liszt was supported by *Le Journal des Débats* and by *Le Monde,* which was not surprising since it was directed by his friend Lamennais. During the spring of 1837 the fortunate music lovers of Paris were able to compare the compositions and performance skills of the two artists in a series of separate concerts which culminated in a double event billed as a musical duel. The final confrontation took place on 31 March in the home of Cristina Belgiojoso, who had planned the silly event. The result was a triumph for the Romantic style and for Liszt. Thalberg's honest merit could not be preferred for a minute when placed beside the intense emotion and rich personality of his rival. Marie could now savor her first public revenge over those members of her class who had mocked her for her elopement with Liszt.

After this success, the lovers went together to Nohant, where George was eagerly awaiting them, having vainly urged them to bring Chopin. They

remained there for three months, enjoying warm hospitality and the pleasures of the Berry province in summer. On some fine mornings the two
women would rise an hour before dawn and ride to the banks of the Indre
when the meadows were still full of mist. One day they waded across the
stream and galloped up a steep track leading through a field of rye, pop-
pies, and cornflowers. She was afraid of falling where the track dropped
sharply toward the river, so George at once jumped lightly to the ground
and led the two horses down by the bridle. They stopped at a mill by the
river, where Marie's horse kept backing away and would not let her mount
him when they wanted to continue. In the end the miller picked her up un-
ceremoniously in his floury arms and quickly placed her in the saddle before
the animal could counter the move. On fine days she and George would sit
after dinner among the roses and listen with rapture to Liszt at the piano.
After one such evening Marie took her diary and wrote a moving homage
to her young genius:

> People think he is ambitious; it is not so, because he knows the limits of all
> things, and the feeling of the infinite carries his soul far beyond all earthly
> fame and pleasure. He is a man of destiny. God has clearly marked him
> with a mysterious seal. With a love full of respect and sadness I contem-
> plate his beauty. What nobility and purity in his features, what harmony
> in the fine lines of his face! His hair is as strong and abundant as the mane
> of a young lion, and seems to participate in his mental life; his burning
> eyes flash like the sword of a cherubim, but even in his most passionate
> moments, when he is full of desires, one feels that there is nothing coarse
> in them. Often these eyes become gentle and look at me with an inde-
> scribable expression of love and tenderness, penetrating my bones with a
> feeling of happiness which is unknown to those who have not been loved
> like this.[14]

When Liszt sat at the piano, he seemed to be invaded by a force greater
than himself. She saw his handsome face become proud and dominant as
the music flowed from his strong hands. Marie watched with emotion, a
mortal under the spell of Orpheus.

George too looked on with fascination. Despite her vigorous activities
and cheerful appearance, she was having suicidal thoughts as she struggled
to recover from rejection. When she considered her friend's position as the

unofficial wife of Liszt, she had secret feelings of envy. Marie was loved by a great artist, yet despite this she found happiness elusive because of her complicated nature. What would George not achieve if she had a man of such genius and passion? Inevitably, Marie began to grow anxious about George's intentions. As was to be expected, the months of cohabitation had allowed her unrealistic enthusiasm to cool. She had been taken aback by her friend's method of recovery from her disappointment with Michel de Bourges, who had rapidly been replaced by Charles Didier. And not long after Didier, the vacancy was filled by the actor Pierre Bocage. The situation drew some jocular comments from Liszt, who was not a model of diplomacy, and George was irritated. In any case, by this time the lovers were intending to leave Nohant to travel to Italy. It was clear because of George's attitude that they should have left earlier. Marie had observed that the woman whom she had idealized as a writer had personal faults. She played tricks; her conversation was sometimes coarse and did not exclude jokes about farts; she was impulsive and possibly unreliable. The speed with which she changed her lovers made Marie wonder if the same fate would befall her friends, and indeed this suspicion would be amply confirmed by later events. For a time their correspondence continued with every appearance of cordiality, providing a valuable record of Franz and Marie's experiences in Italy. Like Goethe and Byron they would visit the land where the lemon tree blooms, the land of passion and of art.

CHAPTER 9

The Lovers in Italy

MARIE and Franz left Nohant in July 1837, George accompanying their carriage as far as La Châtre, where they were to take the stagecoach. Marie reflected that the months in the country had been beneficial to her. Although she did not possess George's playful temperament, she had learned something from her. Her dynamic friend had stimulated her imagination and taught her new pleasures. In addition, the sight of George's shortcomings had enhanced Marie's self-esteem. She was interested to see that this gifted writer also had some characteristics of a willful child. Indeed, her erratic life seemed to be directed by chance rather than by reason. As Nohant faded into the distance, Marie noted in her diary that she had been mistaken in harboring a secret obsession which had begun to nag her in times of depression: the idea that George and Franz were made for each other because of their similar artistic natures and that she was an obstacle in their path. She now dismissed this thought and abandoned herself to the excitement of a journey into unknown regions. She and Franz had a common destiny, she repeated to herself, and she had freely devoted her life to him just as he had given his love to her. In the euphoria of the journey south, he told her that she was his Muse and that he felt the beauty of the landscape only when she was beside him.[1]

Their first notable experience was a visit to the cathedral in Bourges, where Marie contemplated the high Gothic vaults and reflected on her distance from the Catholicism of her youth. Her faith in orthodox beliefs had vanished, as had her acceptance of the social doctrines of the Church. Liszt remarked that the empty churches in France were like the seashore when the tide is low. The salvation of Christianity would be to defend the poor instead of the rich and powerful. When they reached Lyon, they put their principles into practice by paying to see an exhibition called "The Fishermen," by Léopold Robert, knowing that the money would go to the local unemployed. Marie was moved by a portrayal of two men, one in an attitude of energy, the other bent over in despair. It was a spectrum of emotions only too familiar to her. The use of the painting in a humanitarian cause confirmed their belief in the power of art, as did an evening spent with Liszt's friend Adolphe Nourrit. The philanthropic tenor was hoping to wean some of the city's workers away from alcohol by introducing them to the world of music. Artists like this were the true priests of their time, Marie concluded. Only they had the power to celebrate the joy of creation and to save the souls of the nation. Liszt vowed that he too would make his contribution to social progress when they returned from Italy.

They continued to reflect on different forms of religion during a visit to the famous Grande-Chartreuse monastery in the Alps, near Grenoble. For several hours they rode up a steep rocky path in a valley cut by a mountain stream. When their ponies reached their destination, she was struck by the contrast between the beauty of the forest setting and the banality of the buildings. All around were high peaks and a sunlit meadow where cows fed contentedly. Women were not permitted to enter the monastery, but she had no desire to do so. The monks had taken a vow of silence, except for special days, but once a week they could take a walk in the mountains. Why did the Church encourage this sterile life? Marie agreed with Franz that rejection of the world and its pleasures seemed an offense to God. He reflected that a more clever and imaginative pope would make better use of monasteries by turning them into places of industrial activity. This would save them from the hostility of the working class, which saw monks as parasites. By becoming proletarians themselves, they would earn the right to preach Christian morality to the workers. The lovers felt that the idea of shared effort was sound and hoped that communes of artists, scientists, and workers would soon advance the cause of humanity.

Near Geneva they called at the village of Etrembières to see their daughter, Blandine, now almost two years old, and pronounced her to be a beautiful child with a serious and intelligent look. Marie wrote to George that the little girl already loved music and flowers and had been taught to give money to the poor.[2] They decided to pay the foster family to keep her for one more year and agreed that she would join them when their travels were over. Having settled family matters in this simple way, they continued their route through the Alps. After marveling at the Simplon Pass, they descended to the mild and beautiful area of Lake Como and continued on to Milan, where Liszt was to make concert arrangements. He had some fun by arriving unannounced in the shop of Giovanni Ricordi, the leading music publisher in Italy. Without saying a word, he sat at a piano and began to improvise a prelude, whereupon all activity came to a standstill and the publisher quickly appeared in the doorway of his office. Ricordi could not do enough for Franz and Marie and insisted that they use his coach and country home until they had time to set up an establishment of their own in Milan.

Marie's impressions of the city were favorable, and she was relieved to find that Italian women were relatively frank about irregular liaisons. Countess Julie Samoilov, who was the leader of high society, went openly to Trieste to be near the tenor Poggi when he was performing there. It was refreshingly different from France, where Marie's own sister-in-law considered her a moral leper. She was now pregnant with Liszt's second child, and it was a good time to be abroad and far from censorious eyes.

They returned to Como in early September 1837 and took a boat which carried them through vineyards and olive groves to the village of Bellagio. There they rented rooms in the charming Angel Inn, which overlooked the lake. Noting their high, isolated setting, Marie and Franz observed they were living in alto solitudine, a phrase Marie chose as her motto. Liszt, who also liked it, gave her a ring with the Italian words engraved on it. She wrote telling George that they were living in the most beautiful setting she had ever seen. Italy was truly a land for poets and lovers, and a remedy for all melancholy. In her diary she noted details which seemed to indicate a new stage in her life with Franz. Relishing her pregnancy, she felt she never wanted to leave. In the evenings they sat on a balcony festooned with vines and listened to the church bells ring out from the villages around the lake. One day they attended a festival of the Madonna and reflected that this religious tradition was a continuation of pagan customs: the girls bringing baskets of cake and fruit to the statue of Mary were the direct descendants of those who had done the same for Venus. After a blessing from the priest, the baskets were auctioned for the good of the parish. In keeping with the festivities, Liszt bought a large quantity of little cakes and amused himself by throwing them to the children. In the confusion of struggling to catch them, one young boy was knocked down, which greatly irritated his father. In the end the child was found to be upset rather than hurt, and the festival continued. Marie, who did not appreciate naive art, declared the rustic participants to be grotesque. The women in the final procession were mostly old and ugly, and the men bearing candles wore tight red tunics which made them look like umbrellas squeezed into a cover. Even the statue of the Madonna she considered gaudy and tasteless.

On the other hand, life with Franz had never been better. She was surprised to see him so happy in the quiet reclusion of this village inn, so far from the bustle of Paris. All he had was a bad piano, a few books, and serious conversations with Marie, but he was working hard on new compositions. In the evenings they sat and contemplated the changing light of the sun setting over the water. Franz was moved by the beauty of the scene and could feel the inner harmony of the world. He was troubled only by the thought that his effort to express it in music was bound to be imperfect. He felt it was probably the sad fate of all serious artists never to be satisfied.

On 4 October 1837 they celebrated Franz's twenty-sixth birthday by taking an excursion up the hillside. After breakfast a local fisherman nicknamed Roscone brought donkeys, which carried them up among the olive groves, past isolated farmhouses like Swiss chalets and barns packed with maize for the winter. In the fields cows were feeding on grass still lush before the snows. On their return they saw the white villages below them, framed in autumnal colors. That night Roscone took them out on the lake in his boat. In a brazier on the bow, he lit a fire of resinous pine to attract fish and speared them with a long harpoon as the boat glided silently over the water. All this beauty and contentment were an inspiration to Liszt, and on the following day he completed twelve preludes which were to be an introduction to the first major collection of his musical works.

One day he asserted that their future relationship would be like the calm of evening after the heat of the day. When the sun beats down too strongly, the flowers give no perfume and the birds do not sing, he explained. Love too can at first be oppressive but then become serene. As

Marie's body swelled, she reflected that they indeed seemed to have reached that stage as their third year of cohabitation began. She recalled the friction created between them in Geneva, when they had needed time to learn to live together and he had brought Puzzi into their home. In her intellectual life too she was entering a new phase and exploring the works of Goethe with new fervor. How superior was the serenity of his worldview compared to the fevered protests of Byron and Sand! There was something pathological in their works, she concluded, turning her back on the Romanticism of her discontented youth. With Marie's delivery time nearing, they moved from Bellagio to Como in November 1837, and one month later their second daughter was born. Because the town had been known as Cosima in ancient times, they decided to give this name to their daughter. In this way they would perpetuate the memory of a happy stay by the beautiful Italian lake.

Their next move was to Milan, in late January 1838, their new baby having been left with a suitably remunerated foster family. Their departure was dictated by the requirements of Liszt's career, as he could not give concerts in lakeside towns, however beautiful. Far from adopting a low profile in Milan, Liszt acquired a magnificent carriage and a handsome black greyhound named Othello, who went everywhere with him. He was now dressing in the height of fashion and no longer looked the part of the bohemian artist. This attention to his image made him more acceptable to high society, but despite the relative tolerance in Italy, Marie needed a certain courage to go out with him because she was known to be in an adulterous relationship, and the risk of female disapproval could not be ruled out.

Marie's first contact in Milan was with Julia Samoilov, who had first become famous as the mistress of Nicholas I of Russia. After tiring of her, the czar had sent her abroad with a large income; she had settled in Milan, where she was spending it with style. Marie learned that she had had a series of lovers almost all of whom were professional singers, particularly tenors. This had given her a certain reputation among the local ladies, who found it more appropriate to take lovers of their own class, but Julia kept open house, which people frequented because they did not want to miss the entertainment. When Marie met her, she saw a dark, vivacious woman with lots of curls. She quickly sensed that she had little in common with this person of mediocre intellect whose eccentric lifestyle was one of the great themes of conversation in the city. All Milan talked about her lovers, her carriages, her parrots, and her monkeys, and in every boutique Marie was shown the perfumes and the fabrics chosen by this unofficial queen of Lombardy. The status of former royal mistress was still high in Europe four decades after the French Revolution.

In her diary Marie now wrote critically about Milan society.[3] The political situation was a crucial factor, she observed, since the whole of northern Italy was under Austrian rule. The consequence was that Italians of the upper class had a life of indolence in that they were not allowed a political role and they considered it unseemly to train for a profession. The traditional career as an officer did not attract the aristocrat because he did not want to serve in an army which was considered foreign. The marquis of Marignano, for example, was a conceited fool and a prize bore, as Marie noted acidly. She met him because his ugly daughter had a disastrous passion for the piano, and Liszt had been well paid to give the lucky girl ten lessons, which produced little result. Marie described the marquis of Trivulzio as the brainless owner of an excellent library containing notes and drawings by Leonardo. The only man she admired in Milan was Count Gustav Neipperg, a genuine intellectual who was translating Byron into Italian and who had real knowledge of music.

The lovers were also disappointed by the much vaunted musical life of Milan and disliked La Scala. Marie had expected a splendid auditorium with rich draperies but found it to be poorly decorated and ill lit. Yet this famous establishment was the center of social life for the elite, who met there every evening, flitting from box to box for superficial conversations which were impeded by the music and the constant arrival and departure of the participants. They had no interest in serious music, which they rejected as German and alien to their culture. Everyone was charming to Liszt after his concerts, the women in particular finding him witty and handsome. Audiences loved his improvisations, even when they were not very good, Marie observed, but even his Fantasies were considered heavy and too serious.

At this time the dominant musical figure in Milan was Rossini, who was now busy setting up concerts for the winter season. Despite his professional success, the maestro was experiencing some social difficulty because he was living with the Parisian singer Olympe Pélissier and was vainly trying to have her accepted by the ladies of Milan. Even Julia Samoilov had failed to respond to his hints, but Rossini hoped that Marie would do something to retrieve the situation. When Marie refused to meet his mistress, out of concern for her own precarious reputation, the composer took a mild form of vengeance by claiming that Thalberg played with more feeling than Liszt. Such is the power of love to distort truth and threaten friendship. Before leaving Milan, Marie resolved to describe its musical life in a frank article which would tell the truth about the city.

After Milan they set off energetically toward Venice but made the mistake of visiting many cultural sites along the way. Marie felt the most enthusiasm for the Campo Santo cemetery in Brescia, but Liszt expressed a more Romantic preference for isolated tombs among flowers. The funeral theme continued in Verona, where the local tourist industry had invented the tomb of Juliet. Both were disappointed by the ancient arena which featured a puppet show. This comedy, played by grotesque little figures on sites where gladiators had once fought, seemed to reflect the decadence of modern Italy. Up to this point Marie and Franz had found that many works of Italian art had not lived up to their expectations and were often badly placed in dim locations. In addition, Marie was intellectually critical of religious paintings which perpetuated naive traditions about miracles.

They arrived in Venice remembering the words of praise spoken by George Sand, in spite of her recent fiasco there with Musset. Marie's first impressions of the jewel of the Adriatic were very different from conventional ones. The old city had a depressing effect on her imagination, and at first the eerie quiet made her ill at ease. She grew to like the silent progress of the gondolas from which they glimpsed the palaces and churches which spoke of past glory. Although the dirty streets and stinking canals seemed lacking in beauty, they conceded that Venice had a gloomy charm. The Fenice Theatre was less imposing than La Scala but more attractive in its tasteful interior, which was decorated with gilt and light green drapery. They were not impressed by a performance of the opera *Parisina d'Este*, by Donizetti, and thought the music so bad as to be funny. Fortunately the main part was sung by the Hungarian soprano Caroline Ungher, who could move an audience with even the most mediocre music. Once again Marie observed that she should accept the fact that nothing is ever perfect in our aesthetic pleasures: a great singer was performing, but the music was poor; the theater was beautiful, but she could smell the latrines all evening. Was she expecting too much from life, as George had told her?

Liszt too had been impressed by Caroline Ungher but thought that audiences in Paris would find her manner exaggerated. Venice had its own musical style, to which he might have to make some concessions. He was nevertheless taken aback when an impresario offered him a short concert which would be followed by a farce, owing to the difficulty of finding adequate musical performers to fill up an entire evening. How was one to explain the noble function of art to savages like this? The impresario returned with a more acceptable proposition, and it was his turn to be concerned when Liszt said his fee would be the considerable sum of five hundred francs. As he had already played in Milan, he could not longer be billed as a complete novelty, though the fact that he had performed there successfully was reassuring. Marie's disappointment with Venice continued when she declared the contents of the bookshops to be suitable reading for chambermaids. When she asked Countess Polastro to lend her some books, this flower of local society replied that she had no books at all.

Liszt shared Marie's opinion about the lack of new culture in Venice but nonetheless enjoyed their sightseeing, during which they saw famous paintings and many ancient buildings. After observing some instruments of torture in the arsenal, they visited the Palace of the Dukes, where Liszt reflected on the centuries of iron rule which had founded a boring nation of unprincipled traders. During their active social life in Venice, Marie came to the conclusion that the ladies there were appallingly dressed but more intelligent than those in Milan, in spite of the lack of books. Educated men seemed rare, however. Liszt was irritated by the banality of conversation and the constant criticism of individuals who were in any way eccentric. Did it matter that George Sand smoked cigars or that Julia Samoilov kept monkeys? One has the impression that he felt a certain affinity with this likable female whose life was like a minor work of art.

As the winter of 1838 gave way to spring, Marie's diary reflected moments of self-criticism. One evening when Liszt turned up late, she became morose. When would she be more like him, she asked herself? Her love and

admiration were as strong as ever, and she believed that Franz was a second Beethoven, possessing the same genius and strength. How could she be
more worthy of his great love? These diary entries may reveal a latent tension in their relationship, in spite of her lover's charm and affection. In early
April, as if to confirm this, Franz appeared with an Austrian newspaper
bearing news of a devastating flood in his native Hungary. He wanted to
help the victims by going to Vienna to give charity concerts, he explained.
It would be a fitting act of gratitude and humanity for the prodigal son to
return to the city which had launched his career.

From Vienna Liszt sent frequent letters full of affection and expressions
There was no doubt about his generosity, but Marie suspected that Liszt
also wanted time on his own. He advised her to compensate for his absence
by accepting the company of Emilio Malazonni, a young Venetian whom
they had befriended and who was only too happy to accompany Marie as
she continued her study of famous paintings. The study of Italian art had in
fact been one of her main reasons for visiting the country.

From Vienna Liszt sent frequent letters full of affection and expressions
of admiration for her noble character, but to her mind he did not seem to
miss her sufficiently. The imperial city was receiving him with open arms,
he reported, and Thalberg himself had gallantly offered the loan of his piano.
Franz was dining with princes and playing duets with Clara Wieck, a female
musician whose compositions he found superior to those of Thalberg. On
18 April he sent Marie an account of his first concert, which was an enormous success and had earned him eighteen curtain calls. He had been deeply
moved, and Marie would have loved the evening, he wrote. Be happy, he
urged her, be happy. This was the only thing he really wanted.[4] In reality
the letter did not fill her with joy, as he was again forgetting his vow to
turn his back on celebrity and devote more time to composition. And why
the repeated injunction to be happy? She saw it as a hint that she should
take Emilio as her lover so that he would feel free to take a younger and
more entertaining mistress. As she knew well, Franz could turn the heads
of women.

More letters arrived, filled with details of his continued success. He
was the height of fashion, and copies of his portrait by Friedrich Amerling
were selling by the score, though Marie knew that such fanfare would not
go to his head. She was his only passion, the love of his life. Yet she might

have seen an unintended reproach in his comment about a possible invitation to perform in the imperial court, which would dramatically advance his career. The event had been postponed because some wag had informed the empress that Liszt was living with a married woman. Franz may have had no ulterior motive in telling Marie about the circumstances, but saying nothing would have been far more diplomatic. About that time Marie fell ill with a serious gastric complaint, but still he remained in Vienna, explaining that he had given his word for another series of concerts. Why did she not join him in Vienna, he asked, where he was earning vast sums of money?

On his return to Venice, after six weeks away, Marie was convinced that he had been unfaithful. On the other hand, his assertions of undying love bore the stamp of truth. She faced a painful situation, as her idealistic love for Franz adapted to a new reality. In notes written years later, she recorded her version of their discussions during the days following his return from Vienna.[5] He had disarmed her with his frankness: it was true that women had thrown themselves at him and that he had succumbed to temptation. No doubt she was angry and might want more space for herself, he conceded. Besides, would this solution not be better for her too? She had lost contact with her family and had become too dependent on him. She had the talent to make a name for herself in journalism and to silence her critics. Vienna had shown him that in two years as a performing artist he could build up enough capital to secure the future of their children. An artist could not hide away like a monk, and in years to come he would devote himself to composition again. Now was the time for the two of them to be reasonable and think of his immediate career.

Marie listened with shock and disbelief. The man who had sworn eternal love was admitting infidelities and seemed to be preparing her for more of the same! In addition conversations with the democratic Franz were now full of the names of monarchs and princes who were trying to outdo one another in their efforts to invite him to their palaces. In a burst of anger Marie called him a Don Juan and a social climber. Liszt took the insult with restraint and cold irony. In the confusion of her emotions, Marie soon regretted her words and agreed to accompany him to Genoa for his next series of concerts.

They took the steamer from Livorno and on their arrival found a letter in which George Sand took pleasure in reporting that the rumors going around Paris, where their activities were still of great interest, hinted that all was not well between the lovers. Marie replied that nothing was farther from the truth, since they were like prisoners of love who were condemned to be together forever. The choice of metaphor was revealing, and before long George would cruelly use it against her. In the meantime Marie painted a rosy picture of their life in a studiously written account of their time in Genoa. The city was a splendid sight from the shore of the Mediterranean, she enthused. They had gone to Chiavari for the fireworks celebrating the festival of the Madonna and had remained on the beach to enjoy the beauty of the summer night. Franz had fallen asleep with his head in her lap while she happily contemplated the stars and the moon. It was true that in Venice she had been seen in the company of Emilio while Franz was away, and there had been rumors about his alleged activities in Vienna, but it was all too ridiculous. They still loved each other, and if this ever ceased to be the case, George would be the first person informed.[6]

Although this carefully written letter was economical with the truth, it was not totally inaccurate to say that she and Franz needed each other. Their stay in Genoa was relatively happy, despite the recriminations which preceded it, and Liszt was able to devote some time to composition. When they returned to Milan, they were drawn together by a minor drama which could have had a tragic outcome. Marie had written an article on La Scala for *La Gazette Musicale* of 27 May 1838, which reflected the opinions of Liszt and appeared under his signature.[7] The article described the opera house as a business which rented rooms to local ladies who conducted their social lives while scarcely troubling to listen to the artists on stage. The people of Milan liked musical mediocrity and were incapable of appreciating the works of serious composers like Beethoven, Schubert, and Weber, she thundered. Rossini had sacrificed his talent by descending to their level and entertaining them with light melodic pieces. They preferred the song of the lark to the cry of the eagle. Their operas were hurriedly put together and badly rehearsed. In fact they were little more than costumed concerts, with little attempt at emotion or dramatic illusion. Milan was musically ignorant and spoiled operas by continual bursts of applause or abuse.

Copies of the article reached Milan, where it was treated as a declara-

tion of war. Soon it was rumored that someone would challenge Liszt to
a duel in order to defend the local honor. On 18 July, the hotheaded composer told Marie there was no way to avoid the confrontation, because he
would certainly not retract the comments published under his name. That
night she could not sleep, imagining Franz being shot to death owing to
her lack of caution. Liszt finally made a declaration in a local newspaper
that he had not intended to insult Milan society. He was, however, tired of
reading anonymous insults in the press and was ready to fight anyone who
cared to contact him for that purpose. In fact Milan was divided into two
factions, Julia Samoilov and Rossini numbering among his prominent supporters. The main defender of the city was reportedly a certain Vitali, who
had been doing much talking in the cafés. Liszt therefore sent two friends
to call on him in the appropriate manner. No details of the meeting have
survived, but the duel was averted. The incident had three consequences: it
contributed to the Liszt legend, it made Vitali famous for fifteen minutes,
and it showed Marie the alarming power of her pen. Musical criticism, they
concluded, was a thankless task. If a critic is not a qualified musician, his
or her comments will be disregarded unless they are favorable. And if the
critic is a musician, the situation is worse. The musician who dares to express reservations about the talents of a colleague is accused of envy and
seen as a public enemy.

After this brush with danger, Franz and Marie retreated to Lake Lugano
for the remainder of the hot season. When they were alone together in this
beautiful setting, their problems seemed to fade away, and Marie took heart.
They read works by Dante, Shakespeare, and Goethe, discussing them with
animation. In Lugano Franz seemed to have forgotten the adulating audiences and the temptations of the city. Marie happily felt a resurgence of her
admiration for this talented and complex man. He was strong yet receptive to her influence; he was at once proud and humble; he was personally
ambitious yet concerned about the poor; he was absorbed in his creative
power yet generous and loving. She gave herself to him with enthusiasm
and when they left Lugano, she was again pregnant.

The following months saw a return to routine, and the lovers were often
apart while he pursued his career. In early October, while in Bologna, Marie
received a letter from Liszt, who was in the duchy of Modena, a small state

ruled by Francesco IV, a despot who had a bad reputation among progressives. Liszt reported that for his part he had received great kindness from
the duke and had performed in the palace for an audience which included
the duchess of Parma and the Austrian emperor. The impact on his reputation would certainly be considerable. With an engaging touch of self-irony,
he admitted that these performances for royalty did not fit easily with his
political convictions. He also sent the news that Othello, their greyhound,
had been frightened by a stagecoach and had not been seen for days. Saddened by the loss, Liszt hoped the animal would somehow find his way back
to Milan.

Marie too was sad, as her lover still seemed to be intoxicated by the
flattery of dukes and princes. He continued to assure her that she was the
most important person in the world, and she continued to hope that they
could resume their semiconjugal life together. From October until December 1838 they chose Florence as a base from which Marie could continue
her study of Italian painters. Liszt was often away, but he sent her frequent
letters full of details of his life. During these months she busied herself with
more articles for *La Gazette Musicale* about suitable events in Italy, which still
appeared under his signature, although they both contributed to them. She
discussed the contents of them with Liszt, whose opinions about musical
matters were invaluable, dealing with questions of composition and style
herself. One day he had the pleasure of telling her that some people in Bologna had complimented him on them. It was true that Marie was becoming
a confident journalist who knew her subject well.

In February 1839 they moved to Rome, Marie then in the sixth month of
her pregnancy. One of their first visits was to the celebrated French painter
Ingres, who was reputed to play the violin as a hobby. At this time he was
the director of the Ecole de Rome, a French college for artists situated
in the Villa Medicis. The diminutive painter received them graciously and
offered to be their guide during a visit to the Vatican Museums. They were
impressed by his eloquence and knowledge of the ancient statues and paintings. That evening they sat under the trees in the garden and continued an
animated discussion about the evolution of art over the centuries. Liszt had
noticed the music for Beethoven's Violin Sonata sitting on an open piano
and insisted that Ingres play it, to his accompaniment. Ingres performed

with such feeling that at the end Franz rose and embraced him with enthusiasm. It confirmed his belief in a hidden affinity between the arts. Marie and Franz decided that from that day Ingres would be their constant friend.

Meanwhile Marie's relationship with George Sand was rapidly disintegrating. Since their departure from Nohant, Marie had sent long letters about their travels and assured George of her continuing affection, but there had been little response. Marie was perplexed, despite being aware of George's capricious nature. However, she was far from imagining the act which had already been perpetrated against her by her friend. Balzac had visited Nohant, and George had given him a detailed and malevolent account of the situation of Marie and Franz. It was perfect for a novel, she explained, but she could not write it herself for alleged reasons of loyalty. Balzac gratefully noted the facts and later used them in *Béatrix,* the story of a disintegrating relationship between an aristocratic woman and a musician. It bore the ironical subtitle *Prisoners of Love,* a treacherous use of the very expression used by Marie in her letter to George.

Although Marie was as yet unaware of this hostile act, she knew of George's latest escapade, which had been to start an affair with Liszt's friend Chopin and move to the island of Palma. Since Cristina de Belgiojoso was currently involved with the pianist Theodor von Döhler, Liszt had wittily congratulated Marie for having made keyboard players fashionable. Marie expressed some irritation with George in a letter to their mutual friend Carlotta Marliani: "The voyage to the Balearic Islands amuses me. I regret that it did not happen a year earlier. When George was being bled I always used to say: *If I were you I would concentrate on loving Chopin.* She would have had less need of the lancet! Also she would not have written the *Letters to Marcia;* in addition she would not have taken Bocage as a lover and that would have been no bad thing, it is said. Is the stay in the Balearic Islands to last long? As I know them both they are bound to detest each other after one month of cohabitation. They are two contrasting natures. No matter, it is great news and you have no idea how pleased I am for them both." [8] It was an imprudent letter, and one day Carlotta could not resist the perverse pleasure of giving it to George. In the meantime Carlotta wrote a tart reply insinuating that Marie was looking for juicy details to tell her friends. This was indeed part of the truth, and Marie had already told Adolphe Pictet of

a tragicomic incident in which George's former lover Mallefille, suspecting
that he had been replaced by Chopin, had made a scene outside Chopin's
room in the middle of the night. Marie, in her reply to Carlotta, expressed
her loyalty to George and her concern that the writer was dissipating her
energy in serial affairs: "When I was staying in her home I did what I could
in order not to know certain details of her life which have nothing to do
with my feelings for her; later I learned things from public opinion: as you
know it is usually well informed about the business of other people; besides, George likes it this way: for me the only serious thing, which I would
tell her if she were here, is the bad effect on her talent."[9] Thanks to the malevolence of Carlotta, there was now cause for the end of the friendship.
Forgetful of her own greater misdeed, George never forgave Marie for her
flippant comments. Marie concluded that George had let her down and that
their passionate but artificial relationship had been influenced by a mutual
attraction to Liszt.

There was, however, consolation in a new and lasting friendship with
Hortense Allart, whose writings she now knew — though she found them
boring. Hortense had settled in Florence, where she was raising her son,
Marcus, after affairs with a series of lovers that included Chateaubriand. She
too was an emancipated woman, and Marie admired her for her life of quiet
fortitude and intellectual activity, despite her poverty.[10] While in Florence
Marie also met the painter Henri Lehmann, who became another lifelong
friend. Like Louis de Ronchaud, the young man fell completely under the
charm of a woman whose face he would immortalize in several affectionate portraits. Marie was now thirty-three and at the height of her beauty,
though the serenity of her face hid a certain anxiety about the future.

In May 1839, during their stay in Rome, she gave birth to Daniel Liszt,
her fifth child and only son. Some months later she reluctantly agreed that
it was sensible for Liszt to absent himself on a long European tour in order
to provide for their children. He encouraged her to return proudly to Paris
and develop her own career. She could have a literary salon, produce a book,
establish herself as a writer under her own name.

On 19 October she boarded a ship at Genoa, having left little Daniel
in the care of a woman in a village near Rome. Lehmann had promised to
visit the child regularly. Blandine and Cosima were with Marie as she sailed

toward Marseille; from there they would make the long journey to Paris by stagecoach.[11] Liszt had accompanied Marie to Livorno and presented her with a bouquet of flowers before the ship sailed. During the stormy crossing, she had at times wished the sea would swallow her up, but, thinking of her children, she recovered and took Blandine in her arms. Six years earlier Liszt had worried her by saying: "You are not the right woman for me, but you are the woman I want." In her dejection, she reflected that he no longer seemed even to want her.

In reality the situation was more complex than she thought, for she soon received numerous letters in which Franz spoke of his love and his impatience to see her. From Genoa she wrote movingly to thank him for their years of happiness: "How can I leave the dear land of Italy without sending you a last farewell? How can I look back without regret on these two years which were so beautiful and so full? Oh! my dear Franz! Let me tell you again with all the intensity of my soul, you have aroused a deep and unalterable feeling in me . . . a feeling of endless gratitude. A thousand blessings to you!"[12] It was a fitting epilogue to two years of exile which marked them both forever, and the beginning of a new and often painful episode in their lives as they began to move apart. They were bound by their children and by emotions which would live for many years before they faded, if they ever did. When Marie arrived in Paris she courageously admitted her own contribution to their troubles: "In the cruel struggle which we have allowed to exist between us I have sometimes, often, been in the wrong; especially in not wanting to accept the difficulty of living with you or in not knowing how to do so; often I expressed my pain in a bitter and revengeful way. Try to understand this with your reason and to excuse it with your love, because after all my suffering has probably been greater than my errors."[13] She had just taught Cosima to say Liszt, which she did with a charming lisp. Marie reported that the little girl already loved music, and she expressed the hope that Cosima would one day be a famous singer or a great piano player like her father.

CHAPTER 10

The Break with Liszt

ARIE'S account of the separation portrays her as a sad figure clutching her child to her bosom as a storm raged around the ship leaving Genoa, but this was an exaggeration. She certainly had days of melancholy and self-doubt as she set about rethinking her life in the autumn of 1839, but in the end she did it with success. Franz had urged her to be strong and to rebuild her life in Paris, renewing contact with the family. She did not know how she would be received by her mother or whether Charles would let her see their daughter, Claire. Her political principles were now republican, and she would no longer be welcomed by most of her former friends in the aristocracy. Her religious faith, once a solace, had been replaced by a vague existential angst. She would be eagerly courted by men but had no inclination for the bohemian life that Liszt seemed to be planning for himself. After four years spent wandering through Switzerland and Italy, the prospect of settling down had a certain charm, whatever the outcome with Franz. Her installation in Paris was made easy by her comfortable financial situation, and she was determined to create a beautiful home which would become a meeting place for artists and intellectuals. She chose an apartment of moderate size in the Saint-Honoré area, a safe distance from her former residence. Although her establishment included a cook, a groom, and a valet in livery, it was modest compared to her former mansion at Croissy.

At once Marie began to shop, sending copious details to Liszt. She purchased velvet, satin, and silk for the upholstery, paintings for the walls, marble statuettes, china from Saxony, silver lamps for the tables, vases from China, and to crown it all a Venetian chandelier for the drawing room. In

her pursuit of perfection she hired a leading interior designer. The final setting, which was completed early in 1840, was impressive—and a defiant
statement to her class that the errant wife was not going to wear sackcloth
and ashes. In an attempt to reduce the satisfaction George Sand and others
would take at the absence of Liszt, she explained, plausibly, that the demands of his career forced him to be away. Indeed the two continued to
correspond in a manner which was mostly cordial and affectionate, although
it lacked the intensity of earlier times. Over the next few years he was to
send her regular reports of his private thoughts and public concerts in letters which bore the postmark of every major city in northern Europe. He
also commented on her arrangements for their children, agreeing that they
should live with his mother under the care of a nanny and be seen daily by
Marie. She disliked this situation, which was a concession to the Flavigny
family. Her mother and brother did not want her to live with her illegitimate children and thought it less provocative to have them under another
roof.

Remarkably, it had been suggested by Charles that she might return
to live with him, but the mere mention of it had drawn a violent reaction
from Franz, who swore that he would fight him in duel: "If your husband
wants to use extreme measures, I will come at once to Paris and we will
finish matters for good. No matter what the consequences. I am absolutely
determined in this, and not even you could stop me. No doubt according
to the law you are his property body and soul, but things do not happen
like this in the real world. When people detest each other they take some
time, they find a compromise, they make some sort of agreement."[1] The
possibility of her husband and her lover facing each other with pistols in the
Bois de Boulogne—a scene she imagined with horror—was the last thing
she wanted. At least Liszt's jealous reaction had shown her that passion was
not quite dead.

Other letters from Franz gave practical advice about relations with her
family and society in general. Like most men, he suggested, her brother
Maurice would like to be consulted; she should therefore ask his opinion
and appear to value it! Even superior individuals like herself must play these
social games, and it was better to do so with lucidity and grace, making
concessions on minor points. Maurice was a kind man who would offer her

support, in spite of his wife, Mathilde. Marie should above all reject the role of victim, Liszt added. Other women were beginning to emancipate themselves openly and to seek personal happiness as she had done. In two years all of Europe would applaud her; she should hold her head up proudly, trust in herself, know her worth. In his opinion a reconciliation with George Sand would be politic, and Marie could achieve it by encouraging her to talk about her love affairs. Women are like that, he explained helpfully. They want to speak freely about intimate matters without the risk of sarcasm or censure.

Marie put one of Liszt's principles into practice by consulting him regularly about the resumption of a social life in Paris and by sending details of conversations with her brother. Maurice had expressed the opinion that she reacted too angrily to criticism and did not want advice. He complained that in all the time since her elopement she had not sent him one letter suitable for his mother or Mathilde, a paragon of virtue who was beginning to write religious books. If Marie wanted to be accepted by her former social circle, she could not live with her children by Liszt. Maurice understood that this would be hard, but it was the price to be paid if she wished to resume her life in Paris. Everyone was aware of the power of passion and would be willing to show tolerance to a reformed woman who did not pose as a rebel. Her school friend Fanny de Montault, for example, had run off with an actor named Georges Guyon but had nonetheless been accepted back into high society. Even before her elopement, Marie's outbursts against convention and her criticism of her own class had caused irritation. In addition, he explained, her life was too eccentric, in that she smoked cigarettes and was always surrounded by men.

Marie called on Fanny and found her to be different from the cheerful girl she had once known. Fanny was delighted to renew acquaintance with another woman who had risked all for love and experienced social rejection. She surprised Marie by her serenity and pride. Although agreeing to play the role of repentant sinner, Fanny had defiantly told her parents she did not regret running away with a lover and only wished she had chosen better. Marie was reminded that she was not alone in her rebellion against an unhappy marriage.

Her efforts to make her new home into a meeting place for artists and intellectuals were beginning to bear fruit. Her status as a countess gave her a social prestige which she amusingly described to Franz as her bird trap, the first notable victim being the writer Charles Sainte-Beuve. She had always admired his novel *Volupté,* and he had the power to open the doors of prestigious periodicals to newcomers—naturally a useful quality in the eyes of Marie. It was known that Sainte-Beuve had a weakness for the wives of geniuses and had managed to seduce Adèle Hugo a few years earlier. Marie seemed an even more desirable conquest, so her new friend began a long and complicated courtship punctuated by flattering letters and erudite poems composed specially for her. Marie gave an amusing account of events in her letters to Liszt but did little to discourage Sainte-Beuve owing to the prestige which he lent her salon. At last he grew tired of the companionship offered, having concluded, with some justification, that in return he was receiving little except fine dinners and requests for advice about manuscripts. After some years of assiduity which culminated in an open declaration of love, he was formally rebuffed. Sainte-Beuve swore that he would never again court a woman who had literary ambitions.[2]

Marie's old friend Alfred de Vigny was an equally prestigious but less demanding member of her salon. They had much in common, since each had broken with the aristocracy. Meeting again after an interval of several years, they must have asked themselves whether they should have married each other in their youth. Although the works of Vigny had not yet acquired the classic status that comes with the passage of time, her admiration for their creator was sincere. The play *Chatterton* in particular was a Romantic manifesto about the position of the artist in society, a theme dear to her. Like Vigny she disliked the philistine bourgeoisie which was becoming dominant in France. In addition there existed a new bond of shared experience between them, for Vigny had recently broken off a passionate and painful relationship with the actress Marie Dorval and was still nursing his wounds. He too had loved an artist and had tried in vain to bring stability and discipline into her life.

The dream of every Parisian hostess was to recruit some charismatic celebrity who would be the idol of her salon, and Marie was no exception. Madame Récamier had done it with Chateaubriand, but Marie had yet to find a new genius to fill the gap left by Franz. It was a role for which Vigny

was not fitted, so she began to look toward Victor Hugo. Having known
success as poet, playwright, and novelist, he was the most celebrated writer
of the time and had a remarkable talent for self-advertisement. One evening in February 1840 she went to the theater with Louis de Ronchaud,
Henri Lehmann, and her new friend the exiled Polish aristocrat Bernard
Potocki and noticed Hugo in the stalls below her box. At once she had eyes
only for the poet, she confided in a letter to Liszt. What a handsome face
and what a divine smile! She recalled how his poetry had penetrated her
soul in times of melancholy and instinctively disbelieved those who called
him vain and egotistical.[3] Marie finally met Hugo in March 1841 at a dinner given by Delphine de Girardin, which was also attended by Lamartine,
Gautier, and Balzac. That night the poet had obligingly read familiar pieces
from the early *Feuilles d'automne,* which Marie knew. Enchanted by the evening, she wrote to Franz that Balzac had been entertaining and that Hugo
was unpretentious and cheerful.

The next step was to invite him to dinner in her own home. For the
occasion she gathered a small constellation of talent which included Ingres,
Balzac, and the scientist André-Marie Ampère. She could hardly contain
her excitement as she described the evening to Liszt. She thought she had
outgrown her youthful cult of genius, but it was an illusion. As she looked at
Hugo, the emotions of the past came flooding back: she recalled reading his
poems with Franz during sad days in Geneva, when she was torn between
her love for him and the thought of her daughter in Paris. No doubt Franz
would laugh at her fanatical admiration. He replied that her enthusiasm was
a fine emotion, but his own admiration for Hugo had moderated with time.
The man was a brilliant artist with words but could not be taken for a serious thinker, he shrewdly remarked.[4] Decidedly Franz had preceded Marie
in the move away from the heady emotions of Romanticism, having also
ceased to believe in the rebel priest Lamennais as the creator of a new religion which would save society. Unfortunately, Marie failed in her attempt
to recruit Hugo to her salon and began to look elsewhere for the celebrity
who would shine beneath her Venetian chandelier.

Her eyes turned toward Lamartine, whom she had also met in the home
of Delphine de Girardin. The poet of love and nature had been elected
to Parliament, where he supported such humane causes as the campaign

against poverty in France and the drive to end slavery in the colonies. Only the creation of a democratic republic could save France from explosive social forces, he believed. Like Marie he was an aristocrat who had moved away from conservative royalism; in this ideological evolution she saw hope for the future of the country. Lamartine responded to her overtures of friendship and soon joined the cohort of those who came regularly to the rue Neuve des Mathurins, where he too was charmed. He became a loyal friend who would not forget her when he briefly achieved political power after the revolution of 1848.

At that same dinner, Marie had also met Delphine's husband, Emile, who would significantly influence her own future career. It was also an encounter Madame de Girardin would come to regret. Girardin was a remarkable man who had discovered the formula which brought the modern newspaper into existence: his ingenious idea was to use the income from publicity to cover production costs in order to sell the paper cheaply and achieve mass circulation. The illegitimate son of a general, he had overcome this handicap and risen to a position of wealth and power through his commercial genius. Delphine herself was a regular contributor to *La Presse,* for which she wrote chatty articles under the name Vicomte de Launay.[5] Girardin was impressed by Marie's intelligence and at once opened his columns to her. Although her previous articles had appeared under Liszt's name, it was known in the small world of journalism that she had made a contribution to them. She now adopted the pen name Daniel Stern under which she would eventually become well known. The first name was probably an allusion to the biblical story of Daniel surviving among the lions, just as she would have to survive in Paris. The last name of her new persona can be seen as a reference to the belief in protective forces (*Stern* is the German word for star). Marie continued to hope that she might have a lucky star to watch over her, as in her happy days in Italy.

Girardin's motive in offering her a role in his newspaper was a mixture of professional judgment and personal attraction. He was soon courting her earnestly, a fact she took care to report in her letters to Liszt. Remarkably, the brilliant businessman who was said to care only for his printing press had joined the company of her adorers. Marie managed the feat of conducting a sort of love affair with him for four years, during which he published

Emile de Girardin, ca. 1836.

(Bibliothèque nationale de France)

nineteen of her articles without receiving any tangible reward. Girardin did not do things halfway, and on 9 January 1841 he gave her a whole page for her first article, which was an unsigned review of George Sand's novel *Le compagnon du tour de France*. The work was a feeble expression of egalitarian theory dressed up as fiction, and Marie had the pleasure of indicating the shortcomings of a writer in rapid decline.

Vengeance was sweet, but her first article as Daniel Stern also showed an intellectual honesty which would be her hallmark. She followed it with a series on contemporary painting which began on 12 December 1841, with a polite dissection of Paul Delaroche, a specialist in historical paintings who had just completed the large murals which still adorn the Ecole des Beaux-Arts in Paris. The article was sufficiently severe to arouse controversy, which was just what Girardin wanted from his journalists. The soundness of Marie's comments was acknowledged by many, and readers of *La Presse* began to speculate about the identity of Daniel Stern. Marie's career was launched. Her study of art in Italy had given her a broad perspective which enabled her to become one of the more competent Parisian critics. Her main characteristics were her readiness to express a clear opinion and her dislike of mediocrity.

If Marie's first article was an act of vengeance against Sand, she had ample justification. In reality it was a mild retort after the shameful behavior of Sand. For some time she had been wanting to use the story of Marie and Liszt in a novel. This tale of two exceptional individuals in an interesting social and emotional drama clearly had great potential. If their love affair had been cloudless, as they claimed, the story would have had little interest; instead it was a gift for a novelist precisely because tension was beginning to show. George could not use the material herself without openly showing her disloyalty, so she did the next best thing and passed it on to Balzac.

The publication of the novel *Béatrix* took place in 1839, a critical year for Marie in that she was returning to Paris to create a new existence for herself and her children. Sand had evidently given a number of intimate details of her character, appearance, and situation, all of which were cruelly transposed into the novel. The fictional Béatrix is a headstrong lady who abandons her husband and child for a foreign musician she has stolen from

Honoré de Balzac, ca. 1840.

(Photothèque des Musées de la Ville de Paris)

her best friend, a female writer who signs her works Camille Maupin. She is a member of the royal court but has broken with her class and lives openly with her lover. Béatrix is a blonde beauty, but she is thin and her bosom is small. She enters marriage in a state of sexual ignorance and lives unhappily with her husband. At first she seeks compensation in intellectual activity, developing the ability to talk intelligently about literature, music, and art. She is tormented by the ambition to have a salon and become famous. When she falls in love with the singer Conti, she becomes impatient to see him regularly, and one day suddenly orders him to elope with her to Italy. When the action of the novel begins, she is about to be abandoned by her worthless lover and is proudly hiding her wounds.

The portrait of Liszt is even more venomous, since Conti spouts heady nonsense about art being divinely inspired but does not believe a word of it. He has a remarkably fine voice, but his need for applause is insatiable. He charms women with flattery and is attracted to Béatrix mostly because of her social status. When the lovers go to Italy, the heroine sends details of their happiness, but in reality Conti has grown tired of her demands and is being unfaithful. In her letters Béatrix makes false protestations of friendship to Camille, a figure who is a personification of sincerity, intelligence, and generosity, in other words a crudely idealized version of George Sand. The annals of friendship can contain few comparable examples of treachery and self-admiration. Certain details of Marie's appearance and life are so accurate that George must have given them to Balzac in written form. There was sufficient truth in the portrait to make it recognizable, and enough distortion to show real malice.

For Marie and Franz the best policy was silence, as they could not admit that they recognized themselves. The situation was worse for Marie because she was in Paris. It is remarkable that she apparently forgave Balzac for his part in the plot, but her major concern was probably the uncertain state of her relationship with Liszt. As often happens, separation had caused them to miss each other and to recall the good times rather than the bad. He had written affectionate letters from the day he stood waving on the quayside in Genoa. During a storm in December 1839 he had written from Vienna that he was ill. At once she imagined him dead and superstitiously recalled that she had sent him a gold tiepin with the figure of an owl, the bird of graveyards. For days she sat at her fire and held her head in anguish until better news came, but when she revealed that she was being courted by the diplomat Bulwer Lytton she was shocked when Liszt replied by airily giving her permission to be unfaithful. Marie retorted that his attitude was incomprehensible: "I do not want to reproach you, yet I must tell you that you have been imprudent with me. You have not really understood my nature, or you have wanted to distort it and make it like yours. You have done your best to liberate me from notions of duty in love which I needed, which were an ideal which you treated roughly." [6] She did not fail to inform him of the growing number of men who were in love with her, the latest recruit being Bernard Potocki.

Liszt replied from Vienna that he had her portrait by Lehmann in front of him and was contemplating it with sadness and love. He still had faith, he assured her, but disappointingly added that he was capable of loving her like a brother. Marie had no such intention, and after five months of separation her longing to see him was greater than ever. In late February 1840 she wrote to say that no man had been loved as she had loved him. She was certain that when she next saw his powerful hands strike the keys, she would want to run away again and forget the world.

It is strange that an intelligent person could indulge in such illusions, but such is the nature of love. It was difficult for her to admit to herself that they had parted because of a growing incompatibility of character. Franz had been aware of this sad necessity before it had become clear to Marie. Although she was courageously moving ahead, there were days when her autonomy felt oppressive. Her separation from him was a second emancipation, this one more prolonged and painful than the break with her husband. One day she forgot her pride and wrote Franz a letter asking for help: "Think of me; reflect for me. Save me from myself. Make me work like a convict. Create duties for me; enslave me to something. I find freedom hard to bear." [7] She was not devoting herself fully to the role of companion or to maternal duty, and she needed some greater task to restore purpose to her life. All joy and suffering still came from him, she explained.

Other letters between them contained words of advice about their position in society. It was rumored in Paris that success had gone to Liszt's head, she revealed, and he should act to put an end to it. At times Marie expressed irritation because his letters were full of talk about his career and rarely asked about her health or well-being: "What opinion am I to have of myself, when I am full of anxiety thinking of your consumption of coffee and cigars, when I cannot imagine you in the arms of another woman without going out of my mind, when even today I would give up my place in heaven for six happy months with you? You are trying too hard to be superior, you are too much of a philosopher. You are so strong that you do not make allowance for the weakness of others."[8] No sooner had these complaints flowed from her than she asked his forgiveness, saying that all would be well when he returned.

This was another illusion, as they were beginning to fall out even in their correspondence. She knew his pride, and still she sent critical letters, which were not without justification but which she knew would irritate him further. Liszt had spent April 1840 in Paris, and it had not been a happy time. When he left for concerts in London, she broached the subject of his fidelity in a letter, revealing her irritation at the sympathy shown by his friends. Not that she had any pride, she protested. She loved him still, but feared that he would no longer tolerate the truth or listen to advice. He replied in a moderate manner, and she clung to the hope that their present difficulties were just a phase. For the moment it seemed that they could live neither with nor without each other. From London he sent warm letters, in spite of his busy life, for he was being adulated by high society. He had given a private performance for Prince Albert and young Queen Victoria, who had laughed heartily when he made a self-deprecating quip. He was paid a large sum, but life was charmless without Marie. She should spend a month in London, after which they would take a steamer all the way up the Rhine to Baden for his next concert. She was anxious because of their arguments, he conceded, but one must not be fearful of life.

Like the moth to the candle, Marie set off for England. She took the coach to Le Havre, boarding a steamer that arrived in London twenty-nine hours later. The episode was a disaster. At nine in the evening on 3 June 1840, she disembarked hopefully and found that Liszt had sent his servant, Ferco, to meet her because he was performing. When they were together after the concert, she soon forgot her good intentions and accused him of having sunk to a life of celebrity, sex, and money and of turning his back on the only woman who loved him. After this quarrel, she withdrew to her hotel in Richmond, where she received a note saying he was deeply hurt by her words. He did not know if he could talk to her again, but he would not despair.

She returned to Paris, and communication began again in a long series of letters which vividly record the emotional fluctuations of their relationship over the next four years. In intellectual and practical matters, their collaboration continued with calm. During Liszt's almost perpetual absence, Marie loyally played the role of press agent and general adviser. When he needed books or musical scores, she sent them to the distant cities where he was preparing for his next concert. In the autumn of 1840 he entrusted her with the final composition of a letter to be published in the important *Revue des Deux Mondes,* which had declared that performers like Liszt were paid too much, whereas composers were left to starve. From Hamburg he sent an outline of his response to this personal attack, arguing that composers such as Rossini, Donizetti, and Mendelssohn were making a good living. The opposite was true of most performers, however, even though great skill was needed to reveal the qualities hidden in the music of Mozart, Beethoven, and Weber. Please use your diplomatic and stylistic skill to turn my text into one of your finely expressed pieces, he requested.

Franz was attentively reading her first publications in *La Presse* and sent useful advice. From Glascow he wrote to praise her article on George Sand. Do not admit that you are the author, he urged her; wait until you have produced a number of articles and become established as a critic. When *Hervé,* her first story, appeared, he told her frankly it had received more applause than it deserved. She should not let it go to her head, as a first publication is often overvalued in the press. She should always aim at quality, not quantity. That was the way to show her former friends in the aristocracy that she had achieved something. The fact that she was a countess made her a novelty in the world of journalism, he observed wisely, and she should make full use of it.

She reciprocated by giving him sound advice about his career, urging him not to accept a position as professor of music in Brussels. She understood his wish to have some stability, but the post would not suit him. Why put your feet on a ladder when you have wings, she asked? When he wrote enthusiastically that he had been given the Order of the Falcon by the duke of Weimar, her response was so cool that he altered his tone, avowing that he would rather have composed one of Beethoven's symphonies than receive the highest order on earth. In her repeated pleas that he not let his head be turned by royal favors and decorations, Marie was still the voice of conscience. When she spoke to him of artistic discipline, she was still his Muse. In February 1842 he showed that he was ready to reciprocate by giving her active support. On 7 January *La Presse* had published an article by Marie on one of Ingres's paintings, and the newspaper *L'Artiste* had seen fit to make an ironical allusion to her elopement and love affair. Liszt wrote from Berlin that she should let it be known that if any other editor made a similar comment, he would take the first coach to Paris and would challenge the culprit to a duel. The smiles will soon disappear from the faces of Parisian journalists, he predicted.

Their collaboration continued as a new affair developed involving George Sand. Not content with having betrayed her friend's intimate life to Balzac, she had produced *Horace*, a novel containing another malicious portrait of Marie, in the character of the viscountess de Chailly.[9] The fictional Madame de Chailly has a liaison with Horace, an ambitious but untalented writer who wants to penetrate high society. He is selfish, conceited, and incapable of serious work. His aristocratic mistress has a salon, but she lacks spontaneity in conversation and prepares her contribution in advance. She is excessively thin and physically unattractive but makes up for this by her skill as a coquette. When she realizes that Horace is untalented and insincere, she puts an end to their relationship. She maintains appearances after her failure in love, but the true story of her life is one of sexual and emotional frustration.

Horace was a vicious and unwarranted attack by George Sand—indeed it was much worse than *Béatrix*. Marie was taken aback by the cruelty of a former friend who seemed to want to cover her with ridicule at a time when she was vulnerable and reconstructing her life after a traumatic experience. Although the author had deliberately distorted reality in the novel, many readers would penetrate the transparent allusions to Marie and Franz. Sand was publicly mocking their passion, courage, and idealism by portraying them as insincere mediocrities.

Marie consulted Liszt, who wrote from Leipzig agreeing that Sand's intention was malicious. He begged her not to pay serious attention to this latest attack. The more offense she took, the more pleasure for George, he explained. Ronchaud and Girardin had discussed possible forms of vengeance, but Franz urged her to resist temptation. Marie replied that she was not deeply troubled by the situation. There was only one form of vengeance she wanted, and she had already had it, since George had wanted to be loved by Franz and had failed. In the end the episode brought credit to Marie for her patience and dignity and left a serious stain on the record of George Sand.

About the same time Marie and Franz cooperated on two articles devoted to the radical German poet Georg Herwegh, whose work she wanted to introduce to French readers.[10] She was well qualified to do so given her command of German and her knowledge of the national literature. In a letter sent from Nuremberg on 10 October 1843, Franz had expressed some forthright and original thoughts on the poetry of Herwegh, some of which he had set to music. He considered the young man's experience of life and history to be limited. One poem was a trite account of a young man torn between the love of a woman and the love of liberty. This naive cult of liberty had been made unthinkable by the excesses of the French Revolution, said Franz. No society can exist without a balance between freedom and authority, and Herwegh's call for revolutionary violence was unintelligent and dangerous. He urged Marie to end her article with an homage to the political moderation of Lamartine. The defects of Herwegh's theme needed to be highlighted just as much as the good qualities, he asserted. The young writer was posturing and would probably turn into a conservative before long. Liszt's prediction was not inaccurate, since Herwegh soon acquired a liking for the intellectual salons of Paris and duly became a harmless representative of radical chic.

As months went by, Marie continued to receive detailed but censored accounts of Liszt's travels and triumphs. At times she saw with relief that in spite of the difficulties of his life he was continuing to compose new music, some of the most charming pieces being dedicated to her. Only a man of great strength and character could succeed in this way, she told herself. In January 1841 he was on a tour of Ireland and wrote to tell her of the hardships of his work. After a concert in Limerick he had had to join his five companions in their coach and travel all night and much of the next day until they reached Dublin, where they were to perform the same evening. As if that was not enough, they went on to Scotland and shuttled between Glasgow and Edinburgh five times in a week. When sailing from London to Ostend in February they arrived to find so much ice in the harbor that the ship had to return to sea and wait for fifteen hours before it could dock.

Marie read his letters with alternating sympathy and irritation. At times she felt the burden of his vagabond life as heavily as if she were bearing it herself. She asked herself if it was partly her fault that he was trapped in this existence which seemed to lead nowhere. In a letter written to Franz on 12 June 1841 she looked back on their years together and had a superstitious thought about the power of destiny. From 1833 until 1839 everything had brought them closer together, she reflected, but since that date everything had seemed to increase the distance between them. Her summary of the early years shows some idealization of the past, but her perception of their recent years was only too true.

Although their surviving letters do not often speak of the children, which were not their main preoccupation, they did have affection for them. Marie in particular was proud of her good-looking daughters. In early 1843 Daniel was three, Cosima six, and Blandine eight. One day in Berlin Liszt received from Blandine a polite letter which he assumed had been dictated by Mademoiselle Delarue, her nanny. Take her to your home and let her write the next one herself, he said to Marie. I love this child and want her to be natural when she writes to me. Even if she says silly things, it will not matter. He explained that he would be pleased if Blandine became a good pianist but felt there was no point in making children behave in a stiff and erudite way. In this homage to spontaneity lies one of the keys to the character of Franz Liszt.[11]

This exchange of letters about intellectual or practical matters was the peaceful part of their relationship, but ever since their quarrel in London in June 1840 their emotional life had taken on a chronic turbulence, which was to last for some years. Not many weeks had elapsed before Liszt wrote persuasively that he still loved her and expressed the opinion that their troubles reflected the intensity of their passion and the superiority of their

aspiration. They had quarreled more than once, but they had never lied
to each other, he noted. He was still in England, longing for the moment
when he could briefly join her in the country near Fontainebleau, where
she was spending the summer with the children. One day, he assured her,
they would return to Italy and recapture the magic of the past. Then the
discordant notes would be transformed into a sublime harmony. For him,
the beating of her heart was the mysterious rhythm of eternal love.

It was difficult to resist Franz Liszt, and Marie did not try very hard.
Again she abandoned herself deliciously to hope and replied that all anxiety
was behind her, as he had again given her happiness. In November she wrote
to thank him for sending her a letter from the pianist Camille Pleyel, whose
overtures he was politely rejecting: "Your act of trust gives me extreme
pleasure and disarms my jealousy. I believe truly and sincerely that you
have been doing the wrong thing up to now, and with this new method
of complete and instant frankness you will make me patient, understanding, indulgent, possibly even to excess, and above all happy." [12] Her serenity
at this time also reflected the fact that she had actually discussed with her
brother the possibility of marrying Franz, if only Charles would have the
good grace to die. At last things seemed to be progressing, and she reflected
that Franz and she should become more aware of their faults. We cannot
change our characters, she asserted, but it is helpful to understand our individual natures.

Liszt felt that Marie's shortcoming was the need to dominate, and told
her so with cheerful frankness in a letter from Liverpool. It was true that she
was using Bulwer Lytton as a sort of secretary and English teacher, that Lehmann and Ronchaud were ordered around like faithful retainers, and that
even the powerful Girardin did her bidding. [13] To demonstrate his own wish
to abstain from controlling her life, Franz advised her to do what she liked
with the press baron, provided she did not cease to love him. He wanted
her to feel free, both of himself and of others. He hoped she would remain
open and sincere with him, whatever she decided.

Soon after the letter was on its way, he regretted his magnanimity and
two days later sent a jealous missive from Rochdale. It was clear that in spite
of his sexual adventures Liszt was still vulnerable where Marie was concerned. It may make no difference to her decision, he told her, but he was

concerned about the outcome of any intimate relationship with Girardin, a ruthless man who had killed an opponent in a duel and who had the potential of becoming a dangerous enemy. Liszt denied feeling jealous, again declaring that he had no right to rule her life, but explained that the thought of her in the hands of Girardin filled him with anxiety. Marie replied delightedly that she had promised nothing and would never see the man again if Franz so wished. She was in control of the situation and in fact had sent Girardin away that very day in order to reply to her lover. In addition he was not the hard, calculating individual described by others, but respectful and affectionate. In any case, Franz was the man around whom her life revolved.

From Dublin Franz riposted with another outbreak of jealousy. He had guessed that Girardin had publicly accompanied her to the Champs-Elysées to witness the return of Napoleon's body from Saint Helena, and he was displeased. It was inevitable that Girardin and her other adorers should appear to be more tender than himself, he conceded. After all, he was in a state of agitation and irritated by her implicit criticism. Marie quickly wrote to reassure her lover that it was precisely his strong and energetic nature which she preferred. Come back to Paris, she urged him, and we shall be happy. I will not try to direct your life, I shall not argue with you, I shall just love you.

Marie knew that her best policy was to avoid being reproachful, suspicious, or demanding, but this approach was not easy to put it into practice. While they communicated by letter, which was their main form of contact eleven months of the year, there was less cause for friction. Franz was usually a charming correspondent, and on 2 January 1841 he wrote from Dublin saying that he had celebrated her birthday by playing her favorite pieces by Weber, Meyerbeer, and Chopin. The music brought back a flood of memories of their time together. One day it would be like that again, and what a fine life they would have! At other times, Marie and Franz exchanged somewhat critical letters in which they sought a better understanding of their similarities and differences. In one missive Franz expressed the opinion that she did not fully share his sense of the sublime. She replied with good humor that this might be true, but that he did not have her concern for the sensitivities of others. You are sublime and rough like a piece of Alpine granite, she added. In another letter he speculated that she may have expected him to have the feelings of a woman, whereas he had been similarly disappointed because she did not react like a man. He expressed admiration for her character and from Ireland sent proof of his affection by having two elegant poplin dresses made for her. Marie was touched and replied with gratitude: "You think I have charm and grace? Say it to me, say it often; keep on repeating it. Your praise is the perfume of my life. It does not make me more vain, but more joyful in my humility. It does not prove my merit but your love. Oh! Spoil me, flatter me, praise me. What is there in my heart and in my mind that is not yours?"[14] She concluded that they were coming closer together after their problems of recent years and that Franz had learned how to make her happy in their new situation.

It was a theory founded on hope rather than reality. As the winter of 1841 advanced, she looked for an apartment which Liszt would use during a projected visit to Paris and wrote to him in Newcastle saying she already imagined his handsome face in her home and the table piled with music beside his unfinished cup of coffee and half-smoked cigar. This letter seems to contain an allusion to past episodes of sexual impatience and confirms that her attraction to Franz was still far from platonic. As his return neared she wrote to him in Brussels, thanking him for some reassuring words about fidelity:

> Franz, Franz! We have the same ideal; I have always understood that for us there is no possibility of peace, virtue and happiness except in solitude. Will God give it to us? Today it would take almost a miracle because the day of our farewell in Florence we chose to raise mountains between us.
>
> What you tell me about my concerns touches me deeply. I felt much pain. In spite of myself I have remained a woman and in spite of everything I love you, not as a sister but as a passionate and a jealous woman. Stop complaining about it.[15]

In her eagerness to be with him she did her best to repress her fears and doubts and looked forward to the news of his coming.

Liszt returned to Paris in April 1841 and gave several concerts, one of them with Berlioz. He stayed until early May, when his infernal round of

tours began once more. It had been a happy time for Marie, and she accompanied him for the first part of his journey north toward Boulogne and
London. When they parted, he was more pale than usual, and her spirits
were low. With her in the coach were Ronchaud and Liszt's new friend Felix
Lichnowsky, a rich Polish aristocrat. As they reached the outskirts of the
city, they decided to lunch in the garden of a simple restaurant used by the
workers of Paris. During the meal Lichnowsky did his best to cheer them
up by teasing Ronchaud. Fearing that he had gone too far, he then asked
Marie's young friend to forgive him and offered his eternal friendship with
such charm that Ronchaud was moved to tears. Next day Marie wrote happily to Franz to report on events: "Today I have regained full confidence in
your star. We shall soon meet again. And then always. I cannot tell you the
good done me by your stay in Paris! You have been so entirely, so greatly,
so nobly *mine*. I felt that for a second time you were making me the gift of
your soul, your life, your love!" [16] There was reason for her jubilation, for
Franz too had been much affected by their weeks together. From London
he reported that he was working furiously on Fantasies, including *Norma,*
La Somnambula, Moses, and *Don Juan,* and would soon turn to the serious
compositions which would make him more worthy of her.

Liszt's letters from London were music to Marie's ears. Unlike his previous stays in the city, this one was disappointing. It was already May, high
society was leaving for the country, there were no more balls, and income
from concerts was poor. He told her he was longing to return and obsessed
by the thought of staying in her bedroom and having her all to himself. She
replied that he should return incognito so that they could hide in Paris or
in some country retreat if he felt poetically inclined. She happily informed
him that everyone was talking about his being the lover of the singer Sophie
Loewe, but she did not believe a word of it. Franz replied casually that he
often saw Sophie in London, describing her as a decent person with good
manners.[17] The idea of his traveling to Paris secretly was excellent, and he
would soon be on his way: "It will be very easy for me to come incognito. At
last we will have an ideal love-nest! Just try not to have your period! Leave
the rest to me. To spend all my days, all my nights with you alone, to see
you, adore you and lose myself in you and transform myself in you, what a
dream, what happiness! Am I worthy of it?" [18] Having received another let-

ter asking about his relations with Sophie Loewe, he replied that he was not her lover, and never would be. He admired her as a person of distinction who chose her friends carefully. They saw each other frequently, but there had been no loving words, no affectionate looks, no meaningful silences.

Marie did her best to believe his assurances of fidelity and his promises that they would live together when he had achieved sufficient money and reputation. Since he would be traveling into Germany later in the summer, he proposed a meeting on the island of Nonnenwerth, in the Rhine. First he would have to perform in Copenhagen and Hamburg, but at least their reunion was agreed upon, and Marie could look forward to it with the usual hope tinged with apprehension. She was continuing to busy herself with intellectual interests and had completed a long botanical walk in the country. The excursion had been a remarkable effort for a society lady who rarely walked any distance. It had lasted all of seven hours, with some short stops for a rest on the grass, and she had scarcely been tired, whereas Blandine's nanny had been in a state of exhaustion. Decidedly, I am a passionate woman, she told Franz.

She would have preferred to have their reunion somewhere other than Nonnenwerth, a well-known resort where she might be recognized, and she did not want to give people the impression that she was running after Franz. In August 1841 she took the ship from Le Havre to Rotterdam, where she changed to another steamer which took her up the river to Mainz. There she was met by Franz, and they completed the journey in a smaller boat. The hotel in which they stayed on the island of Nonnenwerth was a converted convent. Marie signed the book using a false name and occupied the former apartment of the Mother Superior at the end of a long corridor. The island was small and quiet, with clumps of larch and poplars and a view of mountains across the river. Every day they watched steamers puffing past their peaceful haven.

The arrival of a mysterious lady under a fictional name naturally caused much interest among the residents. A German girl secretly recorded details of the event in her diary, convinced that the newcomer was George Sand.[19] The young resident admired Marie's fine silk dresses and her striking face and noted that she often wore a long shawl around her neck and her magnificent hair in a net. One evening Marie made a dramatic entrance elegantly dressed in a nun's habit, an ebony cross around her neck. Her movements were graceful and her conversation full of charm and wit, the girl observed. For part of their stay the lovers were joined by Lichnowsky, Girardin, and the politician Thiers. One evening after dinner the friends placed a symbolic crown on the head of Liszt. As a sign of gratitude the virtuoso went to the piano and played a series of waltzes and gallops, a lively step which was all the rage that year. The guests rose and danced with enthusiasm. When the party was over, one lady commented on Liszt's melancholy air, a remark which Marie overheard. She replied with a sigh that no earthly happiness is complete.

They had not been together in Nonnenwerth for many days before discord broke out. She had broached the subject of his infidelities, which were becoming an insurmountable obstacle between them. She reproached him not only for his affairs in themselves but also for his lack of discretion. Sexual appetite was one thing, but the role of Don Juan had apparently become part of his public image, the persona which went with his piano playing. Although he described his mistresses as affectionate female friends, Marie decided to present a written ultimatum before they went their separate ways:

> My Dear Franz,
>
> I feel I am going mad and can stand it no longer. I am not able to live in this perpetual agitation. You cannot understand this; so let us put an end to our sad and dismal arguments and let me withdraw because of all these affectionate females who spring up around you. For you I will be a better friend than a lover. I know that I have no reason to reproach you, but I also know . . . I know only that it is painful for me and that I will always make it painful for you if I stay. Therefore, farewell.
>
> We will both use the pretext of a sick child. Public opinion will be satisfied.
>
> Farewell Franz, this is not a final break, but a postponement. In five or six years we will laugh at my sufferings today.
>
> Farewell.[20]

It was a moderate and intelligent proposal, with a word of hope in the conclusion. Franz wrote back saying they were happy in spite of everything and it was their destiny to love each other always.

After the stay in Nonnenwerth, their life continued as before, Marie living in Paris and Franz giving concerts all over Europe. They had occasional meetings, some of them at Nonnenwerth, and Liszt sent letters from all parts recounting his travels and his triumphs. He had been received like royalty at the immense estate of Felix Lichnowsky in Russia, where there had been a whirl of hunting, hot-air ballooning, fireworks, gala dinners, balls, and concerts. The tone of his letters was still loving and enthusiastic, whereas Marie's was more circumspect. Her state of personal and ideological distress was indicated in a letter of 9 May 1842 in which she spoke of making her peace with the Catholic Church. Although she had firmly rejected it as being repressive to women and intellectually weak, she asked herself whether she had any longer the strength to create her own philosophy. She was considering the possibility of repressing her doubts and simply accepting the comfort of established religion. She wanted to discuss the situation with Franz and would go to Nonnenwerth in July that summer.

When the estranged lovers met they again attempted to cement their crumbling relationship. Although Franz was hurt by new reproaches from Marie during their conversations, he showed his usual resilience in subsequent letters and again expressed the hope that fine harmonies might one day grow from their discordant notes. He was on his way to perform before the royal family of Würtemberg, and his mind was full of professional matters, he explained. He nevertheless found time for a new conquest in the person of Charlotte Hagn, a German actress of charm and elegance who played society ladies. Word of the affair unfortunately reached Paris, either through officious friends or through the press, and Marie wrote to him accusingly. In his reply Liszt did not deny the fact that he had a new woman and simply commented on the harm done by gossip. He was writing from Utrecht on a dismal day in the depth of winter and recalled the happy summer days when they used to wake up in Como. The memory of her was the only ray of light in his life, he protested. If they had continued to live together, however, it would have smothered him without profit for her. He sadly admitted that his present life was full of dissipation: "I do not hide the truth from myself. For three years my life has just been a series of feverish excitements which I have often sought and which end in disgust and remorse. I have a compulsion to expend and keep on expending life, strength, money and time without pleasure in the present, and without hope in the future." [21] He was like an addicted gambler, he said. He was like a man walking through the fields picking flowers and fruit and casting them to the winds.

Shortly after this bout of self-criticism, Liszt wrote from Breslau saying he was tempted to undertake a tour of his native Hungary and would like Marie to accompany him, after which they might achieve an old ambition to travel to Constantinople. He added, however, that he might instead go to Russia and would simply decide on the spur of the moment. This new demonstration of the lack of planning in his life drew an angry response from Marie:

> You tell me you act on impulse. That does not surprise me a lot. It seems that this had always suited you, and I do not expect you to do what I wish, but why say it to me? And you do so in the same letter in which you ask me to join you. I will make no reply about Hungary. We will chat about it, as you say, in June, and as I will not have changed nor you either, as you will act on impulse and I will never understand why your impulse never makes allowance for my most reasonable and legitimate wishes, you will break my heart again without great profit for anyone, but it seems to be your destiny and until the end I will enable you to practice your destructive power. That is not easy to understand. I admit that I have always found love and kindness to be better than impulse, but I know nothing about life.
>
> Why did you not let me die? [22]

Liszt responded with more declarations of love and a gold bracelet studded with turquoise. He had just been escorted from Berlin by five hundred students on horseback after his concerts, which had been received with rapture. He agreed to stop seeing Charlotte Hagn, because Marie had protested that she, Marie, was willing to be his mistress, but not one of his mistresses. Swallowing her pride, she replied that she had never loved him more. The sun was going down, she explained, and she wanted to feel its heat while there was still time.

Liszt's problem was that he still had an insatiable hunger for women, especially performing artists like Camille Pleyel or the singer Caroline Ungher. When performing in Munich in October 1843, he also succumbed to the sultry charm of the notorious Irish adventuress known as Lola Montez. This affair between the king of the musical world and the mistress who was busily ruining King Ludwig I of Bavaria was the stuff of dreams for journalists.[23] It was therefore not long before the news reached Marie; in January 1844 she wrote a sad letter asking Franz whether he ever thought of death. He replied that her question gave him a shiver and reminded him of the spooky day when crows had come to peck at his dying father's window.

Her letter had evidently touched a raw nerve. It also contained another plea for discipline in the life of a man who she believed should be remembered for greater things than applause and scandal. She explained with growing irritation that he was aggravating her life because their names were always associated. Her daughter Claire d'Agoult was now fourteen, and finding a husband for her would not be easy if Marie had a reputation and Liszt's behavior created bad publicity: "You have never had a plan, or if you had one you failed completely to put it into practice. What you should do therefore is avoid attention, by being sensible and prudent and showing taste. But I find it hard to hope for this now, as you have grown older without achieving maturity, and all I have gained from trying to reason with you affectionately is that you became angry, then you hid your life from me and abandoned your last virtue with me, which was sincerity." [24] She had heard too much about his dissolute ways and had no faith in him save for his musical genius. Her one request was that he avoid the sort of scandal which would rebound on her. To make matters worse, Puzzi had stolen some of her letters to Franz and was threatening to publish them; she therefore entreated Franz to do his utmost to retrieve them. She would now rely on herself alone, she told him, and would finally shake off the hopes which had followed her for so long like beggars in the street.

Liszt went to Paris in April 1844, and Marie at last found the strength to make the break. In her emotional state she could not yet accept the paradox that his current dissipation and extravagance were a part of his superior nature. Since the beginning of his travels in 1839, he seemed to have become addicted to the stimulus of new places, new faces, new women. Beneath the surface of this chaotic life he experienced the essential solitude of an artist driven by his creative instinct. Compared to the power within him, all else was peripheral: ambition, friendship, even his love for Marie. Inspiration was an intermittent force which came in irresistible surges and gave him only partial satisfaction. Moments of creativity were not enough, because he sought perfection. For a time Marie had brought order and stability into his life, but she could no longer do so. His present existence might be a phase, but there was no sign of its ending. They had been driven apart by friction and hurt pride. When they met, there were more harsh words. For some years they would have little contact except for bitter arguments about the children, and she would react fiercely when he threatened to take them from her. It was the sad finale of one of the great love stories of the time.

Franz, though also deeply shaken, resumed his career after a period of shock and pain. Too honest to deny that he was at fault, he nonetheless felt unable to save himself from his destructive tendency. Marie had already laid the foundations of a new social life and had shown that she had the strength to make her own way forward. Even so, she used Herwegh as her intermediary for a last attempt at a reconciliation.

Balzac had recently published the novel *Honorine,* which seemed only too relevant to her own situation in that it is the story of a wife who leaves an affectionate husband for a man who later abandons her. It carries the bleak message that love rarely brings lasting happiness because there is usually one partner who rules and one who submits.[25] This was true of Marie's relations with the many men who did her bidding, but the dismal theory does not reflect the complexity of her relations with the one who mattered most. She had no doubt played a dominant role in their early days, but their situation had changed dramatically! Despite her disappointment and occasional anger, she would never cease to love the genius to whom she had given so much. She would one day look back with serenity, but in this dark moment it seemed that she had failed both in marriage and in love. Marie reflected on the events of recent years and concluded that she should have broken sooner, but that to do so she would have needed more wisdom and more strength.

CHAPTER 11

The Career of Writer

ARIE remembered the myth of Ariadne, who falls in love with Theseus when he is unarmed and facing the labyrinth. They elope and sail toward Athens, but when they stop on the island of Naxos, she falls asleep and he abandons her. Theseus goes on to other adventures and other women, leaving her to lament her fate, but all ends well when she marries the god Bacchus. Marie reflected that this ancient story of love and separation was like an account of her own life, except for the happy ending.

In spite of this she was soon seeking consolation in the company of Georg Herwegh, who had quickly been charmed by Marie. No doubt the young writer lacked the charisma of Liszt, but he did possess qualities which amply explain her interest. For a start he was an idealistic radical who believed that a democratic revolution was imminent in Europe. At the beginning of his exile in Paris in 1843, he was in close contact with Marx and another advanced thinker named Arnold Ruge, who had arrived from Dresden in a sort of coach into which he had crammed his wife, numerous children, and a leg of veal. On reaching Paris, Ruge had suggested that the three men and their wives create a commune in which the women would take turns running the domestic economy. This rational proposition was quickly rejected by Herwegh's young wife, Emma, who wanted him to herself but soon realized that she was in greater danger of losing him to Marie d'Agoult than to Ruge.

Relations must have commenced before November 1843, because it was at this time that she published the first of two articles on Herwegh.[1] The poet had a great reputation among German youth, especially because of a famous verbal attack on the king of Prussia in an open letter, but Marie expressed considerable reservations about his political radicalism. Society needs a principle of authority, she argued, and one should not be rude to monarchs who have progressive ideas. She reported that Herwegh was normally reserved in manner but that his eyes lit up with passion when he recited his political poems. He lost his temper easily, she added, and then made exaggerated statements which convinced nobody. In her second article, which contained her own French translations of some of Herwegh's poems, Marie was less critical, even quoting his letter to the king of Prussia and stressing the importance of a poet's role in civilized society. Nobody admired Herwegh's poetic genius more than she did, she explained, though she also respected the sincerity of his convictions.[2]

The poet wrote to thank her for the articles and explained that he did not share her moderate principles, because the only hope for Europe was to take all power from the kings and give it to the people, who would bring new energy to society. When Marie eagerly asked Herwegh for information about such German writers as Bettina von Arnim, Brentano, Heine, Hölderlin, Platen, and Marx, he responded with interesting comments. Her overtures became more enthusiastic and culminated in a declaration which revealed her emotional need: she explained that in recent years she had flown on two wings called freedom and love and had fallen into the sea like Icarus. He had appeared just in time to rescue her from despair with his fraternal affection. In this way Marie was turning to idealistic friendship as a compensation for lost love. It was a worthy aspiration which might have succeeded had she not sought perfection; time would reveal that Georg Herwegh too lacked this desirable quality.[3]

In May 1844 she had asked her new friend to act as intermediary between Liszt and herself in a quarrel about the arrangements for their children, perhaps hoping to make the musician jealous. Herwegh reported that there was no sign of Liszt's becoming more moderate. His unprecedented celebrity had apparently distorted his perception of people, and he was suspicious of Marie's motives. Herwegh added that in his presence, one felt Liszt's great power, though it was a force which could destroy his relations with others. It was possible that some deep shock might avert this, and Marie could be the person to achieve it. She replied that she was even more

convinced of the need for a final separation. Liszt had become an idler, a
Don Juan, a social climber, a mere musical acrobat obsessed with applause.
For ten years she had been deceived and could scarcely believe her own
blindness.

Anger, though unjust, has a tonic effect, and Marie began to react with
energy as she emerged from their affair. She would give up self-delusion and
apply herself to political action, she explained to Herwegh as she offered
him a friendship which increasingly looked like something more. She was a
Beatrice without a Dante, and their meeting was predestined. He had the
divine gift of poetry, and she would be his literary adviser and collaborator.
It is clear that Marie's disenchantment with Liszt had not eradicated the
Romantic idealism which was such an attractive part of her nature. Marie
did her best to charm Herwegh's wife, who was naturally observing the approach of this mature beauty with alarm, though some years would pass
before they became friends. Marie had genuine admiration for the young
woman, who had intellectual and musical talent and who shared her husband's zeal for democracy. Emma had more practical ability than her poet
husband, and her day of fame would come some years later when she enabled the Italian revolutionary Felice Orsini to escape from a high-security
prison in Mantua. Through the mail Orsini received from Emma a book
on some high moral theme. Inside the binding were saws of tempered steel
with which he cut through the bars on his window.

Although Marie had not yet succeeded in winning the trust of Emma
Herwegh, she could still count on Hortense Allart, who would remain
one of her few close female friends. Hortense was a woman of real generosity, who forgave Marie for encouraging the courtship of two of her
former lovers, Bulwer Lytton and Sainte-Beuve.[4] Marie admired not only
her kindness, cheerful character, and sincerity but also her ability to converse on any subject. Hortense respected Marie for the audacity of her
elopement and emancipation, a rare example of independence which made
her a model for other women, she believed. Seeing Marie regularly surrounded by men, Hortense had difficulty believing that her relationship
with them was always platonic. The younger ones were a particular source
of curiosity, especially the charming and handsome Henri Lehmann. We
may never know whether Hortense was right in her speculation, but it is

probable that Marie contented herself with the pleasures of friendship and admiration. As her fortieth year approached, she continued to enjoy flirtatious relationships situated in the uncertain territory between friendship and love. She no doubt felt that this strategy gave her control of her life. Her official attitude was that her passion for Liszt had been so important in her life that any sequel would be a lapse into mediocrity. On the subject of Marie's chastity, Hortense remained skeptical, as is the way with friends. Marie was certainly not a lonely woman, though she was seriously frustrated in her maternal affection for Blandine and Cosima, whom Liszt had angrily placed in a boarding school in order to lessen her influence on them. She had seen little of her son, Daniel, who was still with foster parents near Rome. Things were better with her eldest child, Claire, because Charles d'Agoult continued to be a perfect gentleman and encouraged his daughter to see her mother regularly. He took particular pleasure in seeing her elegantly dressed in new clothes chosen by Marie.

Marie began to feel new strength, which she channeled into a major literary project closely based on her experiences. She called the novel *Nélida*, which is an anagram of her pen name, Daniel. The wish to tell a private story in public was a deplorable weakness in the Romantic temperament, and Marie succumbed to it. One motive was to provide a justification of her life and an expression of her progressive social ideas; the other was the wish to establish herself as a novelist. Her great work of fiction would be an eloquent reply to the malicious literary portraits of her by Sand and Balzac.

Nélida appeared in 1846 and attracted considerable interest because of the transparent allusions to Marie's own life.[5] The protagonist, Nélida, is an imaginative and high-minded orphan who is educated in a fashionable convent school; there she responds to the sensual charm of religion and decides to become a nun. She is dissuaded by the Mother Superior, who is frustrated in her situation and describes nuns as a foolish herd of females tormented by intrigue and jealousy. The young heiress leaves the school at sixteen and is introduced to high society by her aunt, who hopes to marry her off without delay. She is courted by Timoleon, a man of experience who charms her and persuades her to become his fiancée. At this point she encounters Guermann, a childhood friend from a lower class who has become an artist. Impressed by his idealism and poverty, she falls in love with him

Marie d'Agoult, engraving by Emile-Pierre Metzmacher,
from a portrait by Henri Lehmann, 1849.

(Bibliothèque nationale de France)

and prepares for a conflict with her family. The innocent girl then learns
that the painter who swears that he loves her has a mistress. This revelation
of male imperfection shocks her, and she decides to marry the aristocratic
Timoleon.

Before long the intellectual young woman is tired of their life of frivolity and pleasure in which she has to compete with other women for the
attentions of her husband. At this point she again meets Guermann, who is
also suffering from melancholy. Soon a new bond forms between them as she
responds to his love and his passionate concept of art. There is something
unruly and extravagant in his behavior, partly because of his enthusiasm
for Romantic literature and the social theories of Saint-Simon. He has a
profound faith in destiny and believes he will achieve fame with Nélida as
his companion and inspiration. He is convinced that their love will overcome the barrier of class and signal a new society in which artists will enjoy
the high status they deserve. After much inner conflict she agrees to elope
with him.

The lovers flee to the mountains of Switzerland, where they have a brief
moment of bliss; when they settle in Geneva, however, Nélida suffers from
the gossip and malevolence of the local ladies. She is coldly disowned by her
family and often left alone by Guermann, who sends her eloquent letters
about his professional and social success. Nélida, who is now working on her
own intellectual development, observes that her lover is failing to produce
any great paintings. Her opinion of him changes, and soon there is serious
tension between them. One day he accuses her of denying him the personal
freedom he needs and announces that he is going to Germany, where he has
been commissioned to do a major work. The task proves too great for him,
and he falls into depression and illness. He is tormented by regret at having
left Nélida, who rushes to his bedside and forgives him before he dies.

As an account of Marie's life, *Nélida* was a strange mixture of fact and
fantasy. With her nobility, intelligence, and beauty, the figure of the heroine
was a highly flattering self-portrait of the author. The figure of Guermann
was of course an attack on Liszt, but it was so crude that he could treat
it with disdain. There were indeed some points of similarity between the
real musician and the fictional Guermann, whom Marie invented and ex-
terminated, yet Liszt's reaction would be remarkably moderate. Her novel

received a surprisingly favorable press in view of its lack of spontaneity and the unsubtle way in which the characters were drawn. It was certainly no masterpiece, but in spite of its shortcomings it remains a fascinating human document which has acquired historical value. Although it shows Marie indulgently portraying herself as a peerless victim of worthless individuals of both sexes, it also expresses interesting themes which were topical during the ferment which preceded the revolution of 1848. Guermann is a failure, but art itself is seen as a noble activity which can contribute to social progress. The female condition is also an important theme, and Marie provides a mordant criticism of a marriage system in which inexperienced girls commit themselves to a lifelong bond with a man they do not know. She provides a brilliant portrait of the sexually ignorant Nélida, who believes she is in love with her fiancé because of the mild excitement caused by the proximity of a man. She poignantly shows the young bride's hopes and illusions and denounces aristocratic marriage as a polite facade hiding a reality of infidelity and indifference.

The subject of social class is the most revolutionary theme in *Nélida,* and it is expressed mainly through the figure of the Mother Superior, who breaks with the Church because of its conservatism and devotes herself to helping workers lead moral lives. The renegade aristocrat wants to unite the proletariat and her own class in a struggle against the bourgeoisie which has dominated France since 1830. Her principles are also explicitly feminist since she urges Nélida to forget the disappointments of love and marriage and join her in a demonstration that women can be strong and active in the cause of progress. It is clear that Elisabeth's credo was nothing less than Marie's political manifesto.

There was little probability of Marie herself going to live among the poor in order to make them sober and prosperous, but her novel was an eloquent contribution to their cause. Encouraged by public response, she produced another highly political novel in the summer of 1847, *Valentia,* an even more critical portrayal of the aristocracy. The heroine, another beautiful orphan with a noble character, is adopted by her dull uncle and his wife, who enjoy high status in the court of Charles X. They quickly arrange a marriage between the innocent young Valentia and Count Ilse, an older man she has scarcely seen. On the wedding night he drugs her and rapes her while she is unconscious. She consults her adoptive mother, who explains that the life of a woman must be one of submission. She is befriended by Rosane, who reveals a policy which will enable a wife to enjoy total sexual freedom while maintaining appearances. For one year she must submit to her husband, but after this period she can use subtle means to achieve independence. Valentia does not apply this method, and soon her health is damaged by her husband's sexual demands. Alone in the mountains, she discovers Homer and Shakespeare and begins her real education. When she falls in love with Ferdinand, a nephew of her husband, she experiences sexual and emotional happiness for the first time. She tries to persuade him to elope and makes plans to earn her living by giving music lessons. Rosane, realizing the danger of Valentia's illusion, warns her that honesty is not the best policy; a cynical priest gives similar advice, pointing out that a return to her husband would cover her in the event of pregnancy. Discouraged by the weakness of Ferdinand, Valentia takes an overdose of opium and dies.

First novels are often autobiographical, but this second fictional work also drew heavily on her own experiences, a fact that underlines the limits of Marie's imagination. Indeed, she seemed to be aware of this shortcoming herself. Even though *Valentia* was to be her last attempt to rival George Sand, the protagonist of the work does interest the reader, who is eager to follow her adventures to the end. Added to the psychological interest of the novella is a socially significant portrait of the French aristocracy. In the month following this literary assault on her class, a tragic event befell Fanny Sébastiani, her old school friend. Fanny had married the duc de Praslin, who brutally murdered his wife on 17 August 1847. Marie's blood ran cold when she learned the details and thought of her shy and affectionate friend. The duke, who had been having an affair with the governess of his children, had apparently stabbed his wife after a violent conjugal row. The duke claimed that an intruder had committed the crime, but the police soon suspected him of being the culprit. To popular opinion it seemed to confirm the truth of contemporary melodramas about villainous aristocrats, and soon a hostile crowd gathered outside the house and shouted for his arrest. Praslin prevented this by means of a timely dose of arsenic, but republican propaganda made good use of the incident. It seemed to further justify Marie's opinion about the decadence of her class, and she told Georg Herwegh that the government had probably supplied the poison in order to avoid the damage of a public trial.[6]

Shortly after the murder of Fanny, Marie published "Thoughts on Women," an article which appeared in the progressive periodical *La Revue Indépendante.* Owing to the ponderous mediocrity of the recent works of George Sand, she had decided to make a contribution to feminist literature in the form of a series of observations on women's social situation and what she saw as their essential nature. Her analysis is primarily concerned with image. The mythical figures of Minerva and Venus are a timeless and valid representation of the power of women, she explained. Her advice to her sisters is a model of positive thinking: "I do not like to see women weeping. They claim they are victims, but victims of what? Only of their ignorance which makes them blind, of their idleness which makes them bored, of their weak character which restricts them, of their frivolity which makes them accept any humiliation for a necklace, and especially a life limited to love affairs and domestic matters."[7] A changing society needs your contribution, she told them sternly. Think! Act! And soon your imaginary problems will evaporate.

Her carefully expressed argument faced an obstacle, however: the lack of equal opportunities for women. They had been perceived as lesser individuals in the past, she readily conceded, and there had been no female Homer or Newton. This could be explained by the inferiority of their education and had no bearing on the future. In spite of unfavorable circumstances, women had achieved high status in certain fields and had made an important contribution to society. They were still a long way from equality and were still excluded from professional activity, but who could doubt that they would achieve it one day? The key was the provision of equal education for boys and girls. This was the fundamental principle of equality from which all others would follow naturally, she concluded. Marie's "Thoughts on Women" is a short, historically interesting text on an issue which was becoming increasingly topical. It contains a barbed reference to George Sand, who is accused of writing in an exaggerated and declamatory way which did a disservice to the feminist cause.

Marie d'Agoult's next significant publication was a prophetic book called *Essay on Liberty*. It appeared in November 1847, just three months before the revolution of the following winter, and clearly bears the mark of its time. It is a radical examination of contemporary French society and makes an idealistic plea for change.[8] Some of Marie's themes were to remain issues for a long time: for example, her plea for the protection of flora and fauna, her attack on the death penalty, and her advocacy of free health care for the poor. Underlying the book is what Musset called the *mal du siècle,* the new existential angst, the feeling that humanity is freeing itself from old beliefs but has not yet established anything to replace them. Marie's book contains a frontal attack on the Catholic Church because of attitudes she had accepted without thought in her youth. She accuses the Church of supporting the obsolete principle of absolute monarchy, thus contributing to the hostility of much of the nation. It taught a puritanical and unnatural distaste and fear of the human body, especially the female one. It had opposed modern science, repeating its famous error over Galileo, and it undervalued reason, as Jesus himself had recommended blind faith and submission. The poor were still instructed to tolerate their misery and passively hope for a reward in heaven. Some still believed in these old doctrines, she commented, and they should continue to follow the priests as the sheep follow the shepherd. Others, however, would see this as an abdication of the intellectual freedom which is the essence of humanity.

The situation of women is another important theme in the *Essay on Liberty,* which complains that every state in Europe had laws which subordinate a wife to her husband. Such laws may have had a certain logic in a distant era, when physical strength was crucial for survival, she conceded, but society had changed. She summed it up in some well-written pages which express the moderate feminist argument as it stood in 1847. With tactical skill she spoke of the disadvantages experienced by man:

> Our laws and customs give him, according to his social rank, no more than a useful servant or a smiling slave. As a consequence, he behaves more like a father or a brother than a husband. Eighteen centuries after

the coming of Jesus, women still show the vices of slaves and the faults of children: a hostile, lying attitude in the lower classes; in the upper ranks frivolous tastes and capricious behavior; a lack of sincerity in both categories. It is quite contrary to conjugal happiness, and to the authenticity of paternity which depends entirely on a wife's loyalty. But the problem is now so deeply rooted that it will take several generations of effort before woman receives her natural place, and nothing shows that there is any serious intention of giving it to her. There have been some isolated protests which few men have troubled to note, some poetical outbursts which have been quickly forgotten, some famous cases which were deemed to be dangerous and which were the subject of idle gossip. But men of intellect and action, philosophers and politicians, those who shape opinion and who change laws have not troubled to debate a question which, in France especially, seems to attract ridicule and frighten even the bravest. . . .

Nothing is more neglected or badly conceived than women's education. What do people want? I do not think anyone has a clear idea. What does reason dictate, and what does tradition enforce? As it is impossible to reconcile them, everything is left to chance. Nothing is done to arm strong characters who are capable of rising to a challenge; weak characters are left to their fate. But by common consent it is demanded that all women, systematically and blindly, whatever their differences of temperament, possess the two negative virtues of chastity and resignation, and no more is required. As no virtue can stand alone, and above all not without the help of reason, the usual consequence is that resignation becomes hypocrisy and chastity turns into sourness, and instead of conjugal peace the usual result is discord, trouble and misfortune.

Women's passions are strong and their knowledge is limited, said Fénelon in his excellent *Treatise on the Education of Girls*. The clarity of his fine mind made him see the cause of the problem, and in his timorous indication of the remedy he was unwittingly following the priestly tradition about Eve and the forbidden fruit, and only giving way step by step and regretfully to the pernicious intrusion of knowledge and liberty into human society, particularly into that half of it which is most enslaved.[9]

Marie's *Essay on Liberty* contains an eloquent plea for equality in education. Do not make girls spend their youth acquiring social talents to the detriment of more essential knowledge, she urges. The belief that strict religious education is good for them, though unnecessary for boys, is also a fallacy. Many believe that their confessors will keep young women on the straight and narrow path, but they could not be more mistaken, exclaims Marie, who wrote from experience. A confessor may be more influential than a husband, but he is never a match for a lover, she adds. Her urgent and heartfelt comments on the female condition also include pages on the need for a reintroduction of divorce, which she persuasively presents as a way to increase the happiness of men as well as women.

Her other main theme was France's need for greater political freedom and for positive action against inequality. She asserted that the great social issue of their time was poverty. People still spoke of society as being divided into three classes, with the aristocracy at the top. In reality there were only two classes: the rich and the poor. The rich enjoyed freedom and the poor were enslaved. Owing to the current recession they did not even have the opportunity to work. The aristocracy, like the Catholic Church, was hostile to political freedom as a matter of principle. The bourgeois, for their part, had quickly forgotten all talk about liberty and equality once they had secured power for themselves in 1830. They now sat in rich homes with chandeliers and Turkish carpets and believed themselves to be intrinsically superior to the rest of the population. Meanwhile the general discontent was being encouraged by radical republicans who preached dangerous utopian ideas to the lower class. The risk of serious violence had been revealed in recent insurrections by urban workers in Lyon and Paris. She concluded that the situation could again erupt unless the government of Louis-Philippe took positive action to increase freedom and equality.

Not all contemporary observers could see the signs of possible revolution with such clarity, and events soon proved her to be right. *Essay on Liberty* is not a faultless work, as it sometimes lapses into verbosity and Marie makes the mistake of using her own life as an example of personal liberation. On the other hand, it had an important theme, ambition, and an interesting historical perspective. Unlike the writings of some contemporary reformers such as Pierre Proudhon, her book is sensible and moderate. It is a call for reform, not revolution. By asserting faith in the decency of human nature and in the power of reason, it shows an essential optimism. Although it was published partly in order to create a public role for

Marie, it also expresses a fundamental altruism, which is one of her finest features.

It was now 1847, and three years had elapsed since the break with Liszt, and there had been significant changes in Marie's life. She had managed to establish herself not as a novelist but as a serious writer within the progressive part of the political spectrum. She had coped with the emotional trauma of separation from her daughters, whom she missed more than Daniel. It seemed that she was less attached to this unfortunate child, perhaps because he was born when relations with Liszt were not good. These difficulties only added to the greater hurt caused by the absences and infidelities of Franz, who had made matters worse by his angry and persistent interference in her relations with the children. He and Marie had exchanged bitter reproaches, and his letters showed an illogical resentment about a situation created mostly by himself.

After two years of separation, they resumed a more normal correspondence; the composer still said, and probably believed, that Marie had been destined to be the love of his life. He persisted in thinking that she should not have examined too closely his personal activities. At times he spoke as if their separation might not be permanent, and he always acknowledged the nobility of her character, though he found her unreasonable, excessively proud, and inclined to pose. In January 1846 he passed her former home in the rue de Beaune and saw that it had been taken over by an agricultural society. If only the emotions of our youth could be kept in bottles like precious liqueurs, he sighed. He knew that Marie continued to read in the press accounts of his concerts throughout Europe, and she was still the person whose esteem he most desired. Perhaps he would never be considered a great composer, he wrote, but he hoped at least to justify the faith of those who had affection for him. Despite their angry exchanges, he avowed, she had remained his inspiration.

As Marie's career as a writer developed, Franz made a point of having copies of her works sent to him in Germany; in a letter written on 26 May 1846 he had the magnanimity to congratulate her on *Nélida,* in spite of her obvious intention to hurt him. His comments express an honest and balanced judgment of the novel: it contained a high level of thought and emotion; there was a certain lack of ease in the way the characters were presented, but it was interesting throughout. As for the intention to portray him in the character of the failed artist Guermann, he reminded her of the similar flurry caused by Balzac and George Sand with *Béatrix* and *Horace*. The allusions to real persons had soon been forgotten, and he did not care what people said about *Nélida*. Although she should not let this early critical success go to her head, she had indeed written a distinguished novel: "Continue in the same vein, and try to improve on it if you can. When you told me: 'You know that I am not a spontaneous and productive genius. The nature of my talent is intellectual, and my style would suffer if I wrote too much,' you summed it up very well, but between excessive haste and your usual idleness there is a middle path which would consist of moderate but persistent work."[10] He congratulated her on the fact that the *Journal des Débats* had devoted no fewer than ten columns to *Nélida,* whereas the first novels of George Sand had received much less publicity, and noted that the article accused Marie of revealing enormous conceit in her idealized self-portrait—a criticism he had often received from her in the past, he cheerfully reminded her.

In a letter written to Franz on 17 January 1848, Marie commented on her writing career and sent him a copy of *Valentia,* which he had requested. An episode in the Alps, she predicted, would bring back vivid memories to him. He had asked for news of her literary reputation, and she reported that it was progressing gradually. Her style lacked color, but it had clarity; she would like to be the literary equivalent of Ingres: "As for my inner feeling, I can tell you that I am now certain that in ten years, if God spares me, the little fish could become a big one. I believe my ideas are acquiring clarity and strength and my expressions becoming more simple. . . . I can feel two fine books ready in my mind, and I think that my late arrival on the scene will have given me the advantage of avoiding the flashy defects which took people in for a while but against which there has been a complete reaction. Romanticism is dead and buried."[11] During 1848 her relations with Franz continued to improve, whereas those with her brother turned bad. Their mother had died the previous year, and Marie had been shocked to discover that Maurice had persuaded her to leave almost everything to him and to his numerous children. By contrast, she appreciated the decent behavior of Charles d'Agoult, and any signs of affection from Franz were welcome in spite of his hurtful allusions to other women. As Marie's anger receded, she reflected on her passion for him and considered whether she should have acted differently. She told herself that love was not necessarily a fleeting and unreliable sentiment and concluded that it was important for a woman to have a sense of her worth. Asking herself if she had lacked that self-esteem in her later life with Liszt, she speculated unconvincingly that had she reacted more energetically to his infidelities she might have salvaged the relationship. Her last surviving letter to him was written on 17 January 1848 and contains an apparently serene but ironical response to the news that he was to marry a rich Polish aristocrat. Marie assured him that she expected nothing less, since his former life of extravagance and dissipation was alien to his superior nature. She now understood that she was the last person who could have reformed his ways: "Your pride was on guard against me, and besides I could promise no more, having given everything. You tell me that a new apparition has taken over your imagination and your heart? So much the better. This woman with the superior character you describe will certainly not agree to share you. She will not want to be *one of your mistresses;* and since the last four years must have brought you not just a surfeit of loveless pleasures but a mortal disgust, you must eagerly seize this thread which will lead you out of the labyrinth." [12] Behind this barbed comment and the carefully measured tone one senses not only hurt pride but an enduring affection for the man who had changed her life. The new woman in his life was Carolyne Sayn-Wittgenstein, who, like Ariadne, was a real princess. Would he abandon her as well?

It is striking that in the years before the revolution of 1848 Marie was becoming progressively alienated from the aristocracy to which Liszt was making overtures. The honorable and kind behavior of Charles d'Agoult represented what was best in the class, but he could also be seen as a symptom of its new passivity in political matters. Aristocrats seemed to have given up hope of a return to power, or else they were counting on some unexpected event such as a foreign intervention like that of 1815. Maurice, on the other hand, represented the less scrupulous segment of the old aristocracy which greedily sought money and position in the new regime. The

condescending attitude of Mathilde and her pious booklets were equally
unpalatable to her sister-in-law. It is therefore not surprising that Marie
preferred the company of her own friends. What was the value of a diplomat
such as Maurice de Flavigny compared to persons like Lamartine, Vigny,
Hortense Allart, the painters Ingres and Lehmann, and the young dramatist Ponsard? The Herweghs had gone to conspire in Zurich, but their place
was filled by the sculptor Pierre Simart, the painter Théodore Chassériau,
and influential journalists such as Anselme Petetin and Eugène Pelletan. In
1847 she made a new friend in the person of Emile Littré, a distinguished
writer who would later produce France's most famous dictionary. She still
had intermittent contacts with Lamennais, whose sincerity and radicalism
she respected. The renegade priest had little time for women and accepted
her invitations to dinner with bad grace because of her occasional services to
him. In addition she was attending the lectures of Auguste Comte, who was
proclaiming the novel idea of studying society through scientific method.
Society was moved forward by certain dynamic forces, he argued, proper
understanding of which could lead to intelligent action. The philosopher
could not fail to notice the attentive figure of Marie and informed himself
of her identity. He may have reflected that this refugee from the aristocracy
was herself a symptom of the very forces he was discussing.

As had previously been the case, Marie still preferred male company,
with the exception of her daughter Claire and Hortense Allart. She had repeatedly shown an inclination for passionate friendships with younger men
such as Louis de Ronchaud, Henri Lehmann, Georg Herwegh, and most recently the playwright Ponsard. These liaisons had resembled platonic love
affairs marked by tiffs and reconciliation. In 1848, at the age of forty-three,
she was still in possession of much of her beauty and all her charm. As conscious of her image as always, she enjoyed dressing elegantly and attending
concerts and theaters in the company of her attentive young men. Although
Marie had already achieved some literary reputation, she may still have held
the secret, and unrealistic, hope that she would one day equal George Sand.
Marie had a lesser female rival in Madame de Girardin, whose opinion was
not important because she had made it clear in *La Presse* that she viewed intellectual women as unfeminine pedants. By contrast, Marie was motivated by
high ambition and wanted to influence minds, even to shape events. She was

in a position to do so not only with her publications but also owing to her relationship with Lamartine. He was the leading orator of the opposition in Parliament and would soon achieve political power.

The revolution of 1848 in France was one of those great upheavals which might have been avoided. In her *Essay on Liberty* Marie herself had expressed the opinion that the government could satisfy popular opinion by increasing freedom and trying to reduce poverty. Louis-Philippe had shown skill and determination in surviving a series of conspiracies and insurrections and could no doubt have done so again, though economic crisis and increasing unemployment had made the social problem more acute. The political situation grew more tense, and throughout France there were meetings of protest which took the form of banquets because of a ban on demonstrations. Still Louis-Philippe refused to make any concessions. His regime was good for a turbulent nation, he sincerely believed, and it was his duty to defend it. High-minded windbags like Lamartine might cause trouble, but Louis-Philippe had a large military force in Paris and a detailed plan to deal with any violence.

Marie followed the events of early 1848 with apprehension. On 22 February a group of moderates planned a demonstration which was at once banned. The leaders decided that it would be folly to go ahead, and when this news reached the king, he congratulated himself on his firm policy. That evening there were minor scuffles, but it was raining heavily and Louis-Philippe laughingly told his entourage that Parisians did not have revolutions in winter. The next day the situation appeared more serious, with reports of fighting between army units and insurgents, who had surrounded isolated groups of soldiers and seized their arms. Suddenly the king's resolution gave way, and he sacked the unpopular Guizot, who had been his most loyal servant in Parliament. At once the streets of Paris filled with triumphant crowds waving tricolor flags, and the danger of violence seemed to have been averted.

Then came the event which turned the insurrection into a revolution. On the evening of 23 February a column of working-class men and women bearing torches and a red flag marched from the suburb of Saint-Antoine to the Ministry of Foreign Affairs on the boulevard des Capucines, which was guarded by two hundred infantry. As the crowd began to press forward, the

Revolution of 1848: Death on the Boulevard.

(Bibliothèque nationale de France)

troops received the order to fix bayonets. Then a veteran republican conspirator named Charles Lagrange deliberately fired a single pistol shot into their ranks. The angry soldiers immediately responded with a massive discharge into the throng. When the smoke cleared, the bodies of a hundred dead or wounded civilians could be seen in the pale light of the gas lamps. After the soldiers withdrew, some of the demonstrators placed a number of corpses in a cart and paraded them by torchlight through the proletarian parts of Paris, arousing fury as they went. Soon the night was filled with the sound of picks breaking up the cobblestone streets, and by the next day large sections of the city were barricaded.

That morning Marie went to the courtyard of the palace, where she saw Louis-Philippe review the troops and the National Guard. He was mounted on a richly decorated horse and accompanied by two generals, but the attitude of the civilian militia was sullen and the monarch soon returned to the palace. The commander of the troops was General Tomas Bugeaud, who had made a reputation fighting rebels in the new colony of Algeria, but this was a new type of conflict and he hesitated to make full use of his regiments against the civilian population of Paris. With remarkable speed the insurgents seized power in a large part of the capital. Inside the palace Louis-Philippe listened as the the gunfire approached, finally reaching the army post in the Chateau d'Eau, near the Palais Royal. There was something unreal about the deadly scene, because cafés in the vicinity had remained open and insurgents could be seen there drinking and joking while they took a rest from the battle. Soldiers inside the palace surrendered when it was set afire with a wagon of burning hay.

The rebels were now close, and Louis-Philippe saw that it was time to abdicate. He exchanged his military uniform for a civilian overcoat and quickly departed with his wife in a coach drawn by a single black horse and accompanied by a small detachment of cavalry. Shortly afterward the palace was invaded by a violent mob who took the throne and paraded it to the Place de la Bastille, where they set fire to it. Meanwhile the royal couple reached the palace of Saint-Cloud, near Paris. He asked for scissors in order to cut off his distinctive whiskers and put on a pair of large green spectacles before heading for Dreux. When he reached the town, he learned that a republic had been declared in Paris. He continued on to Normandy, in the

Revolution of 1848: The Burning of the Throne.

(Bibliothèque nationale de France)

middle of a storm, and hid in Trouville, where his helpers vainly tried to hire a fishing boat to take him to England. His presence in the little port was arousing too much interest, however, and he was forced to steal through a back garden and make his way to Le Havre, where he and his wife furtively escaped aboard a steamer provided by the British consul.

When Marie, in the role of historian, looked back on these events, she did her best to give an objective assessment of the deposed king. In spite of her low opinion of Louis-Philippe's political morals, she refrained from platitudes about poetic justice and portrayed him as a clever and energetic leader who became stubborn and overconfident. She had been frightened by the violence of the Parisian proletariat which had overthrown him, and her record included an account of the wrecking of the Tuileries Palace by a mob. She noted that in the great hall where she had once attended royal receptions a respectful crowd had gathered around a harlot in a red bonnet who was posing as a statue of liberty. Marie concluded, with generosity, that the young woman was a victim of poverty who deserved her moment of glory.

The last detachments of soldiers were withdrawing from the city, where the insurgents had gained power. A delegation of members of Parliament, led by Lamartine, accepted the inevitable and made its way on foot to the rebel headquarters in the Hotel de Ville. There they agreed to proclaim a republic. The streets were stained with blood, and dead horses and over-turned vehicles could be seen throughout the city. A smell of gunpowder lingered in the air, and the great bell of Notre-Dame rang out incessantly. A feverishly excited crowd armed with sabers and guns filled the city center, while the rich waited fearfully in their homes. It was rumored that all the museums and libraries had been wrecked and that a gang of freed criminals was on the rampage. Would the mob take vengeance on the supporters of the fallen regime? Some of the insurgents were talking of burning the city and exterminating the rich. The forces of law and order had disappeared and anything might happen. To Marie's relief, the insurgents behaved with restraint in spite of earlier fears. Her account of the February days contains a homage to a proletariat, which she portrayed as being capable of altruism as well as violence. To her idealistic mind it seemed a Romantic dream come true. The revolution would lead to a new era of reason and liberty, she believed. Amazingly, the leading personality in the provisional government was Lamartine, and his sudden elevation seemed to be a symbolic alliance between the people and a poet. She felt privileged to be a friend of this man of courage and vision who had suddenly come to power.

Such optimism was bound to prove excessive, but Marie was one of many who were filled with euphoria. The new government had pleased progressive opinion by introducing universal male suffrage, abolishing the death sentence for political crimes, and banning slavery in the colonies. It also attempted to solve broader social problems by taking action against the urban poverty which she had herself denounced. She followed events closely as the government announced the creation of a commission to examine solutions and set up national workshops intended to provide jobs for all. The inspiration for these projects was Louis Blanc, considered a dangerous utopian by the rich, though they refrained from expressing this opinion for a while.

When peace returned to Paris after a few days, the upper class put on old clothes and cautiously ventured out into the streets, which were full of enthusiastic supporters of the new regime. Marie, who had already decided to produce a literary account of the revolution, went out to make notes. Whereas George Sand was publishing sentimental articles in praise of the proletariat, Marie was determined to make a more intelligent contribution. Lamartine was too busy to see her at first, owing to his duties as foreign minister, but eventually made amends by dining with her and even asking her for a list of men who might serve the new regime as diplomats. Her new home, in the rue Plumet, had become a center of republican debate in which even Lamennais was taking part. To celebrate the situation Marie went to the theater one evening in a symbolic red hat; her bliss was complete when she heard that Mathilde de Flavigny was talking of going into exile in order to escape the expected persecution of the aristocracy.

Marie could now hope to enjoy real political influence because of Lamartine's key position in the government. In her imagination she saw herself as his trusted friend and adviser. Her admiration for Lamartine had never been more intense, and in truth his courage in front of the mob at the Hôtel de Ville had given him an aura of greatness. In the youthful days as a poet

Alphonse Lamartine, ca. 1848.

(Photothèque des Musées de la Ville de Paris)

he had been inspired by a woman, and what had happened once could happen again. Marie's eagerness may have been overdone, because Lamartine gradually distanced himself from her. He admired her character, intelligence, and social graces, but despite appearances he was a solitary man who valued his independence.

Marie's financial situation at this time was an additional disappointment. Her share of her mother's estate turned out to be six hundred thousand francs, much less than she expected, though it would have seemed a fortune to many. She consoled herself with newfound activities, on 4 May attending with Madame Lamartine the first session of a Parliament elected by universal suffrage. While continuing to work on her history of the revolution, she also produced a series of "Lettres républicaines," published in *Le Courrier Français,* a newspaper situated to the left of center. The first of these open letters was addressed to the prince de Joinville, a son of Louis-Philippe who was intending to stand for election to Parliament. She ironically urged him to go to democratic America and start a new life as a pioneer in the far west. The bourgeois supporters of his father's regime had failed to understand the march of history, she explained, ferociously attacking their lack of principles: "The bourgeoisie, as you well know, does not have any feeling of loyalty to you; it is driven by self-interest alone. It had believed, and will never cease to believe, that the progress which had given it power and wealth was the final step forward taken by the human species. After its defeat it was pale with shock and fear, trembling for its property because it thought the armed revolutionaries were as unscrupulous as itself, so it hypocritically hid its anger and pretended to support the new regime."[13] Her article concluded with an assertion of the idealistic belief that events had demonstrated the superiority and moderation of the ordinary people of Paris. The time of violence and bloodshed was over for good, she ventured.

This proved to be the worst prediction Marie ever made. The euphoria of February soon evaporated in the following months as the hardship of life for the proletariat increased. The *ateliers,* or national workshops, had been established to create employment, but those enrolled were discontented because there was little real work for them and their pay had been reduced. As a consequence they had begun to gather on the boulevards, where they were harangued by agitators calling for a socialist republic. The government acted by announcing that the ateliers would be disbanded and the workers given a choice of joining the army or being sent to work in the provinces.

On 22 June a crowd gathered in front of the church of Saint-Sulpice, its bells silenced by workers who entered the towers. Standing on the fountain was a former theology student named Pujol, a powerful orator who imparted the news that force would be used against the members of the workshops if they did not leave Paris willingly. The government had broken its promise to provide work and wanted to exterminate the proletariat, he warned. From the steps of the Pantheon later that evening he electrified another large crowd with a call to vengeance. The next morning a column of several thousand men with flags and drums marched across Paris to the place where the Bastille once stood. There Pujol ordered them to remove caps and kneel in silent homage to the dead heroes of former revolutions. They too must adopt the slogan "Freedom or Death," he proclaimed. When he had finished his speech, a young woman emerged from the crowd and gave him a bouquet of summer flowers. Pujol's followers then separated into columns which marched away with quiet determination. By noon that day half of Paris was a fortress in their hands.

The National Guard launched its first attack in the Saint-Denis area, where it suffered heavy losses from lateral fire as it tried to storm a huge barricade. At one point in the combat a scantily dressed young woman with a tricolor flag appeared on the barricade to urge the rebels on. Her reckless gesture was apparently inspired by Delacroix's famous painting of Liberty guiding the people — a remarkable indication of the power of art. For a time the militia held fire, but when her provocative gestures continued she was shot dead and the barricade was stormed.

By this time there was fighting over much of Paris as the men, women, and children of the rebel army feverishly melted lead for bullets and fought on with determination. In the fury of battle many prisoners were killed by government forces, and in places there was cheering when insurgents on rooftops were shot and fell to the street. Within hours the city was full of rumors about the rape of convent girls by fanatical socialists and other alleged atrocities. After three days of conflict the rebels had failed to seize power and could hold out no longer. Paris was again a devastated city full of soldiers whose campfires lit up the night.

The Insurrection of June 1848.

(Bibliothèque nationale de France)

This July rising of 1848 was the first class war of modern times. Hatred and hysteria hung in the air, and for days the papers invented crude stories about the cruelty of the insurgents. Marie's republic had survived, but the seeds of its destruction had been sown. Discouraged by recent events, she wondered whether men would ever cease to kill one another. In an article dated 28 June she commented publicly on the insurrection, asking whether it was the fate of her generation to live in eternal violence. The discontent of the workers was justified, she bravely declared, though it had been exploited by ambitious individuals, and the republic would emerge stronger from the experience. Her next articles, however, expressed deep anxiety about the future: the nation must recover from its panic, and repression cannot be an effective method of government, she asserted on 8 July, in an open letter to Parliament. The proletariat could not be expected to accept hardship any longer, and it was wrong for leaders to condemn all socialist theory without knowledge of it. There was indeed a fanatical socialism which preached violent revolution, but there was also the utopian socialism of Etienne Cabet, who was planning a perfect society in the wilds of Texas. In addition the intellectual socialism of Louis Blanc advocated state control of labor and industry. One could add the social theories of Proudhon concerning the organization of finance. Finally she expounded on what she called the socialism of statesmen: the belief that there could not be true freedom and democracy without the eradication of poverty. This intelligent form of socialism was not against property but wished to make it accessible to the proletariat. The government should adopt this principle and take action in order to improve the life of the workers. Whatever the shortcomings of socialist theory, it defined a problem of crucial importance, she added. The recent experience of class war had shaken the nation, and danger lay ahead.

The nation scarcely needed the warning, because the shock of the June insurrection in Paris had sent ripples of fear into every town and province of France. In a series of eloquent articles Marie continued bravely to defend the democratic principle and to plead for reconciliation between the classes. On 5 October 1848 she wrote about the danger of the candidacy of Louis-Napoleon Bonaparte for the new post of president of the Republic. The ignorance of some country voters was so great that they would believe they were voting for Napoleon himself rather than his incompetent nephew, she rightly claimed. In reality this Bonaparte was known mostly for two feeble attempts to start an insurrection under Louis-Philippe; his lack of intelligence was so evident, in fact, that his own party presented him as a harmless candidate who would not disturb the nation. Her article ended with a warning that the Bonapartist party was the real threat to the republic. This ultimately proved to be of no concern to conservative France, which gave Bonaparte a landslide victory in the presidential election. The unfortunate Lamartine, genuine democrat and man of principle, suffered a crushing defeat. The republic Marie had loyally supported had now taken a first step toward political suicide, and time would show that she had seriously underestimated the skill and ambition of Louis-Napoleon Bonaparte.

The Daniel Stern articles written in the momentous year of 1848 show Marie at the peak of her skill in journalism. They deal with the great issues of freedom, democracy, and social justice. Her style in these has become more forceful and incisive, with occasional gems of sarcasm, and she could justifiably feel that her political writing was superior to the diffuse and didactic productions of George Sand. Her portraits of politicians are vivid in physical and psychological detail. Her articles possess an inner coherence as she expresses the belief that political progress, though slow, is inevitable. Although her assessment of Louis-Napoleon was wrong, she was not alone in this error.

Her final article in the series of "Republican Letters" considers the position of women in French society. Political revolutions were insufficient without psychological change, and women too ought to make a contribution to the republic. Recalling the role of Madame Roland in 1789, she asked whether the women of 1848 had lost the ability to give inspiration. No doubt one should not pass harsh judgment on a section of society deprived of elementary rights and a good education, she concedes, but too many women of her generation had lacked ambition. Although unable to alter laws themselves, they could demonstrate the need for change. They might overcome oppression not by the usual female method of coquetry and cunning but by intellectual achievement. This would make them equal partners of men in professional and public life. The gap between intellectual equality and legal equality was smaller than women realized, she argued.

This was especially true in these revolutionary times. The noisy claims of certain feminists, however, had attracted much ridicule and had alienated men and women alike. These radicals had been arrogant and had wanted to move too fast. The traditional female condition of ignorance and frivolity had at least been associated with grace and charm, qualities that feminists should not abandon altogether. Women could enter political life by working for peace between the classes, she concluded. Conciliation was in their nature, and the fragmented nation needed their skills. With this assertion of women's rights and duties Marie ended a series of articles which expressed her idealism and concern for progress.

The next two years brought her nothing but political disappointment as the Republic moved toward doom. Despite his inability as an orator, his mediocre appearance, and his indecisiveness, Louis-Napoleon cleverly gave the frightened nation what it wanted: the belief that it again had a master. An unimpressive sight because of his short legs, he often made public appearances on horseback wearing a feathered hat reminiscent of Napoleon's. With his mistress, his debts, and his extravagant lifestyle, he was not the model of propriety that Louis-Philippe had been, but the nation forgave him in its desire for strong government. With distaste Marie observed the forces of reaction at work. The influence of the Catholic Church was being increased by new legislation, and the royalists were actively plotting to overturn the republic.

The fatal blow came not from royalists but from the president himself. A coup had been expected for some time and finally took place on 2 December 1851, when Bonaparte brought the army into Paris and illegally dissolved the Parliament. During the night the walls of the city were pasted with copies of a presidential proclamation stating that Bonaparte had acted in order to save the republic from anarchy. For two days armed insurrection ruled in Paris, but it was soon crushed with ruthless ferocity.

What most upset Marie d'Agoult about the event was the eagerness of the nation to accept this act of cynical treachery and the destruction of the Republic. It was enough to make her despair of democracy. On 10 December she wrote to her conspirator and friend Emma Herwegh in Zurich that she had no hope left. The coup was welcomed by the bourgeoisie, the shopkeepers, and the provincial population. The workers of Paris, for their part, had not recovered from the massacres of June 1848, and many were now Bonapartist. The coup in France was part of a reaction throughout Europe, she explained to Emma: "It would be madness to attempt a rising now either in Italy or in Hungary. It has all been planned with the agreement of Russia. Everything is ready for a crushing of democracy in Europe. This is all I have time to write today! This letter will reach you only if it is allowed to by those who will read it." [14] The democratic party in France had been led by a band of boastful fools and traitors, she added. Recalling the euphoria of the first weeks of revolution, she reflected that such moments were too beautiful to last. Her opinion of the proletariat had been overly optimistic, she told Emma. Progressives like herself had been intoxicated by their enthusiasm. They had placed too much hope in ideals, whereas most people of their generation had no time for them. Disillusion in politics after frustration in love: it was the second great chagrin in the life of Marie d'Agoult.

CHAPTER 12

Autumn Leaves

MARIE was now in the autumn of her life, and many hopes and
illusions had fallen to the ground. She could certainly draw satisfaction from her career as writer, and the first volume of her
Histoire de la révolution de 1848 had appeared. As a historian of recent events
she had the advantage of knowing a number of well-informed people across
the political spectrum. She had high praise for Lamartine, who, like Marie,
had distanced himself from the aristocracy. She portrayed him as a noble
defender of principles which would shape the modern world: universal suffrage, free education, the ending of hereditary aristocracy, the separation
of church and state, the pursuit of peace, and the protection of the poor. He
stood for lucidity, courage, and generosity, and his rejection by the elector-
ate had been a bitter experience. What hope could be placed on democracy
if the nation cast aside a man like Lamartine? He had once declared that politics should be founded not on force and cunning but on morality, reason,
and virtue. Events had shown this belief to be naive.

The *History of the Revolution of 1848* is Marie d'Agoult's finest work, the
one which has done most for her reputation, and its narrative qualities have
not faded with time. She was faced by the impossible task of giving a complete and objective narration of events which were still recent, but she had
the advantage of direct contact with participants. This immediacy gives
her book a vivid quality which can be seen in her account of the long confrontation between Lamartine and the angry mob he bravely faced when
total anarchy seemed likely: "Twenty times, during these critical hours,
Lamartine's life depended on every word and gesture he made. At one moment someone swung an axe near his head, while the crowd anxiously drew

breath. Whether he did not see it, or whether he coolly reflected that this incident would help him, he summoned up all his strength and continued to speak with consummate eloquence."[1] Marie records that Lamartine was finally embraced with enthusiasm by a ragged man who emerged from the crowd, and she vividly evokes the strange scene as the singing insurgents dispersed into the dark slums of Paris in which they led their miserable existence. Her skill in portraits can be seen in a description of the Blanqui brothers:

> Adolphe Blanqui became well known for his studies of economics whereas his brother Auguste, who was tormented by more furtive ambitions, joined the secret societies which were plotting the overthrow of the dynasty of Louis-Philippe. Nature had intended him to be a leader of conspirators. He had a feverish power of thought and of speech which gave him power over men of revolutionary temperament. He was small, pale, and puny but he had burning eyes. He suffered from a heart condition made incurable by late nights, poverty and prison, and one had the impression that the intensity of his anger was his way of prolonging a life which might end before he could satisfy his ambitions.[2]

She saw this fanatical leveler as a danger to the new republic, which he was already plotting to destroy, but scrupulously noted his intelligence and energy. A famous homage to her narrative skill would later come from Flaubert, who drew on her account of the revolution of 1848 in *L'éducation sentimentale,* his great historical novel.

In March 1851 she purchased a new house in a quiet area near the Arc de Triomphe, at the edge of the city, telling her friends it would be small enough for her to sweep when her financial situation went into terminal decline. This was an exaggeration, as it was a pleasant home with a Renaissance-style facade and stood in an avenue planted with acacias. The interior was hung with her old Italian paintings, and in the small conservatory a fountain bubbled amid mimosas and gardenias. It was an acceptable setting for an intellectual Parisian hostess. Now in her middle forties, and as elegant as ever, she continued to enjoy the autumn of her beauty. Her serenity was disturbed at times by rumors about the impending marriage of Liszt, and she was displeased to learn that he was living in the same house as his new adorer in Weimar. Was there a part of her that still clung to the

hope that he would one day ask for a reconciliation? With all the masoch-
ism of a frustrated lover, she looked for news of his activities and eagerly
noted any reports about possible friction between Carolyne and him. She
reacted with natural indignation on learning that Liszt was describing her
as a bad mother and boasting of the affection shown by Carolyne to their
children. He had harshly ordered his daughters not to visit Marie when they
were let out of their school in Paris. Once in 1850 fifteen-year-old Blandine
had pleased Marie by turning up with Cosima in spite of the paternal edict.
When word of the escapade reached Liszt, he reprimanded the unfortunate
girls so severely that much time would pass before they saw their mother
again.

Four years later he temporarily relented for the sake of their social
education, as he conceded that this was one task to which Marie was well
suited. Blandine and Cosima were soon captivated by this charming and
elegant woman about whom they knew so little. Marie was equally taken
with these two intelligent girls, who met their half-sister, Claire, for the
first time. Liszt's daughters were both musically gifted, and Marie happily
took them to the opera, where Cosima discovered the music of Wagner,
unaware of the role she would one day play in his life. They regularly went
with their mother to the Louvre, where she shared with them her love of
art. The girls were impressed by the people in their mother's circle, where
they met Renan and Littré. In exchange they contributed the charm of their
youth and provided one of the happiest episodes in Marie's life. Her contentment was completed by the visits of her son, Daniel, who was now
attending boarding school in Paris, where he was winning armfuls of prizes.
The boy was fifteen and had seen little of either parent during his childhood. Fortunately he had a resilient nature and seemed to have survived
this regime.

Marie was enjoying the pleasures of parenthood as never before, but
inevitably the situation changed as the children became older. Although she
knew she could not base her life on a maternal role, this thought caused her
sadness. She discussed these emotions in a revealing letter to her friend in
Zurich.[3] Emma Herwegh's own lot had not been easy, having raised numerous children and tolerated a marriage that was far from perfect. She had
expressed the thought that life had given her only a half ration. Marie took

the metaphor a step further and asked Emma if she remembered the ideals of their youth. They had aspired to love and liberty and had received not a half ration, nor a quarter ration, but a twentieth of a ration. Trying to be positive, she went on to show her pride as a mother. Claire had studied science and philosophy and was art correspondent for *La Presse*, where she signed her articles C. de Soult. The financial follies of Claire's husband had obliged her to take legal action in order to save the family from ruin, but she had weathered this storm with serenity. Claire would one day be known as one of the outstanding women of her generation, her mother predicted. Blandine was beautiful and charming, whereas Cosima was more like her father. She had a streak of genius and an inner force which could not be curbed, Marie reported. She had unfortunately entered a marriage in which there was little possibility of happiness.

All this praise of her offspring was expressed in a wistful tone, because Blandine, Cosima, and Daniel were beginning to distance themselves from her after the few years of proximity. Although this change was partly the natural process of achieving independence, Liszt encouraged this alienation. In the summer of 1855 the trio had traveled to Weimar to spend some weeks with a father they rarely saw but whom they revered as a genius. A diplomatic incident occurred when Blandine carelessly left behind some letters in which her mother spoke critically about their father's new companion. Liszt grew angry and did his best to raise a new barrier between the girls and their mother, accusing her of neglect and indifference. This despite the fact that he had always contented himself with very small doses of parenthood and had repeatedly aggravated the situation with his hostility. He added that the day would soon come when they would have to make a choice between Marie and him.

To her dismay, the stay in Germany stretched into months. After three weeks of their visit, Liszt had tired of his daughters and had sent them on an educational trip to Berlin. It was a fateful move for the passionate Cosima, who made the mistake of falling in love with a young man named Hans von Bülow, her father's most brilliant pupil. One day, on hearing Wagner's *Lohengrin* directed by Liszt, he had suddenly decided to abandon his plan to become a diplomat and instead devote his life to music. In the same impulsive way he had asked Cosima to marry him, and she had agreed. When

Marie suspected that something was afoot, she sent stern letters ordering Cosima to return to Paris. Her daughter showed no inclination to obey and instead urged Marie to join her in Berlin. In the end Marie sent Claire to find out the truth, and when the two sisters returned, Marie did her best to persuade Cosima to break off the engagement. She might have reflected on the force of heredity and saved herself the trouble. In the end the head-strong young woman was allowed to marry her musician, and duly lived to regret it.

Daniel too became a source of chagrin for his mother when he obeyed Liszt's order to leave Paris for Vienna, where he was to forget all fancy ideas and study law. What an intelligent decision, Marie wrote sarcastically to Emma: making him quit an enlightened country like France to become the subject of a feudal empire! She had wanted her clever and handsome son to enter the prestigious Ecole Polytechnique and had been hurt by his willingness to leave her. There was some consolation in the fact that Liszt agreed that Blandine at least should spend more time in the company of her mother in the hope of finding a husband among the distinguished men of her circle. Marie was pleased to take on this part of the maternal role but did not go so far as to take her into her small home, as this would have restricted the space needed for social activities. Blandine was offended by this apparent coolness, though her mother had been a much better parent than her father. Blandine's situation was complex. To enhance her marriage prospects, it was important that she not appear to be an abandoned waif; to her mind this mattered more than her illegitimacy, which was redeemed by her personal qualities and the distinction of her parents.

Knowing that she would not have much more time with Blandine, Marie decided they should enjoy a holiday together. In late June they set off by train and coach for the spa town of Divonne, near the frontier of Switzerland. From her window Marie looked across the blue waters of the Lake of Geneva to the snow-capped Alps. Divonne, so peaceful after Paris, was filled with the scents of summer, though, perversely, she sometimes found herself missing the stimulus of city life. Before long they were joined by Louis de Ronchaud. It seems that Marie never for one moment considered the possibility of rewarding her faithful acolyte with the hand of her daughter. Certainly it would not have been right to foist the sexless Ronchaud on

Blandine, though other women of her class might have been less scrupulous than she. But in addition, she would lose his services if he married someone else, even Blandine. Now that Ronchaud was with them, the journey could proceed, and Marie wrote cheerfully to tell Emma that she was leaving Divonne because the chef did not cook lamb chops, without which she could not survive. Their next stop was the little Swiss town of Villeneuve, on the Lake of Geneva. There they were joined by Girardin, who had married after the death of Delphine and was now accompanied by a pretty new wife young enough to be his daughter. The second Madame de Girardin, who seemed to have a frivolous disposition, was said to be the love child of a German prince. The marriage was evidently a remarkable piece of folly on the part of the famously hard-headed Girardin, and in years to come his new wife would present him with children of doubtful paternity. Marie recalled the distant day when she had first met young Delphine as she recited her poetry in the salon of Madame de Flavigny. This new episode made her reflect sadly on the passing of time, the fragility of life, and the errors of love. Twenty years had passed since Marie had visited Italy with Franz, and she was filled with even more melancholy as the group advanced toward the Alps. They had decided not to travel by the easier Simplon route but to climb the high Saint Bernard Pass on mules. After this adventurous journey they slowly descended into the fertile plain of Lombardy.

Before leaving Villeneuve they had been joined by Emile Ollivier, a young lawyer and politician who had arrived on the steamer from Geneva on his way to Florence to see his father, a democrat who had gone into exile because of his opposition to Napoleon III. Marie had known him for several years, and the encounter was not accidental since she had invited him to travel with them. As days went by, it became evident that the young man was attracted to Blandine, and Marie took the precaution of writing to her friend Charles Dollfuss in Paris for advice. Her informant replied that Ollivier had a reputation for fidelity and also a frank and cheerful personality unusual in a lawyer. On the ship from Genoa to Pisa the young couple lingered alone on the deck in the moonlight and were clearly falling in love. After reaching Florence they went for walks among the flowers and wheat fields of the Arno Valley, and their emotional condition quickly became incurable.

Blandine Liszt, by Adam Salomon, ca. 1860.

(Réunion des Musées nationaux)

An early marriage was agreed on, and the wedding was celebrated in the impressive cadre of the church of Santa Maria del Fiore in Florence. Marie was irritated by the fact that Blandine chose her father's birthday for the event, but she was moved by the romantic nature of the ceremony, which took place after dark, the vast church faintly lit by candles and torches. Recalling her own, very different wedding, she fervently wished that Blandine would be happier than she had been. Writing to Emma, she remarked that although it was impossible to predict the success of any marriage, she had high hopes for this one. It was an accurate prediction, though fate would not be kind to Blandine Liszt.

Despite Marie's satisfaction at seeing Blandine suitably married, the weeks in Florence had given rise to friction between her and her new son-in-law, who saw her as a potentially intrusive element in their life and let it be seen that he wanted to keep his distance. She reacted with irrational jealousy when Blandine predictably sided with her husband; the result was a new problem for which Marie was mostly to blame. The situation was made worse by the delayed payment of a dowry of forty thousand francs which she had promised but could not complete at the time. It is interesting to note that in order to amass the sum, she needed the consent of her husband and that Charles agreed to the proposal with his usual nobility in spite of his own financial difficulty. Liszt, for his part, made no contribution to his daughter's dowry. Tragically, the coolness between Marie and her daughter lasted until the premature death of Blandine, whom she never saw again.

Marie was in no hurry to return to Paris, where she would be expected to continue in the pleasant but costly role of society hostess. On her travels she could lead a less expensive life in hotels and enjoy the varied company of the idle but cultivated rich who were avoiding boredom by visiting the cities of southern Europe. She therefore returned to Paris slowly, making a stopover at the Hôtel Victoria in Nice. Although this little town had already been made fashionable by British visitors, it did not find favor in her eyes; she wrote to Emma complaining of the pebbled beach covered in washing and the lack of opportunity for country walks. Her discontent at this time was no doubt the symptom of a more serious problem—her former depression, which was returning to haunt her. Already in August of that year she had spoken to Emma of a worrying mental state but reported that she had placed herself in the hands of a sensitive homeopathic doctor who promised to restore her energy. This talented practitioner had continued to treat her by correspondence during her absence from Paris, she added. There is no doubt that Marie's condition was not one of those recreational maladies which affect the rich, and in the winter of 1857–58 she suffered the most serious recurrence since the time she was living with Charles. One factor may have been a feeling of instability owing to the imminent demolition of her house to make way for a new street in Paris. The whole Haussmann scheme was too geometric, she felt, and would ruin the character of the city as well as making her homeless. More seriously, she was affected by the increasing distance between herself and Liszt's children. All three were showing a growing preference for their father, continuing to see only his musical genius and forgiving him for his neglect. Cosima referred ironically to her mother as the Author, and Blandine felt that Marie had given them little affection. In Blandine's eyes their mother liked them only for their cleverness and social grace and not out of true maternal instinct, and there was probably a grain of truth in her criticism.

One should not condemn Marie for an attitude which was more prevalent in her time than in ours, with its cult of maternal guilt. Liszt was partly to blame for the situation, and it is significant that her relationship with Claire was satisfactory owing to the goodwill of Charles. Despite Marie's bad reputation as a wife, she had found Claire an aristocratic husband named Guy de Charnacé, whose provincial parents were aware of neither the elopement scandal nor her political writings. It was Claire herself who revealed the murky past, upon which they reacted with shock and cut off contact. Guy de Charnacé was a charming young man, though he was somewhat obsessed with improving French livestock. As a consequence, he spent much time in England buying rams and stallions, even when his wife was pregnant with their first child. When Claire naturally complained to her mother, she was disappointed to receive a lecture on the importance of scientific progress. The situation worsened when Guy's agricultural zeal led him to financial ruin; at one point personal relations become so strained that Claire proclaimed that she would rather live in prison than with her husband. On this occasion Marie did the decent thing and provided a tem-

porary home for Claire and her little grandson, Daniel. Some years later
Claire and her husband reconciled and henceforth lived together without
major dramas. Marie continued to like Guy, who was often in her salon.
He belonged to that interesting category of men whose most successful
relationship is with their mother-in-law.

During these family events Marie continued to take an active interest
in politics. Louis-Napoleon Bonaparte's seizure of power in 1851 had been
followed by his elevation to the position of emperor, with the grand title
Napoleon III. Marie's opinion of the new ruler was as low as ever, and her
salon was one of the meeting places of the moderate opposition. Her letters to the Herweghs were regular commentaries on events: she was sad to
report that the majority of the nation supported the new imperial regime
in spite of its illegal origin. The emperor had gained cheap popularity by
military adventures in Italy, Algeria, and the Crimea. The economy was
booming and the nation appeared to be enjoying stability after a period of
turmoil and fear.

The peace had been disrupted early in 1858 by a dreadful assassination
attempt on Napoleon III as he and his wife, Eugénie, made their way to the
opera for a gala performance. The leader was the Italian revolutionary Felice
Orsini, the same man who in 1856 had made a dramatic escape from a prison
in Mantua using the saws sent by Emma Herwegh. During Marie's recent
trip to Italy, she had been amused to see that some newspapers had actually attributed the deed to her, and her denials had only produced knowing
smiles. After his escape, Orsini had settled for a time in London, where he
enjoyed some celebrity and published his memoirs. He then moved to Paris
with the intention of killing Napoleon III because of his support of conservative regimes in Italy. On the evening of 14 January, as the three imperial
coaches drew up in front of the illuminated theater, Orsini and his accom-
plices emerged from the crowd and threw bombs at them from close range.
At once the gaslights were shattered and the street became a scene of dark
horror full of dead and wounded. Although the coach of Napoleon III had
been struck by seventy-six metal fragments, the imperial couple emerged
unscathed. The assassins escaped in the confusion but were captured the
next day.

Orsini behaved with dignity during his trial, which he used to publicize the cause of Italian unity and freedom. On 13 March he was executed, the details of which Marie sent to Emma. The authorities, fearing disturbances, had spread a false rumor that the sentence would be commuted; the guillotine was nonetheless set up in a small square early in the morning while a force of ten thousand soldiers held back the crowd that quickly assembled. Some onlookers climbed trees and relayed news as the event progressed. Hats were removed, and a respectful silence fell when Orsini emerged from the prison van with his arms tied behind him and walked toward his death. Marie reported an unconfirmed rumor that the Austrian ambassador had reserved a good seat and told Emma there was widespread admiration for the courage and idealism of her protégé. Napoleon III had seized power by a similar act of violence, she added sarcastically, and had been absolved because of the form of justification known as success. Despite her preference for moderate methods Marie was attracted to revolutionaries and men of action. She maintained a correspondence, for example, with Louis Blanc, Lajos Kossuth, and Giuseppe Mazzini, whose letters were sometimes read out loud in her salon.

The Orsini drama made her want to renew contact with Georg and Emma Herwegh, and in May 1858 she told them of her intention to spend some time in Zurich. The stay would also be a family reunion, since Claire would stop there on her way to Munich for an art exhibition and Cosima would come with her husband for part of July. Asking Georg for advice about lodgings, Marie claimed that recent events and bad investments had reduced her to poverty. This meant that she would bring only one maid, though she did not envisage actual hardship. She would like three rooms in the Hôtel Bauer, preferably sunny, one being for the maid; she would take breakfast in her own rooms and other meals in the dining room. Her talk of poverty was evidently an overstatement, since she could still enjoy the pleasures of the cosmopolitan rich. This stay in Zurich was significant because it led to her first meeting with Wagner, who was staying in the home of mutual friends; one evening he sat at the piano and entertained them with extracts from the *Ring of the Nibelung*. Marie at first considered him to be charmless and obsessed by his music, but this opinion would radically change one day. The composer endeared himself a little by declaring himself to be an admirer of Blandine, whom he had met in the company of Liszt in

Weimar. Marie observed that he showed little interest in Cosima, which is strange in the light of future events.

Marie's literary output had not ceased, and in 1857 she had entered new territory by composing *Jeanne Darc,* a play on the life of Joan of Arc, a female martyr with whom she felt some affinity. In May of that year the work reached the bookshops — and showed much reluctance to leave them. It was not good enough to be performed in Paris and brought confirmation of the sad truth that nature had not intended her to be either a dramatist or a novelist. At least she could feel confident in her ability as a journalist and historian, and her activity in these areas continued fruitfully with a series of articles entitled "Letters from Italy," which appeared in the influential Paris newspaper *Le Siècle* between November 1859 and July 1860. These articles gave such eloquent support to the cause of Italian unification that on 16 May, when she was in Turin, she was granted an interview with Camillo Cavour, who was already one of the leading political figures in Europe. An audience with Victor Emmanuel II of Piedmont followed on June 10, and Marie was able to converse with a man whom she admired as the embodiment of a modern monarch. Her cup of joy was full when the state theater in Turin staged her play. It ran only two nights, but the first performance was attended by the king himself. This was no bearded and desperate conspirator like Orsini but a powerful ruler who accepted the need for a progressive move toward democracy. It was men like Victor Emmanuel II who would lead to the overthrow of the unenlightened despots of Europe, she felt. Although his sexual appetite was notorious, he was a devout Catholic and could be expected to unseat the pope in a properly respectful manner.

At this time Marie was making a contribution to a new periodical called *La Revue Germanique,* which had been founded in Paris in 1858 by her friends Charles Dollfuss and Auguste Nefftzer. Its aim was to inform readers of the intellectual activity of contemporary Germany, a useful undertaking at a time when the prevailing attitude of the French toward nations across the Rhine was one of disinterest. With her cosmopolitan education Marie was naturally disposed to contribute, as did her daughter Claire. Renan, Littré, and Taine were also willing to participate. Cosima for her part agreed to provide translations, as she did not feel confident in her ability to write articles. Marie's suggestion that Herwegh contribute was politely rejected because of the continuing association of his name with revolutionary activity. She encouraged the review to attack religious superstition and clericalism by publicizing the works of radical German thinkers like David Strauss. It was time to resume the work of Madame de Staël, she told Georg, and to show the French nation that its was not the only literature in Europe.[4] The ideal would be a combination of French elegance and German rigor. In the following years Marie would publish a significant part of her literary productions in *La Revue Germanique.*[5]

Although the period 1858–62 was marked by success in the field of literature and journalism, it was a time of new difficulty in her family life. Emile Ollivier continued to look on her suspiciously and considered her to be calculating, a judgment which he would totally revise in years to come and which evidently owed something to the influence of Liszt on Blandine. Marie would have been horrified had she known that her son, Daniel, had sarcastically described her as Goethe without the genius and had expressed pleasure at the thought that her house in Paris had been flattened by her enemy, Napoleon III. At least Cosima still admired the mother who had defied convention by seeing them openly and by introducing them to their legitimate sibling, Claire.

The first real disaster struck the family in the winter of 1859, when Daniel died at the age of twenty, not having seen his mother for three years. In Vienna he had been a diligent student of law, although he did not like the subject and had announced a vast project which was nothing less than a history of religion. Cosima had found him very pale when he arrived in Berlin for a holiday in the summer of 1859, and soon he began to spit blood and took to bed with the symptoms of advanced tuberculosis. Marie did not go to Berlin, perhaps fearing a rebuff or an encounter with Liszt, who arrived just before the end. The gifted but unfortunate Daniel died quietly in the arms of Cosima.

In spite of her absence from his bedside, Marie was deeply affected by the loss of her son. Indeed the death of Daniel after years of alienation may have been one of the causes of the depression which hit her in the summer of 1860 and lasted several months. It is interesting to note that she experienced it as a physical symptom and recorded its appearance in her diary.

She described it tentatively as a malfunction of the brain caused by either an excess of blood or a lack of blood.[6] She continued to follow the advice of her doctor, Eugène Dally, and eventually made a recovery which was duly attributed to his skill. Marie then followed the tradition of the ailing rich by spending the winter of 1860–61 on the Riviera. She was accompanied by Claire and was disturbed to see that her daughter was having a furtive affair with the appropriately named physician, who had followed her to Nice. Claire was now thirty and did not respond favorably when her mother advised caution, instead reminding her of her own youthful elopement. Marie stressed the social difficulties of a delinquent wife and the impact of a love affair on the reputation of a doctor, but her advice was given in vain and Claire continued to enjoy the pleasures which were clearly not provided by Guy de Charnacé, despite his good manners. One assumes that Marie privately reflected on a characteristic which had driven so many women of her family to defy convention in their pursuit of love.

In 1861 she met Franz for the first time in many years. He was in Paris for the first night of Wagner's *Tannhäuser* and had been shocked when members of the aristocratic Jockey Club had hissed the performance. The prospect of the meeting stirred deep emotions in Marie, and in a series of troubled dreams she relived episodes from their past. The years of separation had raised new barriers between them. For one thing Marie did not appreciate his recent compositions, which lacked the charm of his early music. She was also disappointed by his admiration of the unprincipled Napoleon III and again asked herself what had become of the idealistic and democratic Franz she had once known. She had written to Cosima saying that she would like to see her father during his stay in Paris. Liszt had made it known that he would do so only if he received a direct personal invitation, upon which Marie at once wrote to him.

When he called on her in the apartment she was renting in the Hôtel Montaigne, she noticed that his face had aged but was still handsome and that his movements had remained youthful. His eyes no longer shone with the old passion, however, and there was sadness in his expression. Remarkably, there was no mention of their children during their first meeting. Instead they spoke of episodes in their life in which Puzzi, George Sand, and Lehmann had played a part. He surprised her by claiming that he had always taken her side in her quarrel with George, as a consequence of which his relations with the novelist remained cool. Marie's emotional state was intense when Franz departed, and that night she slept little. They had agreed to have lunch with friends the following week, and when they left the table to go to the salon she linked arms with him. She would never have imagined that one day they would converse politely like mere acquaintances. Perhaps it was the fate of some great passions to end in banality, she reflected. When they met for a third time, the tone was more intimate, and they talked about Cosima and Blandine. She impulsively went and embraced him when he rose to go. After this emotionally charged meeting, Liszt sent Carolyne a carefully arranged version of the event, according to which he had provided Marie with a complete justification of his past actions, personality, and ambitions. He reported that he had asked for God's blessing on her, and that Marie had been in tears when he left.[7]

The next tragic episode in her life occurred unexpectedly in the summer of 1862, when Blandine died at the age of twenty-four, after the birth of a baby boy. She had left Paris and traveled south in order to have the delivery supervised by her husband's brother, who was an experienced doctor. On 3 July she gave birth to a baby she named Daniel, after her brother who had died. Although there had been no apparent problems, after the birth she began to suffer from weakness, insomnia, and fever. In a few weeks her condition became so bad that she was unable to feed the baby. Blandine died in the village of Saint-Tropez two months after the delivery, twice repeating the child's name with her last breath.[8] The impact of the event was all the greater for Marie because of the unfortunate period of discord between herself and a daughter she had not seen for three years. In a flood of memories she recalled Blandine's gentle voice, her charm and beauty, and the brief period when she had graced her home in Paris. For days she remained in bed, lacking the will to face the world, clinging to the hope that somehow the soul of Blandine had survived and that she could feel her mother's love. In the end she went to Vittel to take the waters and was able to recover some of her spirit.

Marie had received an unexpected letter from George Sand expressing affection and saying that she had been moved by the news of her bereavement. It was from true friends like Louis de Ronchaud, however, that Marie drew real comfort. In a letter to Emma Herwegh, she reflected that life is divided into stages: youth is a time that brings people together; then comes a period when they become distant from one another. She wished she could be in Zurich to talk to Emma of the troubles in their lives, but their separation too seemed fated.[9] It was now the summer of 1863, and Marie was again on her way to Italy with a group of friends. She unwisely stopped at Bellagio, which increased her melancholy because of remembrances of her happy days there with Liszt.

In spite of the disenchanted comment to Emma, Marie was far from isolated. Although she still preferred the company of males, she was also in regular contact with Hortense Allart, whose loyalty had been proven over many years. Hortense was probably the only woman to whom Marie spoke openly about her experiences with Liszt. She was one of those friends who give honest advice, and when Marie wrote an article critical of a new composition by Liszt, and encouraged Guy de Charnacé to publish it under his name, Hortense tried in vain to stop her. The fact that Liszt was a swine did not negate his musical genius, said Hortense, and posterity would be severe on his critics. There was much difference of opinion between Marie and Hortense, who had remained approximately Catholic, whereas Marie was strongly anticlerical and leaned toward skepticism. Hortense had also continued to believe in monarchy, quite unlike Marie. Yet she had the rare quality of being devoid of envy, and despite her own obscurity as a writer she did not begrudge her friend's success. In her loyalty she made several attempts to persuade Sainte-Beuve, her former lover, to devote an article to Marie's books, but in vain. This was his petty revenge on the woman who had refused to be his mistress, and the critic would maintain this despicable policy until his death. Hortense had also tried to achieve a reconciliation between Marie and George Sand but had failed because of Sand's reluctance. In addition to her warmth and generosity, the witty Hortense had the ability to make Marie laugh. These two women had much in common: both had infringed upon the laws of society in their love life, and both had known the pleasures and tribulations of a literary career.

Marie had also formed a new friendship with Juliette Lamber, a young woman with literary ambitions who seems to have played the role of substitute daughter for a time. Juliette had published a book that criticized the socialist Proudhon and spoke favorably of the writings of Marie, who consequently invited her to her home, where she soon became a favorite. Juliette too had had an unhappy marriage and had turned to writing as a consolation. Marie eagerly accepted the task of being her literary and personal counselor, encouraged her young talent with practical advice on style, and provided introductions to publishers. Juliette reciprocated with much admiration, even revealing that the novel *Nélida* had had such impact on her that she had considered suicide. Marie advised her wisely about the avoidance of pedantry and the desirability of keeping quiet about books until they had actually been published. Above all, she should not produce her work in a rush. Patience and modesty should be the guiding principles of a serious writer, especially a woman, she told her. It seems that Juliette listened politely to all this good advice and then did exactly as she pleased. She did, however, express her gratitude by dedicating the novel *Mon village* to Marie, and the two remained friends for a number of years. Juliette was later widowed and remarried, as Juliette Adam. Eventually they ceased to see each other because of the political orientation of her new husband.[10]

The period around 1860 was decidedly a good one for friendship in Marie's life, because it was at this time that she met Louise Ackermann, another woman writer to whom she gave generous help.[11] Her attention had been aroused by a collection of stories published by this fortyish widow who lived in Nice and who had been happily married until tuberculosis took her husband, Paul Ackermann, a distinguished scholar. Aware of Marie's reputation, Louise had at first been alarmed by her overtures, but when they met her attitude changed dramatically and a lasting bond formed between them. Their friendship had a partly ideological basis, for Louise was a scientific freethinker who had taken a strongly anticlerical stance and considered God her personal enemy.

Marie expressed her admiration for her robust new friend in an article of 8 June 1863 in *Le Temps*. In fact there were differences of opinion between them. Louise Ackermann's thoughts about the position of women were diametrically opposed to Marie's, as she believed their main function was reproduction and not intellectual activity. Happiness for a woman was to be found in marriage. Her adored husband would never have allowed her to wear a dress which exposed her bosom, she explained, and he would have been even more determined to stop her from publishing poetry, which was another form of self-revelation. Fortunately she did not put these principles into practice but instead went ahead and made for herself a small niche in literature. In this undertaking she was helped by Marie, who introduced the provincial muse into her Paris salon, where she met Littré, whom she admired, and Renan, whom she wittily described as a closet cleric. Louise had a sound instinct and was frank, telling Marie that her correspondent Mazzini was a drawing-room conspirator who sent others to their death. Marie managed to create relations of a sort between her new friend and Hortense Allart, though Louise viewed Hortense as a slave to sensuality, just as Hortense considered Louise to be a sad case of bourgeois convention. Marie and Louise were essentially different personalities. Marie had phases of self-obsession and neurosis, whereas Louise was as solid as a rock and soon became a close and trusted friend.

At this time in her life Marie published an ambitious work which represented her first significant experiment in literary history. After her earlier publications on music, art, social theory, and history, this was a stimulating new venture. Entitled *Dante et Goethe,* the book was a comparative study of the two great writers which required an intimate knowledge of two different cultural contexts.[12] Marie's enthusiasm for Dante was inspired partly by the poetic quality of his language and partly by his treatment of great religious and philosophical subjects. The themes of Italy and love were also of particular interest to her; the story of Dante and Beatrice struck her as a prefiguration of her experience with Liszt. Her analysis of Dante is subjective, since she tends to see him as a freethinker and a defender of political liberty in the modern sense. Her selectivity of argument and mild anachronisms, however, are balanced by the originality of many of her comments on the Italian poet. Her discussion of Goethe is more convincing and added significantly to his growing reputation in France at the time. As she wrote, she remembered with emotion the day in the Frankfurt garden when the famous writer had laid his hand on her head in a sort of benediction. Now Goethe had become her model. He too had experienced a passionate early life followed by a time of serenity. He too had fallen in love with Italy and had celebrated poetically the land where the lemon tree blooms. She admired him for his energy, his love of humanity, his intellect, his tolerance,

and his optimism. Goethe had a high conception of the female role and
knew what it was to be loved and inspired by a woman. In Marie's book one
senses a personal emotion and a wistful recollection of her own brief years
with the wayward genius to whom she had recklessly offered her life. *Dante
et Goethe* bears a moving dedication to her love child, Cosima, an appropriate gesture to the young woman who had been born in the land of Dante
and was now living in the land of Goethe.

Whether driven by temperament or fate, the life of Cosima had begun
to show a remarkable similarity to that of her mother. The circumstances of
her marriage with Hans von Bülow had already shown her to be true to the
family tradition of headstrong women pursuing happiness with unsuitable
men. Cosima's life with her gifted but manic-depressive husband was not
easy, though the marriage had survived for a number of years and she had
borne him several children. Her role seems to have been that of a sister, and
later events suggest that the sentimental young man had not provided sexual
satisfaction. Cosima was irritated by his total devotion to Wagner. It was a
sort of willing slavery shared by Wagner's mild wife and his eccentric mistress, Mathilda Wesendonck. Hans had persuaded Cosima that they should
live in Weimar for greater proximity to his idol. So they moved there. One
summer, Marie rented a house in Zurich and joined the group. While there
she met Wagner again and enjoyed several evenings of musical entertainment by these outstanding performers. Wagner, who had been impressed
by Marie's intelligence and distinguished manners, provided an account of
the meeting in a letter to Liszt.[13] The attraction between them was mutual,
though the composer did not mention to Liszt that he had willingly accepted her invitation to see her during future visits to Paris. The attraction
between Wagner and Cosima was even greater, and they became lovers.

One wonders if Marie sensed that her daughter had fallen for the devi-
ous but manly genius. In 1865 Cosima bore Wagner a daughter, whom they
called Isolde, and the following year she continued in her mother's footsteps
by leaving her husband and living openly with Wagner. Their situation was
made easier by the fact that they were not in a Catholic country and could
obtain a divorce by consent. Cosima kept the Bülow children and married
Wagner in 1869, after which she bore him two more children. The two continued happily together for years. Unlike her mother, Cosima had found it

Cosima Liszt.

possible to live with the eccentricity of genius. Wagner never ceased to admire Marie, in spite of the influence of Liszt, and would always send her first editions of his works. She made frequent visits to their home in Bayreuth, and Cosima remained loyal in her affection. Marie was sorry to observe that her daughter was becoming progressively Germanic in attitude, and their different reactions to the Franco-Prussian War would cause disagreement between them.

During the decade 1860–70 Marie's salon continued to be a center of intellectual opposition to Napoleon III, and she noted with satisfaction that, except within rural France, the regime was losing popularity. Among intellectuals and the industrial proletariat discontent grew steadily like a rising tide, and clever satirists like Henri de Rochefort exerted considerable influence, despite restrictions on the press. In response to the increasing unpopularity of his regime, Napoleon decided to reject the opinions of his wife and other reactionaries and play the liberal card. He consequently invited Emile Ollivier to form a cabinet. Marie's son-in-law had already alienated himself from her political friends by his gradual acceptance of the detested regime and now fully expected to be despised as a renegade. On his way to Compiègne for furtive meetings with the emperor, Ollivier removed his glasses and hid his face with a scarf to avoid recognition. A deal was finally struck, and he became prime minister of France in January 1870. He could have chosen a better moment, as the regime was about to collapse like a pack of cards from the onslaught of the Prussian army. Ollivier imprudently earned himself a niche in history by telling Parliament he awaited the war with cheerful confidence.

The defeat of France in 1870 was a bitter experience for Marie because of her family background and cosmopolitan culture. She also suffered psychologically during this time: the previous autumn she had had a fit of depression so severe that her daughter Claire had feared a lapse into madness. The political events of 1870 at least had the merit of distracting her from her personal troubles. When war broke out in July, she was staying at the country estate of Louis de Ronchaud in Saint-Lupicin, in the Jura region. Marie was following her usual custom of rising early to enjoy the birds and trees in the gardens. As she strode the country lanes, she exchanged greetings with workers in the fields. Apparently serene and at peace with the world, by summer she showed no sign of her recent depression.

She learned of the war from the French newspapers, most of which had encouraged patriotic sentiment and war fever. As a consequence the streets of Paris had been full of intoxicated crowds certain that the French army would soon make a triumphal entry into Berlin. Marie had a more accurate sense of Prussian power, and the defeat of France did not cause her great surprise. To her mind there were two Germanies: Beethoven's and Bismarck's, and the northern warlike nation was now alarmingly dominant. Letters brought news of life in the capital as Paris prepared for a siege. Anxious residents of the suburbs were flocking inside the fortifications, and herds of sheep and cattle grazed in the elegant Bois de Boulogne, in the expectation of hungry days ahead.

She naturally decided to remain in Saint-Lupicin during the conflict, though she commented publicly on events in an article of 13 September 1870 in *Le Temps*. Enlightened opinion held that war between France and the German states had become a thing of the past, she reflected, but the old fatality still pursued them. Despite her links with Germany she felt passionately French in this time of crisis. Prussia had no justification in prolonging the war once it had deposed Napoleon III, she argued, with more hope than logic. Her article also expressed the optimistic thought that Britain, Italy, and Austria might intervene to save France from humiliation. In the *Journal de Genève* of 30 October she published a second article stressing the peaceful intentions of Ollivier and blaming the conflict completely on Bismarck and Napoleon III. French pride had deserved punishment, but it was now urgent to stop the fighting and make a peace treaty which would not itself become the cause of a future conflict, she shrewdly argued.

During the siege of Paris she was shocked by reports of the violence of the Paris Commune, a recklesss attempt to impose a socialist government on France. In early 1871, she moved to Divonne, in the vicinity of neutral Geneva, where she could obtain reliable news. She discussed events with her old friend Adolphe Pictet and continued to correspond with acquaintances on both sides of the Rhine. Wishing to express an opinion about the political regime best suited to France, she published another article in *Le Temps* on 13 March. What an astonishing variety of systems France had known between 1792 and 1871, she observed. Far from having acquired wisdom, the nation was again adrift, and one could only hope for a new generation of moderate politicians. Napoleon III had used plebiscites in a manner which stultified public opinion. A democratic regime offered hope because it wanted public opinion to be truly informed, she argued persuasively. Returning to Paris in September, she had the satisfaction of seeing that the new republic had survived for a year. She was worried, however, by the efforts of the Catholic Church to regain lost ground and by the possible return of Napoleon III from England. Another dangerous exile was the comte de Chambord, who was also conducting negotiations in the hope of returning to a throne which he still claimed by divine right. Marie need not have feared this outcome, because the grandson of Charles X had inherited all the political ineptitude of his grandfather and soon alienated public opinion with his fanaticism.

When Marie returned to Paris, the Republic had defeated the Commune, whose leaders had either been shot or put in prison, and had obtained peace by sacrificing the provinces of Alsace and Lorraine to the new German empire. She observed the continuing survival of the precarious regime with anxious relief. The new prime minister, Adolphe Thiers, had wittily asserted that monarchists like himself were the best managers of a republic, and there seemed to be much truth in his statement. He was the perfect pragmatist, untroubled by theories or principles. Marie was still worried about the new clerical offensive based on the cult of the Virgin Mary. Ambitious priests were encouraging pilgrimages to Lourdes and making much of the allegedly miraculous cure of a baker's wife from Champdeniers. How could people believe such things in the day of Cuvier and Darwin?

After an absence of seventeen months, it was not possible for her to reestablish a salon immediately, and she accepted a temporary home with her daughter Claire. In letters to Ollivier, who was now residing in Italy under a false name, she told of the remarkable recovery of France from defeat. Although Paris was full of ruins because of the Commune, the people seemed full of vitality and were quickly repairing the damage. After a year of anxiety and shortages, they were eager to enjoy life again. Some had expected hunger and bankruptcy, but the harvest had been exceptional, the war indemnity was being paid, and the streets were free of trouble. Political power was in the hands of moderates, and there was hope that the nation would resist the intrigues of priests and communists.[14] Even though the war had affected the stock market, and therefore her income, she was able to resume her role as a hostess. The list of distinguished visitors now included a rising political star named Jules Grévy, soon to become prime minister. Once again, her home had become one of the significant centers of intellectual life in Paris. In the rue Malesherbes, near the fashionable Parc Monceau, Marie could be seen walking beneath the chestnut trees in her black silk dress. At sixty-six, she still gave an impression of youth and energy as she strolled in the park where mothers watched their children play.

The political opinions she had expressed in 1848 seemed less radical since the return to a republic, and as a consequence the French Academy saw fit to honor her with a literary prize in 1872. The award was given for *Histoire des commencements de la République aux Pays-Bas, 1581–1625,* a historical study of the first Dutch republic, published that same year. This recognition of her status as a historian gave her much satisfaction, not least because she knew that some members of the highly conservative institution still considered her *History of the Revolution of 1848* to be dangerously subversive in its sympathy for democracy and the proletariat. A study of events in the sixteenth century was clearly less controversial, even though it recorded the fanaticism of the Catholic Inquisition in Holland. For the most part Marie's new book had a favorable reception by the press, though it drew a tasteless attack from the reactionary Barbey d'Aurévilly, who sprang to the defense of Phillip II and claimed that Marie reminded him of some dessicated and pedantic English governess.[15] Women should not be anticlerical or support female emancipation but should stick to making jam, and if they could not contain the literary urge, they should limit themselves to novels, he advised. Eager to add a touch of personal insult, the critic went on to express his astonishment at the number of men who had admired Marie's cold beauty and to speculate that she must have been a difficult mistress. One can imagine the delight that Liszt and Carolyne would have taken in this ridiculous article—and it is more than likely that one of their friends in Paris sent it to them. Marie could console herself with the thought that a despicable attack brings no credit to its author.

Marie d'Agoult, by Adam-Salomon, 1861.

(Réunion des Musées nationaux)

Pleased with the generally positive response to her new book, she resumed work on a historical study of a very different nature. She had started writing her memoirs several years earlier, having been encouraged to do so by several friends, including Hortense Allart, who had already published a version of her own adventures.[16] Hortense had tried to help Marie's personal literary project by repairing her old friendship with George Sand, after a long period during which they had done nothing more than exchange formal notes. Louis de Ronchaud, who was also involved, was sent to ask if George would collaborate in the publication of correspondence exchanged with Marie during their time of intimacy. The novelist refused and sent him away, falsely claiming that she had burned all her letters in case they fell into the hands of the Prussians. To make her feel better, Marie's friends told her George was jealous, old, and fat. Her way of dressing was as bad as ever, they reported, and she now looked like those bulky ladies who sold canaries in the Paris bird market.

It seemed that former friendship could not be revived, any more than lost love, and the aging Marie reflected deeply on past events as she planned her memoirs. With the death of her daughter Louise so long ago, followed by the loss of Blandine and Daniel, three of her five children had gone before her into death's dark region. She had also lost her loyal friend Alfred de Vigny, and the next leaf to fall from the tree was her brother, who died of cholera in October 1873. Maurice de Flavigny, who placed personal advancement above all other considerations, had served a series of regimes as diplomat and politician. He had cheerfully accepted the lion's share of their mother's fortune; that Marie forgave him this is another indication of her generous nature. Despite Maurice's conventional and superficial character, she had always appreciated his charm and affection, qualities which had remained constant since the happy days of their country childhood.

Around this time she received news from Cosima and other sources of new escapades by Liszt. To the astonishment of those who did not know him well, the composer had entered holy orders and made vows of chastity and obedience. With a wry smile Marie reflected on the changes brought by time. She had become Daniel Stern, and Franz was now Father Liszt. Just as Marie had predicted, Carolyne had been made an unwilling member of the Ariadne club. Remarkably, Carolyne too had taken to literature and now sat smoking cigars and writing volumes critical of the pope. Liszt was sharing himself between the Vatican and the Budapest Conservatory of Music, where he gave master classes to a cosmopolitan group of young pianists. He nevertheless had enough time and energy for a new series of sexual adventures, notably with an enterprising harlot named Olga de Janina, who quickly seized her chance to make money by publishing, under a pseudonym, a lurid account of her experiences with Liszt.[17] Her story confirmed Liszt's incorrigible character, but the ridiculous affair can have given Marie no pleasure.

She felt very different emotions in March 1875, when news came of the death of Charles d'Agoult. To her old friend Pictet in Geneva she wrote movingly about the character of her husband: "I have just been shaken by one of those events which stir one to the depths of one's thoughts and conscience. M. d'Agoult passed away on March 18 in his eighty-fifth year. For some time he knew his end was near, and awaited it with the simple patience of a soldier and with Christian resignation. But he was spared the anguish of the final hour. Neither he, nor anyone, not even the doctor, saw it coming. He showed no sign of suffering or final convulsion. To all who knew him he leaves the memory of a perfect gentleman. In difficult situations I have always found him loyal, decent, generous. I mourn him with respect and my deep regret is that I could not equal his spirit of abnegation and loyalty."[18] Not many months later came the news that Adolphe Pictet himself had died, another reminder that her turn might come soon. Although she had little time for conventional religion, she believed in the existence of a God and was not without hope that the soul might live on. She had an irrational fear of falling into a deathlike coma and being buried alive and thought that a bell should be placed beside all corpses so that they could ring for help. The idea never became common practice, although one ingenious British inventor did design such a coffin. It seems that Marie was not alone in her anxiety and her lack of faith in doctors.

By the start of 1876 she had completed the biblical span of seventy years and still showed considerable energy when not suffering from her recurring bouts of depression. She was looking to the future and working on new editions of her *Esquisses morales* and her *Histoire de la révolution de 1848*. Her memoirs still needed to be completed, in particular the moving episodes of her years in Italy with Liszt and possibly the account of their separation. These pages were destined to remain unwritten, because death struck her down on the sixth day of March in the year 1876. Marie was working quietly in her study on this spring day when she was suddenly affected by a pulmonary congestion which killed her in a few hours.

In a gesture to the religion of her childhood, she had expressed the wish to have a Lutheran minister at her funeral, which was granted. Her body was buried in the Père-Lachaise cemetery, with Ernest Renan and Emile de Girardin among the mourners. She was missed most by Claire and Cosima but also by Louis de Ronchaud, to whom she left all her papers. She had asked him to look after her affairs, which he did with his usual dedication. In her will she asked Claire to make certain she was actually dead before they buried her and also requested that Claire pay forty thousand francs to her half-sister, Cosima, who, as an illegitimate daughter, had no formal rights. Marie d'Agoult was regretted by the group of friends she had created. She had demanded much and had given them much in return. When news of Marie's death reached Liszt, he made an ungracious comment about the pains she had caused him. The woman who had loved him lay in the grave, and even now he could not find a generous word to honor her memory.

Much of the French press paid tribute to the female writer who, after George Sand, had contributed most to contemporary French literature. It was clear that Marie's historical and social writing would remain important works. Her *Histoire de la révolution de 1848* had several editions in her lifetime and became a minor classic. Her *Essai sur la liberté* and her *Esquisses morales* have an enduring interest. They reflect the idealism of 1848 and express an essential optimism based on a future society liberated from the political and religious dogmas of the repressive past. Traditional Christianity had made the mistake of denouncing the body, she believed, and the Catholic Church in particular had allied itself with superstition and reaction in every field. A new and more rational system of belief was needed. It was not enough to proclaim that humans were led by self-interest, virtue, or vice: love of beauty should be added to the list of important motives. The ability to speak the immortal language of art, music, and literature was a superior gift, a power that elevated the state of civilization. The rise of the bourgeoisie had

hindered this upward progression, she asserted, because it was more interested in money than in higher things. The literary taste of this class did not
go beyond moral comedies and trashy novels.

As for the old aristocracy, Marie never forgave it for withdrawing from
affairs after the revolution of 1830. In the new industrial society, she asserted, it could have found a respectable role as protector of the weak. In
times past the nobility had served in the armies of the king, but now it
needed to seek new avenues and become active in the universities, in industry, in Parliament. Instead, the men of this class seemed to be wasting their
time with racehorses and loose women. The old system of arranged marriages had prevailed among the aristocracy, producing cold unions which
provided neither emotional nor sensual satisfaction. In addition, the women
of that class had failed to embrace the new ideas about a more open society
which had been so influential around 1830. They spoke sarcastically of the
overdressed females among the newly dominant bourgeoisie and looked
down on these wives of bakers and industrialists who had more money than
style. Marie hoped for a collaboration between the women of the aristocracy and those of the new social elite, one in which some degree of past
elegance might be regained.

Marie still believed that the improvement of conditions for the proletariat was the crucial challenge of the century. The rich had little knowledge
of this large section of society, and the literary works which portrayed it
were either crude denunciations or sentimental idealizations. The modern
worker operating a machine was no better than a slave—and was indeed
less fortunate than the slaves of antiquity, who were at least fed and clothed
by their masters. The provision of regular work, decent housing, education:
Was this a dream?

This question placed her firmly among the progressive thinkers of her
time, as did her call for female emancipation. Men and women were intrinsically different, she believed, and were designed by nature to play com-
plementary roles. The male mind was often attracted by abstract thought,
whereas females looked for tangible reality. Furthermore, there was an affinity between women and artists, as both had imaginative and emotional
natures. Marie felt that women understood men better than men understood women, because women were naturally perceptive and the centuries

during which love and marriage were their main concern had made it necessary for them to observe men closely. She also believed that women were
usually more faithful in love but thought it possible that in the future men
would emulate women in this area and add to the sum of happiness by
treating them as equals. To Marie's mind, platonic love was nothing but a
compromise, since real love involved body and soul, as had her passion for
Liszt. The most perfect sentiment is the friendship which can follow early
love, she thought wistfully. Its only rival is the affection which can exist
between a brother and a sister, a bond sealed by childhood memories, pleasantly tinged with the natural attraction of the sexes, yet free from the sense
of duty which can affect relations between a husband and wife.

As for friendship with men — her greatest success in the realm of human
relations — Marie considered few women of her time capable of it, because
they were accustomed to a relationship in which one partner or the other
held power. She was convinced that social equality and female emancipation would one day be achieved in France, though it would take time. The
process would necessarily start with the provision of proper education for
girls, who must be freed from the influence of nuns in convent schools,
where they were taught the ideal of a sexless woman who was fearful of
hell, ashamed of her own body, obedient to priests, and ready to be their
agent even in the conjugal bed:

> But the laws and customs which do not give women a reasonable role
> in social life have not destroyed the instinct which tells them they too
> are free creatures. Having been refused legitimate ways win to indepen-
> dence, and the road to intellectual emancipation being closed, they have
> been thrown into the devious method of coquetry. Among women in
> civilized society it had become a science as profound as politics. Because
> they have much time on their hands they have learned to use the desires
> of men in order to enslave them, at least for a time, and all their faculties
> of observation and calculation are used to inspire love without sharing it,
> to arouse passion without satisfying it. . . . Men complain bitterly about
> this coquettry from which they suffer, at least in their youth. But they
> alone have caused the problem. They would like loyal behavior, and they
> are right, because loyalty is the basis of domestic virtues; but one cannot
> have loyalty without strength and reason, and they have kept women in
> a state of puerile weakness. Coquettry is their revenge. Give women a

proper way to satisfy their just desire for intellectual equality, and they will take it.[19]

It was not enough to teach young women music and social graces or to encourage a blind piety which was not expected from young men, she added. If women were offered a full education, they could progressively enter professional and political life. All reasonable men understood this premise, she claimed, though the radical theories of some feminists like Saint-Simon and Fourier had harmed the cause. Freedom was one of the great sources of happiness in society, and men had much to gain from the emancipation of women. Delilah was not a suitable model for the female of the future, she asserted with some humor.

Marie's memoirs, entitled *Mes souvenirs, 1806–1833,* contain a softened and indirect version of this feminist argument, though her major subject is her childhood and youth. After a charming evocation of the time in Frankfurt and the French countryside comes a critical account of her years in the Paris convent school and the sad story of her arranged marriage. Her comments on the old aristocracy and her description of the court of Charles X are an elegant piece of political subversion. The aristocracy, which had awaited the publication of the memoirs with trepidation, was much relieved when they read a book which, though critical of blind conservatism and social abdication, spoke of its traditional ethic of sociability, loyalty, and courage. This was a sincere homage from the countess who had rejected her class and transformed herself into an advocate of democracy and the proletariat.

Readers of the memoirs were disappointed not to find an account of her elopement and the years with Liszt. She had intended to relate the great drama of her life in a later volume, but death cut her down before she could complete it. Her papers contained fragments of the story, which were eventually published by Blandine's son, Daniel Ollivier, long after her death.[20] Marie carefully explained for posterity the cultural context in which she had recklessly left her husband and child in order to dedicate her life to a musician. In France the decade 1830–40 was marked by upheaval and renewal, by doubt and idealism, by dissatisfaction and ambition. The passion of Marie and Franz reflected the emotions of the era. His music too showed the Romantic spirit: intense, wayward, lyrical, and dramatic. In their happy years it reflected his love of Marie as they explored the mountains of Switzerland and the lakes of Lombardy. During this period of their lives they had believed in their lucky star.

Although disappointed by Franz, Marie had forgiven him much. The unfinished fragments of her memoirs show that she intended to give a moving and generous account of their life together. It was to be a story devoid of bitterness, a tale touched by the hand of art. The hardest part had been his later hostility and cruel efforts to alienate her children. She believed the story of their love was timeless, despite its sad ending. Like the tale of Heloïse, it had lifted her above the common destiny, bringing celebrity and drama. After the break with Liszt, she had created another life as a writer of serious literature and had won respect as one of the leading historians of the time. In spite of this one senses she would have given it all up for the love of Liszt, and secretly she probably never ceased to relive the years of passion. After her death she was overshadowed by Liszt and repeatedly denigrated by his admirers. It can be said that Marie d'Agoult was less tender and emotional than some women. She was also very proud, but this was part of her strength. The daughter of Flavigny had remained true to her nature and had based her life on more than motherhood. She had been born rich and talented, seemingly destined to a life of ease, but her adult years had been marked by disappointment and adversity. Marie d'Agoult had fought through it with courage, and in the end she died at her desk like a soldier in battle.

Notes

CHAPTER 1: *A Soldier's Daughter*

1. *Mémoires, souvenirs et journaux de la comtesse d'Agoult,* ed. Charles F. Dupêchez, vol. 1 (Paris: Mercure de France, 1990), 48. The memoirs of Marie d'Agoult were first published as *Mes souvenirs, 1806–1833* (Paris: Lévy, 1877). Future citations refer to the Dupêchez edition.

2. *Campagne in Frankreich,* in *Goethe Werke,* vol. 10 (Munich: Beck, 1982), 235–36. See also Ramsey W. Phipps, *The Armies of the First French Republic* (London: Oxford University Press, 1926), 111–35.

3. A. B. Rodger, *The War of the Second Coalition, 1798 to 1801* (Oxford: Clarendon Press, 1964), 247–48.

CHAPTER 2: *The Fall of Napoleon*

1. The mansion in which Marie lived was demolished by its owner in the late nineteenth century and replaced by a new house, which is not open to the public.

2. Interesting details are given by Laure d'Abrantès in her *Mémoires* (Paris: Ladvocat, 1831–35).

3. George Sand, *Histoire de ma vie,* vol. 1 (Paris: Gallimard, 1970), 739.

4. Walter Scott, *Life of Napoleon Buonaparte,* vol. 8, 162. The first edition of this biography appeared in 1827, and the work is included in *The Miscellaneous Prose Works of Sir Walter Scott* (Edinburgh: Robert Cadell, 1835). The title of Chateaubriand's pamphlet is *De Buonaparte et des Bourbons.*

CHAPTER 3: *The Ways of the World*

1. *Goethe et Bettina* (Paris: Gosselin, 1843). Correspondence translated into French by Hortense Cornu. Letter written on 7 August 1808 and quoted by Marie d'Agoult, *Mémoires,* 1:69–71.

2. Jean Lucas-Dubreton, *La Restauration et la monarchie de juillet* (Paris: Hachette, 1937), 21–22.

3. Joseph Lancaster (1778–1838) was a pioneer in teaching methods that he applied to the poor of London, where the good order and cheerfulness of his schools made an impression. He attracted the support of powerful patrons, and his system was much copied. Fame proved to be too much for him, however, and he became vain and reckless, eventually going bankrupt. In 1818 he emigrated to the United States, where he enjoyed early success before falling into debt again. His life ended dramatically when he was run over by a carriage in New York City.

4. Jacques Vier, *La comtesse d'Agoult et son temps* (Paris: Armand Colin, 1955–63), 18–19.

5. Théodore Leclercq, *Proverbes dramatiques* (Paris: Le Normant, 1823–26). There were many editions of these popular works. Joseph Fiévée was the author of a very successful novel: *La dot de Suzette* (Paris: Maradan, 1798). He also published a number of other books, including serious works on political themes.

6. *Mémoires,* 1:120.

CHAPTER 4: *Adolescence*

1. George Sand left an eloquent account of the impact of Chateaubriand on her own young imagination: "I felt that René was me. Although I had no comparable anxiety in my life, and did not inspire any passion which could cause me horror and despair, I felt weighed down by a weariness with life which seemed to have sufficient justification in the nothingness of human concerns. I was already sick; I then experienced what happens to people who look up their illness in medical books. In my imagination I was infected by all the maladies described in this cheerless story" (*Histoire de ma vie* [Paris: Gallimard, 1970], 1092).

2. There is a similarity between Marie's account of convent school and that of her future friend George Sand, who claimed that she too had a phase of religious fervor. Her autobiography relates a mystical experience in the dim light of the chapel in her convent school: "It was getting late, the bell had been rung, and soon the church would be closed. I had forgotten everything. I do not know what was happening inside me. The air I was breathing was full of indescribable sweetness, and I was breathing it with my soul more than with my senses. Suddenly there was some change in my whole being and I had an impression of dizziness and felt that I was surrounded by a white glimmer. I thought I heard a voice whispering in my ear: *Tolle, lege*" (*Histoire de ma vie,* 1:953). The Latin words were heard by Saint Augustine on the day of his conversion, telling him to pick up the Bible and read it.

3. François de Coessin expounded his ideas in *Les neuf livres* (Paris: Leblanc, 1809).

CHAPTER 5: *Marriage French Style*

1. By this time Sophie Gay had published *Laure d'Estell* (1802), *Léonie de Montbrise* (1813), *Anatole* (1815), *Les malheurs d'un amant heureux* (1818). The poems of

Delphine Gay included *Les soeurs de Sainte-Camille, Amélie, Mademoiselle de La Vallière,* and *La vision de Jeanne Darc.* Her *Oeuvres complètes* were published in 1856.

2. A detailed account of the relations between the poet and the two women can be found in Lamartine, *Souvenirs et portraits* (Paris: Hachette, 1872), 1:375, 378–402.

3. Saint-Simon, *Mémoires* (Paris: Gallimard, 1953), 1:116.

4. It seems that most young people accepted arranged marriages quite readily, despite prolonged criticism of the system by a series of sentimental novels. In a diary entry made in November 1809, Stendhal recorded a discussion on the subject while he was vainly trying to seduce the happily married Mme Daru. She fended him off by expressing a dislike of young men and the opinion that marriages based on love did not last. These two considerations had led her to follow the established custom and accept, without question, the husband chosen by her parents. It was of course essential to consult the future bride about her preference for one or another suitor, but often this was done at a late stage, when there was already pressure to accept. Parents who did not listen to sincere objections would have been thought both unkind and imprudent. The obvious fact that willingness was better than coercion was illustrated not only by novels but also by some celebrated cases of family conflict. One striking example is illustrated by the aristocratic Cour Breton family, who tried to make their daughter marry an unwanted suitor. After endless conflict, the spirited girl allowed a date to be fixed and actually went to the church for the ceremony. When the priest at the altar asked the ritual question whether she accepted the man standing beside her as her husband, she replied with a resounding no! The episode won her sympathy and admiration, and she was eventually allowed to marry the man she loved (Stendhal, *Oeuvres intimes* [Paris: Gallimard, 1953], 1:894). Arthur Young, *Travels in France* (London: Maxwell, 1929), 167.

5. Charles d'Agoult gave a written account to his daughter, Claire. Extracts of these unpublished memoirs and letters are reproduced by Vier, *La comtesse d'Agoult,* 1:347–48. See also his study *Marie d'Agoult, son mari, ses amis* (Paris: Editions du Cèdre, 1951).

6. Vier, *La comtesse d'Agoult,* 1:84.

7. Honoré de Balzac, *La comédie humaine* (Paris: Gallimard, 1980), 11:95. *Physiologie du mariage* was published in 1828 and *La femme de trente ans* in 1834. George Sand too spoke of the problem of sudden sexual initiation. In a letter to Hippolyte Chatiron in 1843 she wrote: "See that your son-in-law does not treat your daughter brutally on their wedding-night. . . . Men are not sufficiently aware that their pleasure is our pain. Tell him to control his desire and wait until he can gradually bring his wife to understand and respond. Nothing is more terrible than the horror, the pain and the revulsion felt by a poor child who knows nothing and sees herself raped by a brute. We try to bring them up like saints, and then hand them over like fillies" (G. Sand, *Correspondance* [Paris: Garnier, 1969], 6:43).

8. *Valentia,* novella by Daniel Stern (pen name for Marie d'Agoult), first pub-

lished in the newspaper *La Presse* in 1847, then in *Nouvelles* (Paris: Michel Lévy, 1883).

9. Letters from Charles d'Agoult to Mme de Flavigny, quoted by Vier, *La comtesse d'Agoult,* 1:348, 86. The painting by Gérard was shown in the Paris Salon of 1822.

CHAPTER 6: *The Wind of Revolution*

1. Marie d'Agoult, *Mémoires,* vol. 1 (Paris: Mercure de France, 1990), 264–65.

2. Ibid., 1:244–58; Théodore Anne, *Mémoires sur l'intérieur du palais de Charles X* (Paris: Werdet, 1831); Amable de Barante, *Souvenirs* (Paris: C. Lévy, 1890–91); Odilon Barrot, *Mémoires posthumes* (Paris: Charpentier, 1875–76); Simon Bérard, *Souvenirs historiques de la révolution de 1830* (Paris: Perrotin, 1834); Jean Lucas-Dubreton, *La Restauration et la monarchie de juillet* (Paris: Hachette, 1937); Jean Lucas-Dubreton, *Le comte d'Artois* (Paris: Hachette, 1928); José Cabanis, *Charles X, roi ultra* (Paris: Gallimard, 1972); Alexandre Mazas, *Mémoires pour servir à l'histoire de la révolution de 1830* (Paris: Urbain Canel, 1832); Armand de Pontmartin, *Souvenirs d'un vieux critique* (Paris: Calmann-Lévy, 1882); Sébastien Charléty, *La Restauration* (vol. 4 of E. Lavisse, *Histoire de France contemporaine* (Paris: Hachette, 1921–22); David H. Pinkney, *The French Revolution of 1830* (Princeton: Princeton University Press, 1972); Vincent W. Beach, *Charles X of France* (Boulder: University of Colorado Press, 1971).

CHAPTER 7: *Elopement*

1. Prince François de Joinville, *Vieux souvenirs, 1818–48* (Paris: C. Lévy, 1894), 177.

2. Polignac was sentenced to life imprisonment and sent to the Ham fortress, in which he had already served time under Napoleon. He was released after six years.

3. Paul Dermoncourt, *La Vendée et Madame* (Paris: A. Guyot, 1834). Alfred Nettement, *Mémoires historiques de S.A.R. Duchesse de Berry* (Paris: Allardin, 1837). Hippolyte Thirria, *La duchesse de Berry* (Paris: Plange, 1900).

4. Memoirs of Charles d'Agoult, recorded by Claire de Charnacé, Bibliothèque municipale de Versailles, Fonds Feliciano de Oliveira, ms. f. 859, p. 189.

5. Ibid.,187.

6. *Mémoires,* 1:298–305.

7. *Correspondance de Liszt et de la comtesse d'Agoult publiée par M. Daniel Ollivier* (Paris: Grasset, 1933), 1:54.

8. Ibid., 54. *La captive* is a poem by Hugo set to music by Berlioz. The music of *Die Abgeblühte Linde* is by Schubert. *Bénédiction de Dieu dans la solitude* is a poem by Lamartine which Liszt set to music some years later.

9. Ibid., 56.

10. Ibid., 57.

11. Ibid., 49.

12. Ibid., 73.

13. Ibid., 74.

14. Ibid., 76.

15. Ibid., 80.

16. Ibid., 102. The work by Hugo is *Claude Gueux.*

17. Ibid., 85.

18. Ibid., 100.

19. Ibid., 108.

20. Ibid., 112.

21. *Mémoires,* 1:359. The women who best fit the description are George Sand and Maurice de Flavigny's wife, Mathilde.

22. *Correspondance de Liszt et de la comtesse d'Agoult,* 1:132.

23. George Sand wrote as follows about her illegitimate half-brother, Hippo-lyte Chatiron: "Hippolyte would have lacked gratitude if he has posed as *Antony.* . . . In some milieux, the love child gets so much attention that he becomes almost the king of the family, or at least the most active and independent member of it, the one who does what he likes and who is forgiven everything because there is an in-stinctive wish to compensate for his social isolation" (*Histoire de ma vie,* 2:432). The play *Antony* (1831), a Romantic drama by Dumas, contains a sympathetic portrayal of the bastard Antony, a protest against social convention, and a plea for free love.

24. "Love is woman's virtue; it is for love that she proudly accepts the conse-quences of her acts, it is love which gives her the heroism to face her remorse. The greater the cost of her misdemeanor, the more she deserves from the man she loves" (George Sand, *Indiana* [Paris: Garnier Frères, 1962], 281). The theme of female emancipation was in the air, and also featured strongly in Balzac's novel *La femme de trente ans* (1834). The unhappy heroine suffers from sexual incompatibility with her husband and takes a lover, with disastrous consequences.

25. Letter quoted by Vier in *Marie d'Agoult, son mari, ses amis,* 22.

CHAPTER 8: *Life with Liszt*

1. Marie d'Agoult later gave an idealized account of this episode (*Mémoires,* 1:318–20).

2. Letter dated 3 July 1835, Daniel Ollivier archives. The emphasis is Marie d'Agoult's.

3. *Correspondance de Liszt et de la comtesse d'Agoult,* 1:138.

4. Ibid., 154.

5. Ibid., 173.

6. *Marie d'Agoult, George Sand: Correspondance,* ed. Charles Dupêchez (Paris: Bartillat, 1995), 20.

7. Ibid., 28.

8. Ibid., 45. Hortense Allart had just published *La femme et la démocratie de nos temps* (Paris: Delaunay, 1836). Her earlier publications included the novels *Gertrude* (Paris: Dupont, 1828) and *L'indienne* (Paris: Vimont, 1833).

9. *Marie d'Agoult, George Sand: Correspondance*, 55.

10. "Lettre d'un voyageur: A Charles Didier." This long and entertaining account appeared in *La Revue des Deux Mondes* on 15 November 1836. It is included in volume 15 of *Oeuvres de George Sand* (Paris: Bonnaire, 1838–42). Another version of the excursion was provided by Adolphe Pictet in *Une course à Chamounix* (Paris: Duprat, 1838).

11. *Marie d'Agoult, George Sand: Correspondance*, 120.

12. Ibid., 128.

13. Ibid., 164.

14. *Mémoires*, 2:114.

CHAPTER 9: *The Lovers in Italy*

1. *Mémoires, souvenirs et journaux*, 2:131–33.

2. *Marie d'Agoult, George Sand: Correspondance*, 172.

3. *Mémoires*, 2:159–62.

4. *Correspondance de Liszt et de la comtesse d'Agoult*, 1:218.

5. *Mémoires*, 2:250–53.

6. *Marie d'Agoult, George Sand: Correspondance*, 2:209–22.

7. It was not until 1912 that the articles written by Liszt or composed in collaboration with Marie d'Agoult were published as a collection. The titles included "De la situation des artistes," "Lettre d'un voyageur à M. George Sand," and a series of "Lettres d'un bachelier ès musique." In the 1912 volume edited by Jean Chantavoine, the articles are attributed to Franz Liszt alone and given an artificial title: *Pages romantiques* (Paris: Félix Alcan, 1912).

8. *Marie d'Agoult, George Sand: Correspondance*, 218.

9. Ibid., 222.

10. See Vier, *Marie d'Agoult, son mari, ses amis*.

11. *Mémoires*, 2:251–52.

12. *Correspondance de Liszt de la comtesse d'Agoult*, 1:262.

13. Ibid., 291.

CHAPTER 10: *The Break with Liszt*

1. *Correspondance de Liszt et de la comtesse d'Agoult*, 1:295.

2. Vier, *Marie d'Agoult, son mari, ses amis*, 61–118.

3. *Correspondance de Liszt et de la comtesse d'Agoult*, 1:395.

4. Ibid., 2:127–28, 154–55, 160, 197.

5. See Henri Malo, *La gloire du vicomte de Launay* (Paris: Emile Paul, 1925).

6. *Correspondance de Liszt et de la comtesse d'Agoult*, 1:365–66.

7. Ibid., 398–99.

8. Ibid., 412.

9. George Sand, *Horace* (Paris: de Potter, 1842).

10. *La Presse,* 17 November and 28 December 1843.

11. *Correspondance de Liszt et de la comtesse d'Agoult,* 2:251.

12. Ibid., 51.

13. Ibid., 60.

14. Ibid., 109.

15. Ibid., 126–27.

16. Ibid., 132.

17. Sophie Loewe, a proud beauty with a superb voice, arrived in Paris in 1841 but left without achieving full success. She went on to London and then to Italy, where she broke the heart of Donizetti. Eventually she married the prince of Lichtenstein and quit the stage.

18. Ibid., 147.

19. A. de Hévésy, "Liszt et Madame d'Agoult," *La Revue Musicale,* June 1928.

20. *Correspondance de Liszt et de la comtesse d'Agoult,* 2:175–76.

21. Ibid., 242.

22. Ibid., 255–56.

23. See Bruce Seymour, *Lola Montez: A Life* (New Haven: Yale University Press, 1995).

24. *Correspondance de Liszt et de la comtesse d'Agoult,* 2:328.

25. Balzac, *Honorine,* 1843.

CHAPTER 11: *The Career of Writer*

1. "Georges Herwegh et les hégéliens politiques," *La Presse,* 17 November and 28 December 1843. Relations between Marie d'Agoult and the Herweghs can be studied in the correspondence published by a son of the poet: Marcel Herwegh, *Au printemps des dieux: Lettres de Marie d'Agoult et de Georges Herwegh* (Paris: Gallimard, 1929).

2. Ibid., 19.

3. Ibid., 48.

4. See Léon Séché, *Hortense Allart de Méritens* (Paris: Mercure de France, 1908).

5. Daniel Stern, *Nélida* (Paris: Michel Lévy, 1846). There is a modern edition, with notes by Charles Dupêchez: *Nélida* (Paris: Calmann-Lévy, 1987).

6. Herwegh, *Au printemps des dieux,* 145.

7. "Esquisses morales: Pensées sur les femmes," *La Revue Indépendante,* 25 September and 10 October 1847. Feminist ideas had already been expressed by Saint-Simon, Fourier, Leroux, Sand, Flora Tristan, and Hortense Allart, among others.

8. *Essai sur la liberté* (Paris: Amyot, 1847).

9. Ibid., 99–103.

10. *Correspondance de Liszt et de la comtesse d'Agoult,* 2:362. Liszt had some fun pretending to believe that the figure of Guermann was a portrait of Lehmann: "Poor Lehmann!" (letter from Marie d'Agoult to Henri Lehmann in *Une correspondance romantique,* 226). It is interesting to note that Jules Sandeau wrote a novel which Marie saw as an answer to her own: "Have you heard about *Madeleine,* an anti-Nélida novel which has just been published by the Catholic bookshop? I am honoured!" (Marie d'Agoult to H. Lehmann, ibid., 229).

11. Ibid., 415.

12. Ibid., 416. The words underlined by Marie are an allusion to the complaint made by her in 1843.

13. "Lettre à François d'Orléans, prince de Joinville," *Le Courrier Français,* 25 May 1848.

14. Herwegh, *Au printemps des dieux,* 158.

CHAPTER 12: *Autumn Leaves*

1. *Histoire de la révolution de 1848,* 1:361.

2. Ibid., 365.

3. Herwegh, *Au printemps des dieux,* 166.

4. Ibid., 195.

5. Notably "Vingt-cinq ans de l'histoire des Pays-Bas (1584–1609)" in 1863 and some of her "Dialogues sur Dante et Goethe" in 1864.

6. 25 June 1860. Quoted by Charles Dupêchez in *Marie d'Agoult* (Paris: Perrin, 1989), 261. This manuscript diary is in the archives of Mme Daniele Jeanson de Prévaux, Paris.

7. Liszt, *Correspondence* (Paris: Lattès, 1987), 436.

8. Daniel Ollivier, *Autour de Madame d'Agoult et de Liszt* (Paris: Grasset, 1941), 67.

9. Herwegh, *Au printemps des dieux,* 201.

10. The works of Juliette Lamber (later Juliette Adam) included *Blanche de Coucy* (Paris: Vanier, 1858), *Mon Village* (Paris: Michel Lévy, 1860), *Idées anti-proudhoniennes sur l'amour, la femme et le mariage* (Paris: Dentu, 1861), and *L'éducation de Laure* (Paris: Michel Lévy, 1869).

11. The works of Louise Ackermann included *Contes* (Paris: Garnier Frères, 1855), *Contes et poésies* (Nice: Caisson, 1862), and *Poésies philosophiques* (Nice: Caisson, 1871). See Vier, *Madame d'Agoult, son mari, ses amis,* 119–23.

12. The study was first published as articles in *La Revue Moderne* and *La Revue Germanique* in 1864 and 1865. It later appeared as a book: *Dante et Goethe: Dialogues,* by Daniel Stern (Paris: Didier, 1966).

13. Richard Wagner, *Sämtliche Schriften und Dichtungen* (Leipzig: Breitkopf und Härtel, 1912), 11:17; letter written in September 1858.

14. Ollivier, *Autour de Mme d'Agoult et de Liszt,* 111, 124.

15. *Le Constitutionnel,* 14 April 1873. This article by Barbey d'Aurévilly was later incorporated in *Les oeuvres et les hommes* (Paris: V. Palmé, 1878).

16. Hortense Allart, *Les enchantements de Mme Prudence* (Sceaux: Dépée, 1872).

17. Robert Franz (Olga de Janina), *Souvenirs d'une Cosaque* (Paris: Lacroix, 1874).

18. Letter dated 5 April 1875, in the Daniel Ollivier archives.

19. *Essai sur la liberté,* 102.

20. *Autour de Mme d'Agoult et de Liszt* (Paris: Grasset, 1941).

Bibliography

Books by Marie d'Agoult

Nélida. Paris: Amyot, 1846.
Essai sur la liberté. Paris: Amyot, 1847.
Lettres républicaines. Paris: Amyot, 1848.
Esquisses morales et politiques. Paris: Pagnerre, 1849.
Histoire de la révolution de 1848. 3 vols. Paris: G. Sandré, 1850–53.
Jeanne Darc. Paris: Michel Lévy, 1857.
Florence de Turin: Etudes d'art et de politique. Paris: Michel Lévy, 1862.
Dante et Goethe. Paris: Didier, 1866.
Histoire des commencements de la République aux Pays-Bas, 1581–1625. Paris: Michel Lévy, 1872.
Mes souvenirs, 1806–1833. Paris: Calmann Lévy, 1877.
Oeuvres de Daniel Stern. Paris: Calmann Lévy, 1880.
Valentia. Hervé. Julien. Paris: Calmann Lévy, 1883.

Select Articles by Marie d'Agoult

"De la situation des artistes." *La Gazette Musicale,* 3 May 1835.
"Lettre d'un voyageur à M. George Sand." *La Gazette Musicale,* 6 December 1835.
"Lettre d'un bachelier ès musique à M. George Sand." *La Gazette Musicale,* 16 July 1837.
"La Scala de Milan." *La Gazette Musicale,* 27 May 1838.
"De l'état de la musique en Italie." *La Gazette Musicale,* 28 March 1839.
"Lettre d'un bachelier de musique: Venise." *L'Artiste,* 16 June 1839.
"Lettre à Hector Berlioz." *La Gazette Musicale,* 24 October 1839.
"Le concert de Chopin." *La Gazette Musicale,* 19 September 1841.
"La nouvelle salle peinte par M. Paul Delaroche." *La Presse,* 12 December 1841.
"Portrait de Chérubini par Ingres." *La Presse,* 7 January 1842.
"Le salon de 1842." *La Presse,* 8 March 1842.
"Georges Herwegh et les hégéliens politiques." *La Presse,* 17 November 1843.

"Pensées sur les femmes." *La Revue Indépendante,* October–December 1847.
"Lettres écrites d'Italie." *Le Siècle,* 29 November 1859.
"Lettres écrites d'Italie." *Le Siècle,* 14 January 1860.
"Lettres écrites d'Italie." *Le Siècle,* 23 January 1860.
"Le comte de Cavour." *Le Siècle,* 14 February 1860.
"La persécution religieuse." *Le Siècle,* 3 July 1860.
"Madame Ackermann." *Le Temps,* 7 June 1863.
"La guerre et l'opinion politique." *La Liberté,* 5 July 1866.
"Laurette de Malboissière." *Le Temps,* 28 July 1866.
"République ou monarchie." *Le Temps,* 13 March 1871.

Manuscript Sources, France

Douai, Bibliothèque municipale:
    Letters from Marie d'Agoult to the writer Marceline Desbordes-Valmore.
Paris, Bibliothèque de l'Institut:
    Letters from Marie d'Agoult to Sainte-Beuve and George Sand.
Paris, Bibliothèque historique de la ville de Paris:
    Letters from Marie d'Agoult to the historian Jules Michelet.
Paris, Bibliothèque nationale de France:
    Diaries and notebooks of Marie d'Agoult and correspondence with Louise Ackermann, Hortense Allart, Charles d'Agoult, Claire d'Agoult, Christina de Belgiojoso, Hector Berlioz, Louis Blanc, Hans von Bülow, Guy de Charnacé, Marceline Desbordes-Valmore, Delphine de Girardin, Emile de Girardin, Georg Herwegh, Emma Herwegh, Victor Hugo, Dominique Ingres, Alphonse de Lamartine, Franz Liszt, Emile Littré, Jules Michelet, Emile Ollivier, Adolphe Pictet, Louis de Ronchaud, Sainte-Beuve.
    Daniel Ollivier Archives: Diaries of Marie d'Agoult (1835, 1836, 1842, 1843, 1847, 1848, 1850, 1851, 1852)
Versailles, Bibliothèque municipale:
    Letters from Hortense Allart, Christina de Belgiojoso, Guy de Charnacé, Marceline Desbordes-Valmore, Mathilde de Flavigny, Maurice de Flavigny, Jules Grévy, Blandine Liszt, Emile Littré, Pauline Roland, Sainte-Beuve, Flora Tristan, and others. Letters from Marie d'Agoult to her daughter, Claire d'Agoult, and others. Manuscripts and fragments by Marie d'Agoult.

Major Private Collections

Avignon, Archives of M. Josserand de Saint-Priest d'Urgel:
    472 letters to Claire d'Agoult, 19 letters to Guy de Charnacé, 11 letters to Mme de Flavigny, 3 letters to Cosima Liszt, 52 letters to Emile Littré.
Château de Bois-Montbourcher, Maine-et-Loire, Archives of Guy de Girard de Charnacé:

105 letters from Marie d'Agoult to Maurice de Flavigny; 19 letters to Mme de Flavigny, 3 letters to Charles d'Agoult, 1 letter to Cosima Liszt. Letters to Marie d'Agoult from Mme de Flavigny, Mathilde de Flavigny, Maurice de Flavigny, Charles d'Agoult, Claire d'Agoult.

Château de Riblaye, Tarn-et-Garonne, Archives of M. and Mme Raymond de Bengy:

95 letters from Marie d'Agoult to Louis de Ronchaud.

Geneva, Archives of M. Pierre Pictet:

84 letters from Marie d'Agoult to Adolphe Pictet.

Paris, Archives of Mme Daniela Jeanson de Prévaux:

Diaries of Marie d'Agoult.

Published Sources

LETTERS AND MEMOIRS

Au printemps des dieux: Correspondance inédite de la comtesse d'Agoult et du poète George Herwegh. Edited by Marcel Herwegh. Paris: Gallimard, 1929.

Autour de Mme d'Agoult et de Liszt: Lettres publiées avec introduction et notes par Daniel Ollivier. Paris: Grasset, 1941.

Correspondance de George Sand: Textes réunis et annotés par Georges Lubin. Paris: Garnier, 1966.

Correspondance de Liszt et de la comtesse d'Agoult publiée par M. Daniel Ollivier. 2 vols. Paris: Grasset, 1933–34.

Correspondance de Richard Wagner et de Franz Liszt. Paris: Gallimard, 1943.

Une correspondance romantique: Mme d'Agoult, Liszt, Henri Lehmann. Edited by Solange Joubert. Paris: Flammarion, 1947.

Daniel Stern: Lettres républicaines du Second Empire. Edited by Jacques Vier. Paris: Editions du Cèdre, 1951.

Franz Liszt. Correspondance: Lettres choisies et annotées par Pierre-Antoine Huré et Claude Knepper. Paris: Lattès, 1987.

Marie d'Agoult, George Sand: Correspondance. Edited by Charles Dupêchez. Paris: Bartillat, 1995.

Mémoires, souvenirs et journaux de la comtesse d'Agoult. Edited by Charles Dupêchez. Paris: Mercure de France, 1990.

Sand, George. *Histoire de ma vie.* Paris: Marcel Lévy, 1856.

HISTORICAL AND LITERARY WORKS

Abensour, Léon. *Le féminisme sous le règne de Louis-Philippe et en 1848.* Paris: Plon, 1913.

Abrantès, Laure d'. *Mémoires sur la Restauration.* 6 vols. Paris: Henry, 1835–36.

Ackermann, Louise. *Pensées d'une solitaire.* Paris: Lemerre, 1903.

Adam, Juliette. *Mes premières armes littéraires.* Paris: Lemerre, 1904.

Allart de Méritens, Hortense. *Gertrude*. Paris: Dupont, 1828.

————. *La femme et la démocratie de nos temps*. Paris: Delaunay, 1836.

————. *Les enchantements de Mme Prudence*. Paris: Michel Lévy, 1872.

————. *Lettres inédites à Sainte-Beuve*. Paris: Mercure de France, 1908.

Anne, Théodore. *Mémoires sur l'intérieur du palais de Charles X*. Paris: Werdet, 1831.

Apponyi, Rodolphe. *Vingt-cinq ans de Paris*. Paris: Plon, 1914.

Aragonnes, Claude. *La comtesse d'Agoult, une destinée romantique*. Paris: Hachette, 1938.

Arnadu, René. *La Deuxième République et le Second Empire*. Paris: Hachette, 1948.

Balzac, Honoré de. *Physiologie du mariage*. Paris: Didier, 1828.

————. *Scènes de la vie privée: La femme de trente ans*. Paris: Béchet, 1834.

————. *Béatrix ou les amours forcés*. Paris: Souverain, 1839.

Barante, Amable de. *Souvenirs, 1782–1866*. 5 vols. Paris: C. Lévy, 1890–91.

Barbey d'Aurévilly, Jules de. *Les oeuvres et les hommes: Les bas bleus*. Paris: Palmié, 1878.

Barrot, Odilon. *Mémoires posthumes*. 4 vols. Paris: Charpentier, 1875–76.

Beach, Vincent. *Charles X of France*. Boulder: University of Colorado Press, 1971.

Bérard, Simon. *Souvenirs historiques de la révolution de 1830*. Paris: Perrotin, 1834.

Berlioz, Hector. *Mémoires*. Paris: C. Lévy, 1878.

Berthier de Sauvigny, Guillaume. *The Bourbon Restoration*. Philadelphia: University of Pennsylvania Press, 1966.

Bory, Robert. *Une retraite romantique en Suisse: Liszt et la comtesse d'Agoult*. Paris: Attinger, 1930.

————. *Liszt et ses enfants*. Paris: Corrêa, 1936.

Broglie, Victor de. *Souvenirs, 1785–1870*. Paris: 1886.

Cabanis, José. *Charles X, roi ultra*. Paris: Gallimard, 1972.

Castille, Hippolyte. *Histoire de la Seconde République*. 4 vols. Paris: Lecou, 1854–56.

Chantavoine, Jean. *Pages romantiques de Liszt*. Paris: Alcan, 1912.

Charléty, Sébastien. *La monarchie de juillet*. Paris: Hachette, 1921.

Collingham, H. A. C. *The July Monarchy*. London: Longman, 1988.

Crétineau-Joly, Jacques. *Histoire de la Vendée militaire*. 4 vols. Paris: Hivert, 1840–42.

Dansette, Adrien. *Louis-Napoléon à la conquête du pouvoir*. Paris: Hachette, 1961.

Daudet, Ernest. *La révolution de 1830 et le procès des ministres*. Paris: Hachette, 1907.

Delvau, Alfred. *Histoire de la révolution de Février*. Paris: Blosse, 1850.

Dermoncourt, Paul. *La vendée et madame*. Paris: Guyot, 1834.

Desanti, Dominique. *Daniel, ou le visage secret d'une comtesse romantique, Marie d'Agoult*. Paris: Stock, 1980.

Dupêchez, Charles. *Marie d'Agoult*. Paris: Librairie Académique Perrin, 1989.

Girardin, Delphine de. *Lettres parisiennes*. Paris: Charpentier, 1843.

————. *Oeuvres complètes*. Paris: Plon, 1860–61.

————. *Lettres parisiennes du vicomte de Launay*. Paris: Mercure de France, 1986.

Guillemin, Henri. *Le coup du 2 décembre*. Paris: Gallimard, 1951.

Haraszti, Emile, *Franz Liszt*. Paris: Picard, 1967.

Howard, Michael. *The Franco-Prussian War*. London: Hart-Davis, 1961.

Hugo, Victor. *Les feuilles d'automne*. Paris: Ladvocat, 1831.

————. *Choses vues, 1847–1848*. Paris: Gallimard, 1972.

Joinville, François de. *Vieux souvenirs, 1818–48*. Paris: C. Lévy, 1894.

Lamartine, Alphonse de. *Méditations poétiques*. Paris: Nicolle, 1820.

————. *Souvenirs et portraits*. Paris: Hachette, 1872.

Legouvé, Ernest. *Histoire morale des femmes*. Paris: Didot, 1856.

Liszt, Franz. *Pages romantiques*. Paris: Félix Alcan, 1912.

Lucas-Dubreton, Jean. *La Restauration et la monarchie de juillet*. Paris: Hachette, 1937.

————. *La France de Napoléon*. Paris: Tallandier, 1981.

Luna, Frederick. *The French Republic under Cavaignac, 1848*. Princeton: Princeton University Press, 1969.

Maigron, Louis. *Le romantisme et les moeurs*. Paris: Champion, 1910.

Malo, Henri. *Delphine Gay et sa mère*. Paris: Emile Paul, 1924.

Mazas, Alexandre. *Mémoires pour servir à l'histoire de la révolution de 1830*. Paris: Urbain Canel, 1832.

Mazzini, Joseph. *Lettres de Joseph Mazzini à Daniel Stern*. Paris: Germer-Baillière, 1872.

Ollivier, Emile. *L'empire libéral, études, récits, souvenirs*. 18 vols. Paris: Garnier, 1895–1918.

————. *Lettres de l'exil, 1870–1874*. Paris: Hachette, 1921.

Pictet, Adolphe. *Une course à Chamounix*. Paris: B. Duprat, 1840.

Pinkney, David. *The French Revolution of 1830*. Princeton: Princeton University Press, 1972.

————. *Decisive Years in France, 1840–47*. Princeton: Princeton University Press, 1986.

Pommier, Armand. *Madame la comtesse d'Agoult*. Paris: Dentu, 1867.

Pontmartin, Armand de. *Souvenirs d'un vieux critique*. Paris: Calmann Lévy, 1882.

Ramann, Lina. *Franz Liszt als Künstler und Mensch*. 3 vols. Leipzig: Breitkopf und Härtel, 1880–94.

Rémusat, Charles de. *Essai sur l'éducation des femmes*. Paris: Ladvocat, 1824.

————. *Mémoires de ma vie*. Paris: Hachette, 1962.

Rials, Stéphane. *Le légitimisme*. Paris: Presses Universitaires de France, 1983.

Robin, Charles. *Histoire de la révolution française de 1848*. 2 vols. Paris: Penaud, 1849–50.

Rocheblave, Samuel. *Une amitié romanesque: George Sand et Madame d'Agoult*. Paris: Imprimerie de Chaix, 1894.

Sand, George. *Indiana*. Paris: Gosselin, 1832.

————. *Horace*. Paris: de Potter, 1842.

————. "Lettres d'un voyageur." In *Oeuvres de George Sand*. 27 vols. Paris: Bonnaire, 1881.

————. *Histoire de ma vie.* 2 vols. Paris: Gallimard, 1970–71.

Séché, Léon. *Hortense Allart de Méritens.* Paris: Mercure de France, 1908.

————. *Delphine Gay.* Paris: Mercure de France, 1910.

Seymour, Bruce. *Lola Montez.* New Haven: Yale University Press, 1995.

Tocqueville, Alexis de. *Souvenirs.* Paris: Gallimard, 1964.

Thureau-Dangin, Paul. *Histoire de la monarchie de juillet.* 7 vols. Paris: Plon, 1884–92.

Tulard, Jean. *La vie quotidienne des Français sous Napoléon.* Paris: Hachette, 1978.

————. *Les révolutions.* Paris: Fayard, 1985.

————. *Dictionnaire du Second Empire.* Paris: Fayard, 1995.

Vier, Jacques. *Emile de Girardin inconnu.* Paris: Armand Colin, 1949.

————. *Marie d'Agoult, son mari, ses amis.* Paris: Editions du Cèdre, 1950.

————. *Lettres républicaines du Second Empire.* Paris: Editions du Cèdre, 1951.

————. *La comtesse d'Agoult et son temps.* 6 vols. Paris: Armand Colin, 1955–63.

Vigier, Philippe. *La vie quotidienne en province et à Paris pendant les journées de 1848.* Paris: Hachette, 1982.

Williams, Adrian. *Portrait of Liszt.* Oxford: Clarendon Press, 1990.

Zeldin, Theodore. *The Political System of Napoleon III.* London: Macmillan, 1958.

Index

Numbers in italic indicate illustrations.